The
Committed
Enterprise

Praise for *The Committed Enterprise*

'Ambitious in intent, meticulous in detail and penetrating in analysis, this book is alive with ideas and hard experience. Anyone who is serious about leadership in an age of uncertainty will benefit from it.'

Sir Brian Pitman, Chairman, Lloyds TSB Group (1997–2001)

'This excellent book describes how the right vision and values, well implemented, create strong commitment inside and outside organizations. Unusually for a "soft" topic, it is highly practical, covering design, communication, embedding and measurement of vision and values. Essential reading for all leaders or would-be leaders.'

Professor Gordon Conway, President, The Rockefeller Foundation

'*The Committed Enterprise* is a must for all business leaders who want to move their organization into the future. Professor Davidson uses relevant business cases and interviews to illustrate the importance of moving beyond the words "vision" and "values" and toward systemic and actionable change.'

Faye Wilson, Senior Vice President, The Home Depot (world's second most profitable retailer)

'Here is a highly readable book on how to manage vision and values in a scientific yet creative way. It's built around seven best practices, full of examples, based on over a hundred interviews with successful leaders, and equally relevant to companies and non-profits.'

Douglas Blonsky, Chief Operating Officer, New York Central Park Conservancy

'*The Committed Enterprise* is a must read handbook for all levels of management. Its unique format makes it easy to read and retain the key ideas.'

Leonard A. Lauder, Chairman, Estée Lauder

'This deeply impressive and original work is a "must read" for all senior managers, whether in public or private sector enterprises, since it has been meticulously researched, concisely written and provides a compelling analysis of best practices that can readily be adopted and implemented. Read *The Committed Enterprise* before your competitors do!'

Professor Simon Knox, The Cranfield University School of Management

'Professor Davidson has captured, with a practical approach, the key to differentiation and sustainability in today's complex marketplace.'

Jack Duffy, Senior Vice President, Strategy, United Parcel Service (UPS)

'Upbeat, well illustrated, forcefully written and thoroughly practical, Davidson shows how to develop vision and values to create a winning combination. This book is a gem.'

Dr Frank Rhodes, President Emeritus, Cornell University

'It has been said that without vision, the people perish. Business leaders recognize this same imperative. Based on examples from the world's leading enterprises, *The Committed Enterprise* offers the reader many creative and validated approaches on how to put value-based principles into action. This book is very through and well-researched.'

Joel Allison, President and CEO, Baylor Health Care System, Dallas

'*The Committed Enterprise* is a thoughtful and practical guide that can help an organization clearly establish its vision and values. Equally important, Professor Davidson uses real-world examples to demonstrate how those ideals can be turned into tangible benefits.'

**Edward Whitacre Jr.,
Chairman and CEO, SBC Communications (major telecom company)**

'Hugh Davidson's latest book takes high level organisation theory and turns it into effective practice. It translates vision into action and should be essential reading for anyone aspiring to lead a dynamic organisation in any sector – public, private or voluntary.'

Barry Clarke, OBE, Chairman of Save the Children (UK)

The unique structure of *The Committed Enterprise* makes it an excellent teaching tool. For a free downloadable version of all the left-hand charts in the book, along with access to other supporting information and resources, please log on to:

www.bh.com/companions/0750655402

To my father, Alec Davidson, who, as an architect and surveyor,

sustained the highest standards of integrity and professional conduct

The
Committed
Enterprise

How to make vision and values work

Hugh Davidson

OXFORD AMSTERDAM BOSTON LONDON NEW YORK PARIS SAN DIEGO
SAN FRANCISCO SINGAPORE SYDNEY TOKYO

Butterworth-Heinemann
An imprint of Elsevier Science
Linacre House, Jordan Hill, Oxford OX2 8DP
225 Wildwood Avenue, Woburn, MA 01801–2041

First published 2002

British Library Cataloguing in Publication Data
Davidson, J. H. (John Hugh), 1935–
    The committed enterprise: how to make vision and values work
    1. Organizational effectiveness   2. Business ethics   3. Success in business
    I. Title
    658.4

Library of Congress Cataloguing in Publication Data
A catalogue record for this book is available from the Library of Congress

ISBN 0 7506 5540 2

For information on all Butterworth-Heinemann publications visit
our website at www.bh.com

Internal page design by Claire Brodmann
Printed and bound in Great Britain

Contents

Preface

This book was almost completed before the tragic events of 11 September 2001 which shocked the world, but out of this horror came global admiration for the heroic values of the rescue services, especially the people of the Fire and Police Departments of New York. They demonstrated in extreme circumstances how strong values work.

The purpose of this book is to help guide organizations to future success with attitudes and behaviours they feel proud of. It is about how to get good results in the right way, so that they are sustainable

The book is written for current and future leaders of every kind of organization, and is as relevant to senior people in education or hospital management as to business leaders, entrepreneurs and leaders of police forces, or charities.

There is much good writing about vision and values but little on how to make them work in practice on a day-to-day basis. This book aims to fill that gap, and to establish vision and values as a continuing management process, not a single, soon forgotten exercise.

To earn its place on the shelf, any book should be different. This one is distinctive in three ways:

- **Accessible format.** Charts or illustrations occupy the left-hand pages (fast track) and lead you to read the main text on the right (scenic route). The left-hand pages comprise a complete chart presentation, and may be read on their own or together with the linked right-hand pages.
- **Depth and breadth of research.** There are now many books based on interviews with CEOs, usually conducted by a team of researchers. I did all 136 interviews for this book personally, ensuring consistency of approach and comparison. The task required 40 000 miles of travel to 45 different locations. Criss-crossing the USA for almost 80 days beneath a carapace of five suitcases full of interview data, background files, running gear, interview suits and leisure wear was a unique challenge.
When I give talks, the most frequent question is 'How do you know whether the people interviewed were telling the truth, or giving an unduly favourable view?' My answer is that you can never be sure, and organization leaders tend to give a favourable gloss. That is why, for this kind of research, face-to-face interviews are vastly superior to telephone contact or mailed questionnaires. I have been very conscious of this issue from the outset, researching each organization beforehand, and searching for signals when I'm there. So I talked to my cab drivers, and to receptionists, security officers, and secretaries. I visited canteens, arrived early to study people passing the reception area, observed the behaviour of children walking to school, and requested relevant documents (e.g. 5-year plans, appraisal formats). All interviews were confidential, the questions probing, the answers apparently candid. My legal training, decades of interview experience, and familiarity with many industries also helped.
- **Full coverage of companies and non-profits.** Of the organizations seen, 57% were companies and 43% non-profits. The same questions were asked of both. This produced, as expected, a great deal of cross-learning, which is detailed in the book. One of my private conclusions is that the two most difficult types of organization to manage successfully are police forces and symphony orchestras.

The book was technically challenging to develop, since left- and right-hand pages have to be continuously aligned. My wife, Sandra, applied her skills in layout and editing to make this difficult task feasible. She was also responsible for the creative brief for all left-hand pages and developed initial computer graphics for each one. Sandra worked closely on the book throughout the 2 years it took to complete, and made a major contribution to it, not least as a steady source of encouragement.

Another significant challenge was to arrange interviews with difficult-to-see people. Cold contact proved ineffective and I was only able to set up interviews through personal introductions. The starting point was the good fortune of having some effective friends and contacts. They led me to others and the process became self-sustaining.

In the critical early stages, Sir David Barnes opened doors to global CEOs he knew, and Sir David Ramsbotham introduced me to military and police leaders in the USA and UK. Charles Strauss, David Lewis (Senior Partner at Norton Rose) and Professor John Quelch (Professor of Business Administration at Harvard Business School) were also extremely helpful, while Philip Carne enabled me to connect with leading American hospitals via Johnson & Johnson.

I am most grateful to all 136 organization leaders who were good enough to see me. Apart from the minor plus of appearing in the book, there was no benefit for these very busy people in being interviewed. Most did so because they were obviously committed to making vision and values work, and wanted to contribute to the topic. They all gave generously of their time and thinking, and most of the interviews were very lively. Only one person did a 'no show', and only one cancelled at short notice. This is a measure of the commitment to vision and values found during this research.

The book is full of quotes and examples from the interviews. To use them all, this book would have had to be enormous. Those unquoted provided valuable thinking, and contributed importantly to the conclusions drawn.

A number of people kindly read early drafts. My brother, Ewan Davidson, who has extensive senior management experience in both major companies and non-profits, and Professor Simon Knox, of Cranfield University School of Management, read the first draft. Both made valuable comments on structure and content, resulting in a change of chapter sequence, and re-writing of the earlier chapters. Professor Malcolm McDonald, also of Cranfield, has been consistently encouraging, making many constructive suggestions.

Peter Jensen, formerly Senior Vice President at SmithKline Beecham, now with a wide portfolio of business interests, and Jack Duffy, Senior Vice President Strategy at United Parcel Service (UPS), both read the final draft, and their comments improved the book significantly.

Two landmark works – *Built to Last* by James Collins and Jerry Porras, and *Competing for the Future* by Gary Hamel and P.K. Prahalad – greatly stimulated my interest in vision and values and helped inspire this book. I also found Stephen King's book *On Writing* indispensable and have tried to follow his advice about simple sentences and avoidance of adverbs.

At Butterworth-Heinemann, Tim Goodfellow, publisher, has supported the book strongly from the outset, and, together with Neil Coffey and Margaret Denley, confronted the challenges of the unique format in a positive and skilful way.

Summary of organizations interviewed

	Business	Education	Hospitals/Police/Military	Arts, Charities, Religion	Total
UK	44	15	3	3	65
USA	26	12	9	13	60
Total	70	27	12	16	125

Note: 136 people from 125 organizations were interviewed.

Business organizations

Note:
People whose names are starred have moved since the date of the interview. Their title and organization is shown as at the time of interview.

Name	Title	Organization	Location
USA			
Ray Anderson	Chairman/CEO	Interface	Atlanta
Richard Antoine	Vice President	Procter & Gamble	Cincinnati
Dick Brown	Chairman/CEO	EDS	Dallas
Harold Burlingame Jr	Executive VP	AT & T	Basking Ridge
Robert Darretta	Chief Financial Officer	Johnson & Johnson	New Brunswick
Stephen Demeritt	Vice Chairman	General Mills	Minneapolis
David Deming	Managing Director	JP Morgan	New York
Jack Duffy	Senior VP Strategy	United Parcel Service	Atlanta
Robert Eckert	CEO	Mattel	Los Angeles
Michael Hawley*	Chairman/CEO	Gillette	Boston
Charles Holliday Jr	Chairman/CEO	DuPont	Wilmington
Durk Jager*	CEO	Procter & Gamble	Cincinnati
Charles Knight	Chairman/CEO	Emerson Electric	St Louis
Leonard Lauder	Chairman	Estée Lauder	New York
John Pepper	Chairman	Procter & Gamble	Cincinnati
Lewis Platt	CEO Former Chairman/ CEO	Kendall Jackson Hewlett Packard	Santa Rosa
John Powers	Managing Director	Goldman Sachs	New York
Steven Rogel	Chairman/CEO	Weyerhaeuser	Seattle

Name	Title	Organization	Location
USA (continued)			
Lewis Rudin	Chairman Co-Chairman	Association for a Better New York Rudin Management	New York
Frederick Smith	Chairman, CEO	FedEx Corporation	Memphis
Dr William Stavropoulos	Chairman	Dow Chemical	Midland
Charles Strauss	Chairman	Unilever USA	New York
Douglas Sweeney	VP Strategy	IBM	Armonk
Troy Todd	Executive VP	EDS	Dallas
Joe Weller	Chairman/CEO	Nestlé USA	Glendale
Edward Whitacre Jr	Chairman/CEO	SBC Communications	San Antonio
John Whitacre Jr*	CEO	Nordstrom	Seattle
Faye Wilson	Senior VP Values	Home Depot	Atlanta
CANADA			
Richard Currie	President Former President	George Weston Ltd Loblaw Companies	Toronto
UK			
Sir Michael Angus*	Chairman Former Chairman	Whitbread Unilever	London
Brian Baldock	Director and Acting Chairman	Marks & Spencer	London
Sir David Barnes*	Deputy Chairman	Astra Zeneca	London
Robert Bauman	Former Chairman Former CEO	British Aerospace SmithKline Beecham	London
Pauline Best	Director, HR	Vodafone UK	Newbury
Peter Blackburn*	Chairman	Nestlé UK	Croydon
Lord Blyth*	Chairman	Boots	Nottingham

Name	Title	Organization	Location
UK (continued)			
Adrian Bourne	Chairman	G Costa & Co	London
Lord Browne	CEO	BP	London
Philip Carne	Former President	Ethicon	London
Sir Robert Clarke	Formerly Chairman	Thames Water	London
Sir Anthony Cleaver	Chairman	AEA Technology	London
Sir Peter Davis	Chairman Former Chairman	J Sainsbury Prudential UK	London
Chris Gibson-Smith	Managing Director	BP	London
Martin Glenn	President	Frito-Lay UK	Reading
Sir Stuart Hampson	Chairman	John Lewis Partnership	London
Tim Harrabin	Director, Strategy	Vodafone UK	Newbury
Andrew Harrison*	Marketing Director	Coca Cola UK	London
Kenny Hirschhorn	Executive VP Strategy, Imagineering and Futurology	Orange	London
Keith Holloway	Chairman	OneClick HR	London
John Hooper, CBE*	Director General	ISBA	London
Tony Illsley*	CEO	Telewest	Woking
Peter Jensen*	Senior Vice President	SmithKline Beecham	London
David Kidd	Partner	Egon Zehnder	London
Terry Leahy	CEO	Tesco plc	Chesham
Allan Leighton*	CEO Europe	Wal-Mart	Leeds
John McGrath*	CEO	Diageo	London
Charles Miller-Smith	CEO	ICI	London

Name	Title	Organization	Location
UK (continued)			
John Murphy	Chairman	Plymouth Gin	Plymouth
John Neill, CBE	CEO	Unipart	Oxford
David Pearson	CEO	NXT	London
Sir Michael Perry	Chairman Former Chairman	Centrica Unilever	London
Howard Phillips	Former CEO	Perkins Foods	Peterborough
Sir Brian Pitman*	Chairman	Lloyds TSB	London
Sir Alan Rudge, FRS	Chairman	WS Atkins	London
Ian Ryder	Brands Director	Unisys	Uxbridge
Lord Sheppard	Former Chairman	Grand Metropolitan	London
Sir Brian Smith	Former Chairman	British Airways Authority Cable & Wireless	London
John Steele	Director of HR	British Telecom	London
Liam Strong*	President, International	Worldcom	London
Hamish Taylor	Managing Director	Eurostar	London
John Taylor*	CEO	BNFL	Riseley
Paul Walsh	CEO	Diageo	London
Nigel Worne	Managing Director	Denby Pottery	Denby
Robert Youngjohns	Vice President	Sun Microsystems	Camberley
GERMANY			
Dr Holger Hätty	Senior Vice President	Lufthansa	Frankfurt
SWEDEN			
Percy Barnevik	Chairman Chairman	Investor AB ABB	Stockholm

Non-profit organizations: education

Name	Title	Organization	Location
USA			
Angela Addiego	Principal	Bel Air Elementary School	San Bruno
Doris Avalos	Principal	North Campus Continuation School	San Pablo
Robert Berdahl	Chancellor	University of California	Berkeley
Gini Dold	Reform Co-ordinator	ER Taylor School	San Francisco
Dary Dunham	Headmaster	Indian Mountain School	Lakeville
Dr Tom Everhart	President Emeritus	Caltech	Pasadena
Mary Hurley	Teacher Leader	Oaklands Arts School	Oakland
Dr Gerald Lynch	President	John Jay College of Criminal Justice	New York
Robert Mattoon	Headmaster	Hotchkiss School	Lakeville
Frank Perrine	Head of School	Fessenden School	Boston
Dr Frank Rhodes	President Emeritus	Cornell University	Ithaca
Eitan Zemel	Vice Dean	Stern Business School, NY University	New York
UK			
Dr Eric Anderson	Provost	Eton College	Eton
Stephen Baldock	High Master	St Paul's School for Boys	London
Prof. Sir Alec Broers	Vice Chancellor	Cambridge University	Cambridge

Name	Title	Organization	Location
UK (continued)			
Carole Evans, CBE	Head Teacher	Priory School	Slough
Prof. Mary-Jo Hatch*	Professor of Organization	Cranfield University	Cranfield
Jim Hudson, OBE	Head Teacher	Two Mile Ash School	Milton Keynes
Ani Magill	Head Teacher	St John the Baptist School	London
Michael Murphy*	Head Teacher	Hurlingham & Chelsea School	London
Sir Peter North, CBE, QC	Former Vice Chancellor Principal	Oxford University Jesus College	Oxford
Claire Oulton*	Head Teacher	St Catherine's School	Bramley
Lord Oxburgh, KBE, FRS*	Rector	Imperial College	London
Christine Peters	Head Teacher	Parliament Hill School	London
Susan Scarsbrook MBE	Head Teacher	Sudbourne Primary School	Brixham
Roger Trafford	Headmaster	Dragon School	Oxford
Chris Woodhead*	Chief Inspector of Schools	OFSTED	London

Non-profit organizations: hospitals, police, military

Name	Title	Organization	Location
USA			
Joel Allison	President and CEO	Baylor Health Care System	Dallas
Philip Edney	Specialist	FBI	Washington
Barry Freedman	President	Mount Sinai NYU Health	New York
Dr Toby Gordon	Vice President	Johns Hopkins Health System	Baltimore
Dr Michael Karpf	President	UCLA Medical Center	Los Angeles
Pancho Kinney	Director of Strategy	Office of National Drug Control Policy	Washington, DC
Dr David Lawrence	Chairman, CEO	Kaiser Health Foundation	Oakland
General Barry McCaffrey*	Director	Office of National Drug Control Policy	Washington, DC
Ronald Peterson	President	Johns Hopkins Health System	Baltimore
Howard Safir*	Commissioner	New York Police Department	New York
Dr Hugh Smith	President	Mayo Clinic	Rochester
Rex Tomb	Unit Chief	FBI	Washington
UK			
Simon Corkill	Superintendent	Metropolitan Police	London

Name	Title	Organization	Location
UK (continued)			
General Sir Michael Jackson, KCB, CBE, DSO	C-in-C Land Forces	Army	Wilton
General Sir David Ramsbotham, GCB, CBE*	HM Chief Inspector of Prisons	Prisons Inspectorate	London
Sir John Stevens, QPM	Commissioner	Metropolitan Police	London
David Veness, QPM	Assistant Commissioner	Metropolitan Police	London

Non-profit organizations: arts, foundations, charities, religion

Name	Title	Organization	Location
USA			
Dr Eugene Bonelli	President	Dallas Symphony Orchestra	Dallas
Douglas Blonsky	Chief Operating Officer	Central Park Conservancy	New York
Prof. Gordon Conway	President	Rockefeller Foundation	New York
Ralph Dickerson Jr	President	United Way – NY City	New York
The Very Revd Alan Jones	Dean	Grace Cathedral	San Francisco
Paul Guenther	Chairman	New York Philharmonic	New York
Charles Lyons	President	UNICEF USA	New York
Dr Charles MacCormack	President	Save the Children USA	Westport
Dr Jonathon Schmick	Pastor	Marine View Presbyterian Church	Tacoma
Shelton Stanfill	President and CEO	Woodruff Arts Center	Atlanta
Rev. William Tully	Rector	St Bartholomew's Church, Park Avenue	New York
Merrill Vargo	Executive Director	Bay Area School Reform Collaborative (BASRC)	San Francisco

Name	Title	Organization	Location
USA (continued)			
Mark Volpe	Managing Director	Boston Symphony Orchestra Inc	Boston
UK			
Barry Clarke, OBE	Chairman	Save the Children UK	London
Lord Peter Melchett*	Executive Director	Greenpeace UK	London
Sam Younger*	Director General	British Red Cross	London

Chapter

The new challenge for organization leaders

Overview

Choose how to read this book
- Fast Track or
- Fast Track and Scenic Route

Defining and prioritizing stakeholders
- Who are they?
- Main ones are customers, finance providers, employees
- How prioritize?
- How link?

Managing conflicting stakeholder needs
- There's a natural conflict
- It needs to be managed
- Relative importance of stakeholders is changing
- Customers becoming most important

Meeting the challenge – the Committed Enterprise
- Committed Customers + Motivated Employees = Satisfied Resource Providers
- This formula links stakeholders
- Vision and values drive it

Example of Committed Enterprise – Mayo Clinic
- The Mayo prioritizes and links stakeholders
- Its strong vision and values are driving force

Learning from 125 organizations
- 125 organization leaders in USA and Europe interviewed on vision and values
- Companies and non-profits covered

CHART 1.1 Distinctive format of this book

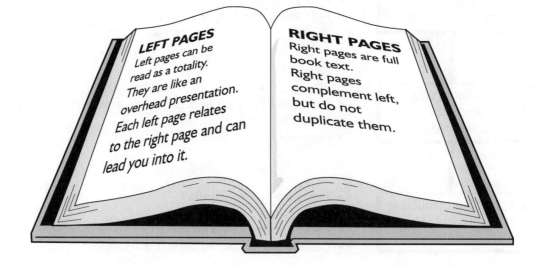

LEFT PAGES
Left pages can be read as a totality. They are like an overhead presentation. Each left page relates to the right page and can lead you into it.

RIGHT PAGES
Right pages are full book text. Right pages complement left, but do not duplicate them.

CHART 1.2 Two ways to read it

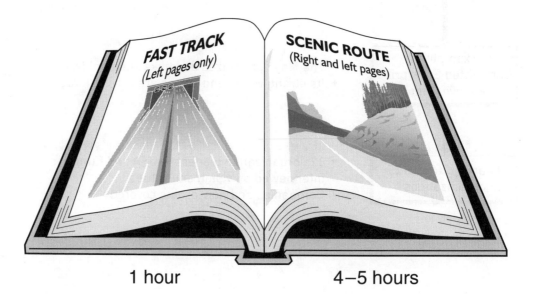

FAST TRACK
(Left pages only)

SCENIC ROUTE
(Right and left pages)

1 hour

4–5 hours

How this book will deliver reader value

This book is aimed at leaders and senior managers of every type of organization, from global companies to schools, police forces to small businesses, and will enable them to do two things very well:

- Establish a strong set of vision and values
- Make them work in practice at all levels

The first is less important, yet absorbs most of their time on this task. Typical practice is to spend months crafting a set of vision and values statements, communicating them through seminars, meetings, posters, booklets, intranet and plastic cards, before breathing a sigh of relief and getting 'back to work'.

Based on anecdotal evidence, there is a mismatch between relative importance and time allocation, as shown in Table 1.1:

Table 1.1

Mismatch of priorities (read across)		
	Developing vision and value statements	**Making them work**
Relative importance	15%	85%
Time allocation by leaders	80%	20%

Results, unsurprisingly, are often depressing. This book therefore focuses on implementation, outlining seven Best Practices for making vision and values work, and taking a hard-edged approach to a soft topic. Creation of vision statements is included because *exciting* visions work better.

Companies and non-profits are given equal attention, since each has much to learn from the other. Non-profits often have superior skills in developing vision and values, living them and branding them. Companies are usually better at building systems to embed and to measure vision and values.

Most business book buyers don't finish their books. To avoid this, *The Committed Enterprise* has a fast track on the left-hand pages. These make a complete presentation, taking an hour to read. This distinctive format recognizes that you are short of time, and more accustomed to scanning charts than reading blocks of text.

Once the charts catch your attention, however, they will divert your eyes to the right-hand pages, thus getting you involved in the book. Reading the whole thing should take about 4 hours, which is feasible on, say, a flight across the Atlantic.

CHART 1.3 Stakeholders have an economic interest or impact on your organization

Economic interest **and** impact	• Employees • Shareholders • Suppliers	• Distributors • Partners • Trade unions
Economic impact	• Customers • Pressure groups • Regulators	• Legislators • Communities • Media

CHART 1.4 Stakeholders have conflicting needs

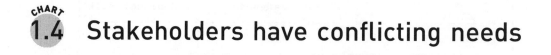

The new challenge – gaining commitment from all stakeholders

Strong vision and values, effectively practised, build commitment among stakeholders. Many leaders said this was their most important task. It's also one of the most challenging. The various stakeholders have powerful needs, which often conflict, as Chart 1.4 demonstrates. They are difficult to win over yet easy to lose, and reluctant to subordinate their interests to those of the organization.

So what exactly does this ugly but useful word 'stakeholder' mean?

A stakeholder has an interest in, or impact on, an organization. Chart 1.3 gives examples of each type. The first group has a vested interest. It includes employees and finance providers. The second has an economic impact and includes customers.

There have been three big stakeholder changes in recent decades: more types, greatly increased power and a rise in the importance of customers. To bring clarity to this complex situation, organization leaders need to find convincing answers to three questions:

- Who are our stakeholders?
- What is their relative priority?
- How can their interests be linked?

These questions were included in the research described later in this chapter (p. 14). Results highlighted significant differences between businesses and non-profits. For companies, shareholders were No.1 stakeholder, for non-profits, the customer dominated (Table 1.2):

Table 1.2

Prioritization of stakeholders (%)			
No. 1 stakeholder	Companies	Non-profits	Total
• Finance provider	50	4	29
• Customer	33	70	50
• Employee	17	19	18
• Other	—	7	3
TOTAL	**100**	**100**	**100**

Source: 96 of the 125 organizations interviewed in 1999/2000

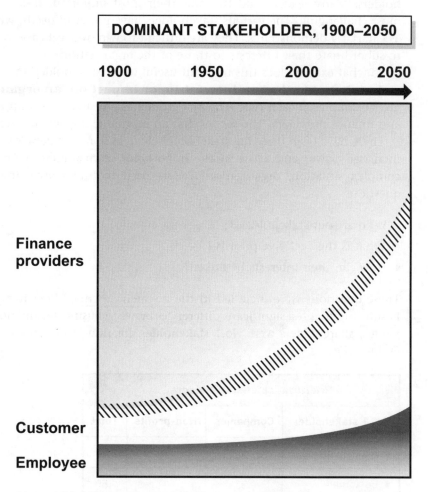

CHART
1.5 Customers will be tomorrow's dominant stakeholder

DOMINANT STAKEHOLDER, 1900–2050

| 1900 | 1950 | 2000 | 2050 |

Finance providers

Customer

Employee

Note: This chart is illustrative of trends, not based on quantified research

__THE SOURCE__

1 Notably the Service profit chain concept, developed by researchers at Harvard Business School. See James L. Heskett, W. Earl Sasser Jr and Leonard A. Schlesinger, *The Service Profit Chain* (Free Press, 1997).

2 Conversation with American Airlines.

3 Data from Alliance and Leicester Car Price Index, based on estimated actual prices paid. A Competition Commission Enquiry, criticizing car price levels, and activity by the media and the Consumers Association also influenced this price decline.

Managing conflicting stakeholder needs

It's the job of senior management to anticipate and resolve conflicts between stakeholders. Otherwise their organization will resemble a rowing eight with oars all pulling in different directions. The boat will eventually crack under the pressures and break up without going anywhere.

Half the organizations interviewed actively aligned their stakeholders. A typical CEO comment was, "To achieve value for shareholders, you must have very satisfied customers and employees." A non-profits leader said, "You must link stakeholders, but in doing so you have to establish a priority starting point. In our case, it's people's needs." Now academic research[1] is establishing robust linkages between customer commitment, employee motivation and shareholder value, something many business leaders already understood. However, understanding stakeholder linkages is not enough. They must be **managed** and aligned.

To successfully manage conflicting stakeholder needs, organization leaders need to unite them through strong vision and values, and recognize how they are changing. We have already seen that customers are the most important stakeholder in the non-profits researched, and in business they should continue to gain at the expense of finance providers, as **Chart 1.5** forecasts.

The development of customers as key stakeholders has not reached fruition. From the moneychangers of Greek/Roman times to the second half of the twentieth century, finance providers have been the dominant stakeholders in business. As Table 1.2 above shows, the balance of power is moving rapidly towards the customer. In the 1980s and 1990s increasingly informed customers exploited overcapacity in most markets.

Today's consumers pick and choose, discriminating on price or quality. Pan American and TWA were America's largest international airlines in the 1970s, but are now history. Pan Am's demise was hastened by poor customer service. TWA was dominated for long periods by financial stakeholders and neglected customers. It's now been acquired by American Airlines and its brand name will be discontinued.[2]

Consumers activated the past decade's low inflation. For instance, in the UK, supported by politicians and the media, they questioned why prices for similar car models were much higher than in continental Europe. Faced by hollow answers, they pressed harder for good deals and cut back on purchases. The pressure worked, and by December 2000 new car prices had fallen by 10.4% against the previous year.[3]

Consumers also punish poor quality through publicity or legal action. Producers adopt a moral tone in describing them as disloyal or promiscuous, but consumers are merely leveraging their growing strength. Value comparisons from the Internet, active consumer groups and continuing overcapacity in goods and services, will make customers the dominant stakeholder in future decades.

CHART
1.6 **The Three Legs of the Committed
Enterprise**

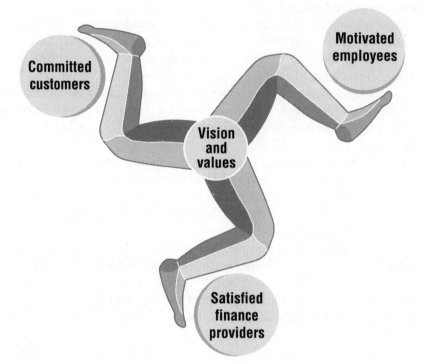

- The Three Legs of Mann is the ancient national symbol of the Isle of Man

- Its motto is, 'Whichever way you throw me, I stand'

- All three legs are connected and balanced

- Vision and values move the legs in the same direction

THE SOURCE

4 Interview with Percy Barnevik, Chairman of ASEA Brown Boveri and Investor AB.

5 Sir Michael Perry, Chairman of Centrica and former Chairman of Unilever, first suggested the Three Legs of Mann as a symbol for the three major constituents of organizations.

6 For simplicity, we have excluded other constituents, like communities, regulators, suppliers and legislators. They could be grouped under a fourth leg called 'external constituents'.

Meeting the challenge – the Committed Enterprise

Chart 1.6 summarizes the formula for the Committed Enterprise:

Committed Customers + Motivated Employees = Satisfied Resource Providers

It aligns the needs of stakeholders, and enables them to move forward together. Customers are the crucial leg, since they generate benefits or wealth for all the others, as Percy Barnevik points out:

The customer is the beginning and the end. The main constituent is the owner or shareholder, but he will only succeed if customers are satisfied and employees motivated.[4]

Chart 1.6 uses a visual symbol dating back to Roman times.[5] The Three Legs of Mann represent motivated employees, committed customers and satisfied resource providers. We are calling this ideal the Committed Enterprise, because it succeeds in generating a high level of commitment from all main stakeholders.[6]

Table 1.3 illustrates the criteria for the Committed Enterprise, and enables you to appraise present and past employers.

Table 1.3

Criteria (max. 10 points for each)		Score
Vision	Is it memorable, motivating, customer-based?	
Values	Are they simple, memorable, measurable, linked to vision?	
Buy in	Do most people understand/agree with the vision, values?	
Action	Are vision and values practised in everyday decisions and behaviour?	
Customers	Are they committed rather than just satisfied?	
Employees	Do they like coming to work? Is turnover low?	
Resource providers	Do they believe future results will be positive?	
Other constituents	Do they feel emotional attachment?	
Employee atmosphere	Is it distinctive? Is there laughter and pressure?	
Measures	Are vision and values defined, measured and constantly reinforced?	
Your employer's (or former employer's) total score (max. 100)		

CHART
1.7

Example of a Committed Enterprise – the Mayo Clinic

1. Description	**Mayo Clinic.** Non-profit foundation, dating from 1889. Seven hospitals, integrated with medical research and education centres
2. Key stakeholders	Patients first, employees a close second
3. Hallmarks of Committed Enterprise	• Committed customers. Ranked second (after Johns Hopkins) in *US News Best Hospitals Survey, 2000* • Motivated employees. Staff turnover of nurses 4% p.a. versus 13% national average; physicians 3% p.a. • Satisfied finance providers. These are government, state, foundations and individuals
4. Vision	'The best care to every patient every day'
5. Values	Primary value is 'The needs of the patient come first.' Others include teamwork across disciplines, mutual respect, and commitment to quality
6. Brand proposition	'The needs of the patient come first'

THE SOURCE

7 Interview with Dr Hugh Smith, President, Mayo Clinic.

8 Article in *Mayo Today*, April 2000. For consistency, the word 'mission' in the statement has been replaced by 'vision'.

A Committed Enterprise – the Mayo Clinic[7]

Chart 1.7 illustrates the key elements of the Committed Enterprise, using the Mayo Clinic as an example. There is a clear definition of the key stakeholders and their linkage. The Mayo is single-minded about putting patients first. High calibre and well-motivated employees are the primary means for achieving this. Mayo's finance comes from four sources – paying patients, state or government payments through Medicare, the Mayo Foundation, and private donors. One of the myths about the Mayo is that most of its patients are rich and famous. In fact one-third are on Medicare, and costs are similar to other health care providers.

The three hallmarks in Chart 1.7 cover the main stakeholders. Customer commitment is based on the *US News*, *Best Hospitals Survey*, conducted annually. In this survey 2550 certified specialists are asked to identify the five US hospitals they consider the best, ignoring location and expense. Hospitals are ranked on reputational score, mortality rate, technology services, nurse-to-bed ratios, and facilities. Mayo Clinic and Johns Hopkins have shared the top two places in recent years. Patient satisfaction surveys are also done at the Mayo.

Level of employee motivation is measured by staff turnover, and regular employee surveys. Another useful measure is percentage of job offers accepted by physicians – in Mayo's case, around 90%.

The Mayo vision dates back to its guiding principle, articulated by co-founder, Dr William Mayo: 'The best interest of the patient is the only interest to be considered.' It also emphasizes the integration of patient care, research and medical education. The three interlocking Mayo shields symbolize this. There are no names on the shields, underlining co-operation across functions.

An important value is teamwork, both across departments, and between different types of staff. It is built into the Mayo's system in a number of ways:

- **Remuneration**. Physicians are rewarded by salaries only. There are no incentive or productivity bonuses.
- **Board members** are elected as individuals. There is no representation based on function.
- **No star system**. When professors are appointed, there is no tenure or extra money.
- **Recruitment.** Most new physicians are selected from Mayo Medical School, having already absorbed the Mayo vision and values. Last year there were 3500 applications for 42 places at Mayo Medical School.

As Dr Michael Wood, President, Mayo Foundation, has stated: 'Our vision and values affect all that we do – our patient encounters, our decision-making, our planning and our goal setting.'[8]

CHART
1.8 **Organization leaders interviewed on vision and values**

	UK	USA	Total
Business	44	26	70
Education	15	12	27
Hospitals/police	3	9	12
Arts/charities	3	13	16
Total	**65**	**60**	**125**

Learning from 125 organizations – the research base

To extend this book's base of evidence, leaders of 125 organizations were interviewed, using 18 open-ended questions on 'making vision and values work'. Of these, 18 were applicable to all organizations, 3 were not. Interviews lasted 45–60 minutes on average, and took place in 45 different locations, between August 1999 and October 2000. The author conducted 90% face to face, and the rest by phone. In most cases the head of the organization was interviewed. **Chart 1.8** gives a breakdown of companies seen, by sector and country.

Objectives of the research were fourfold:

- To identify how vision and values were managed.
- To establish best practice.
- To evaluate how well organizations performed by type of best practice, and by companies and non-profits.
- To obtain examples and insights.

The author targeted organizations with above average performance, aiming for a reasonably even split between the USA and UK, and companies versus non-profits. Most US companies were in the top quartile of *Fortune* magazine's 'Most Admired Companies', while colleges and hospitals scored well in *US News* surveys. Many of the UK companies were international, e.g. BP, AstraZeneca, Diageo. Capitalization of all companies interviewed was $2.6 trillion, equivalent to over 20% of American GNP.

State schools visited in California and Southern England tended to be good performers in difficult socio-demographic areas. Some organizations could not be ranked, but had global reputations, e.g. New York Philharmonic, Rockefeller Foundation, Save the Children, New York Police, FBI, the Metropolitan Police (Scotland Yard), and the Red Cross.

Obtaining the desired interviews proved difficult and time-consuming. It rapidly became apparent that cold call approaches generated a low response, especially from CEOs. Interviews were therefore conducted with personally known leaders of effective organizations, who recommended others meeting the specification.

Those interviewed are listed on pages xii–xxi. The Appendix shows the questions asked. Since questions were open-ended, spreadsheets were constructed for over 200 hours of content analysis. This evaluated type of vision and values; processes used; linkages between vision and values, key success factors and brand propositions; methods of communication; type of measurement; integration of activities, and other practical topics.

Results of the research are summarized in Chapter 3 and quotes from interviews are spread throughout the book.

Did everyone tell the truth as they saw it? Yes, I think they did, with two exceptions.

Chapter

How vision and values create Committed Enterprises

Overview

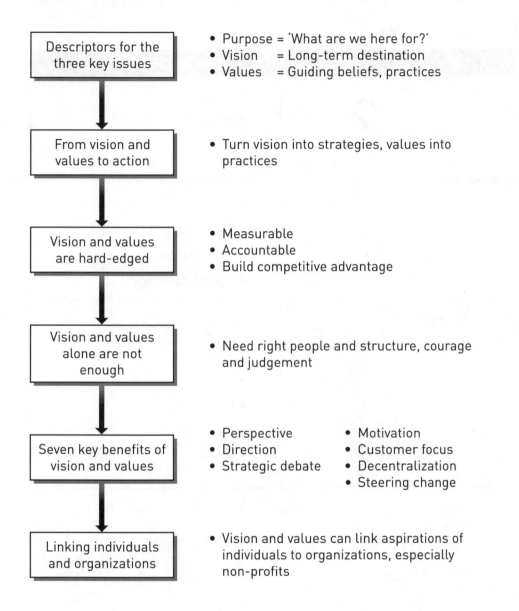

Descriptors for the three key issues	• Purpose = 'What are we here for?' • Vision = Long-term destination • Values = Guiding beliefs, practices
From vision and values to action	• Turn vision into strategies, values into practices
Vision and values are hard-edged	• Measurable • Accountable • Build competitive advantage
Vision and values alone are not enough	• Need right people and structure, courage and judgement
Seven key benefits of vision and values	• Perspective • Motivation • Direction • Customer focus • Strategic debate • Decentralization • Steering change
Linking individuals and organizations	• Vision and values can link aspirations of individuals to organizations, especially non-profits

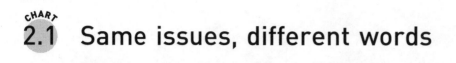

CHART 2.1 Same issues, different words

Issue		Possible descriptors
What are we here for?	**?**	• Purpose • Mission • Aim
Where are we going?		• Vision • Goal • Strategic intent • Destination • Future direction
What beliefs will guide our behaviour?		• Values • Credo • Ethos • Principles • Guidelines • Rules

What's the meaning of all this?

In the past two decades, organization leaders have begun to speak with religious zeal, using words like 'mission', 'vision' and 'values'. They refer to 'purpose', 'strategic intent', 'practices', as **Chart 2.1** shows. But still they hang on to the simple 'goals', 'objectives' and 'strategies' of earlier times. Some of these terms are used interchangeably. Most are ill defined. This section establishes how they will be used in this book.

Based on interviews with 125 organization leaders, there was broad agreement on three issues for every organization. These are also the fundamental questions of life:

- What are we here for?
- Where are we going?
- What beliefs will guide us on the journey?

That's where the consensus ended. The fun began in selecting the words to describe the answers. Many people cringe at the word 'mission', preferring 'purpose'. 'Mission' and 'vision' are often confused or combined. Life would be a lot simpler if there were fewer words to choose from and Chart 2.1 illustrates some of those in use. However, as long as all three fundamental questions are addressed, the words chosen don't matter. Each organization should adopt those it feels most comfortable with.

For consistency, this book will use 'purpose', 'vision' and 'values' to describe the three fundamental questions, as follows:

- **Purpose** covers 'What are we here for?'
- **Vision** handles 'Where are we going?' in the long term.
- **Values** answers 'What beliefs will guide us on the journey?'

Over 90% of organization leaders interviewed felt comfortable with these words, although they didn't always use them.

Purpose and vision have to be deliberately created by management. Values always exist, good and bad, in every organization. They circulate like air. The most difficult of the three to develop is the vision, because it requires imagination and a bold view of the future. Perhaps that is why some organizations combine purpose and vision into a single statement. This is often 95% purpose, and neatly side-steps the demanding challenge of developing a vision.

Once vision and values have been agreed they can be translated into action through **objectives**, **strategies**, and **plans**. **Branding** the organization's vision and values, so that their internal and external expression are inseparable, is also crucial, and this is covered in Chapter 10.

CHART
2.2 Linking purpose, vision, values and brand

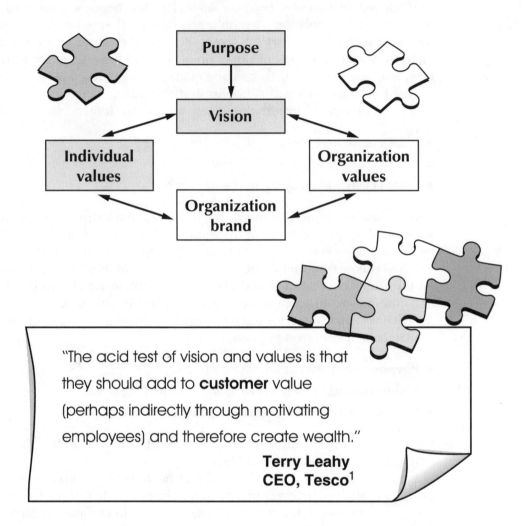

"The acid test of vision and values is that they should add to **customer** value (perhaps indirectly through motivating employees) and therefore create wealth."

**Terry Leahy
CEO, Tesco**[1]

The brand connects our employees, our customers, our products and our core values.[2]

The problem with 'mission', 'vision' and 'values' is their emotive and trendy connotations that repel business people in particular. By contrast, words like 'objectives', 'strategies' and 'plans' sound practical and emotionally neutral. When you say, "I've got a strategy", people respond, "Fine, let's see it!" They know what you're talking about and what to expect. But, try saying, "I've got a vision!" and watch people edge away.

Vision has been enshrined in academic literature as a magic potion. Yet, like strategy, it's neither a good nor a bad thing. It is neutral, requiring more perspiration than inspiration, and can be well or poorly designed. It doesn't protect organizations from competitive or performance pressures and is no substitute for good judgement, smart people or excellent execution. Vision is just another management tool for giving an organization a sense of future direction. It may help or hinder, just like strategies.

Objectives, strategies and plans meet vision and values and convert them into action. So **Chart 2.2** is incomplete. It should continue on from 'organization brand' as in Figure 2.1 on the left.

Objectives and targets plot how to reach the vision, in a series of 3-year steps. These point in the general direction of the vision, but rarely follow a straight line. They are precise and quantified. **Strategies** provide the 'How' – the specific means for meeting the objectives and targets. **Structures** should facilitate achievement of vision and values, encouraging cross-departmental cooperation, as in the case of the Mayo Clinic (pages 11 and 12). **Plans** turn strategies into detailed action, to be **implemented and measured**. Every step is imbued by values, which govern behaviour and decision-making.

Figure 2.1 From vision and values to action

THE SOURCE

1 The world's most profitable grocery retailer.

2 Howard Schultz, *Put your Heart into It* (Hyperion: 1997). Schultz, Chairman and CEO, Starbucks, uses the word 'partners' – Starbucks' word for employees. Because 'partners' has such a wide range of meanings, it has been replaced by 'employees' in the quote.

CHART
2.3
The vision and value drivers are hard-edged

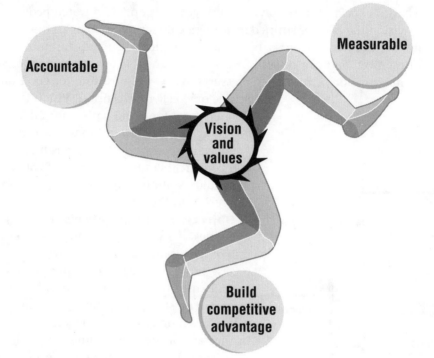

- Committed Enterprises are tough in implementing vision and values
- This benefits all their constituents
- Vision is the navigator of the Committed Enterprise, values are its motor

The vision and value drivers are hard-edged

As the Three Legs of Mann symbol indicates, the Committed Enterprise is driven by vision and values. Vision pictures a future destination, and the route is charted through strategies. Values define the principles guiding the organization on its future path. Both determine how people behave and make decisions every day.

Words like 'vision and values' may conjure up images of nice people, cosy places to work, or impractical aspirations. **Not so**. Committed Enterprises are challenging to work in, full of hard-driving people, wedded to their customers and insistent on getting results.

A Committed Enterprise is tough to work for. Individuals have demanding performance targets, exciting futures and the opportunity to realize their personal vision and values through a like-minded organization. It is invigorating and satisfying to work with such companies as a customer – the Chairman and CEO of Jaguar said that in meetings with Unipart, a major supplier: "You wouldn't know who was on the Unipart side and who was on the Jaguar side. I believe that both organizations feel that they are as one."[3]

And Committed Enterprises make formidable competitors, because they are dedicated to providing superior customer and shareholder value.

So how can vision and values, which sound so soft, be hard-edged and practical? In stepping forth into the unknown, future visions require imagination, faith, and courage. Crafting the Vision Statement is only the beginning. Visions become real when the statement is imprinted in the minds of members of the organization, and translated into hard-edged objectives and strategies. Values, too, remain mere words until translated into measurable practices. These become the benchmark for behaviour and decision-making, the basis for appraisal, promotion and rewards.

A Committed Enterprise with strong vision and values is principled yet hard on performance, like Johnson & Johnson:

"We believe nothing is to be gained by short cuts. People at J&J are here for the long term and you reap what you sow – that is the core of the company. Values lead to long-term results. Some companies are driven by results or values – you must get both, and there is zero tolerance at J&J for not reaching targeted commitments."[4]

The real test of vision and values lies not in the statements agreed by senior executives, but in the actions of people way down the organization. Vision and values are sometimes a figment of management's imagination. If your service engineers, telesales people and receptionists don't know what your vision and values are, then they don't exist.

THE SOURCE

3 Comment by Nick Scheele, then Chairman and CEO, Jaguar Cars, now COO, Ford USA.
4 Interview with Robert Darretta, Chief Financial Officer, Johnson & Johnson.

CHART
2.4

Vision and values are not the only thing

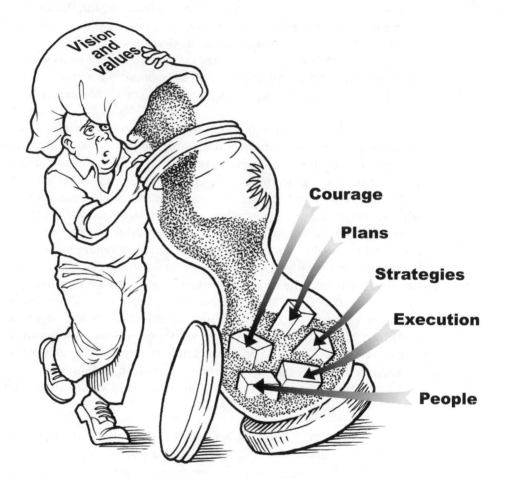

Vision and values are not the only thing

Management books tend to offer quick-fix solutions to everything, pandering to the ready market for miracle cures. Just as the best solution to obesity is to eat less, so success in management is dependent not on fancy techniques, but on good judgement, courage, determination, hard work and enthusiasm.

While the application of compelling vision and values will increase any organization's chance of success – this alone is never enough. Other things are necessary, in addition to the personal qualities already described. Things like the right kind of people, the ability to make things happen, structures that encourage teamwork, and a culture which accepts change, as **Chart 2.4** illustrates.

The experience of Harley Davidson demonstrates that while vision and values are great drivers, they need to be instilled into everything. They are the beginning not the end. They depend for their success on courage, strategies, and excellent implementation.

Harley Davidson virtually owned the market for high-powered motorcycles in the 1960s, but by the early 1980s its market share of 650cc+ machines had plummeted to 15.2% from over 70%.

In the 1970s, it endured the travails of top-down fixes, lack of cash, a leveraged buyout and downsizing, with a 40% workforce cut in 1982. Quality, morale and performance had sagged.

In 1982–6, the blood loss was staunched. Some recovery began. Costs were cut, quality and productivity improved. Cash pressures were reduced by a public flotation in 1985. Market share started to climb up – a little.

In 1987, a new CEO, Rich Teerlink, was appointed, determined to move from survival to renewal. The story of the subsequent transformation is inspiring. By 1999, market share had raced up to 49.5%.

How? Not by vision and values alone. Paradoxically, the vision developed in 1989, and revised in 1994, was not exactly enthralling: 'To be a leader in continuous improvement in mutually beneficial relationships with all our stakeholders.'

Five values were agreed in 1989:

- Tell the truth

- Be fair

- Keep your promises

- Respect the individual

- Encourage intellectual curiosity

Five issues were also selected – quality, participation, productivity, flexibility and cash flow. It was recognized that Harley Davidson would have to succeed on all these issues in order to reach its vision.

CHART
2.5

Emotional commitment is based on belief and hope

MEN WANTED for hazardous journey. Small wages , bitter cold, long months of complete darkness, constant danger, safe return doubtful, honour and recognition in case of success.

- Job advertisement for Shackleton's 1914 Antarctic Expedition
- 5000 applied, 27 chosen
- Expedition failed, yet became legendary

The key to Harley Davidson's success was the way in which it implemented its vision and values. Linking to **Chart 2.4**, this included:

- The belief and resilience of its leaders, who had the courage to persist with the vision and values, through setbacks and disappointments.

- Strong and continuous communications with all stakeholders, creating trust and confidence.

- Complete overhaul of information systems, appraisal and rewards, and new product development.

- Structural change from top-down management to individual enterprise.

- Emphasis on processes and behaviours, to bring the vision and values to life on a daily basis, for every employee.[5]

How emotional commitment differs from mere satisfaction

Harley Davidson is a Committed Enterprise. Employees appreciate its values, reputation and products, and like working there. Customers are committed to the brand, and many are members of the Harley Owners Group, the world's largest motorcycle club. And shareholders, some also employees, have achieved good returns.

There's a big difference, though, between the emotional commitment people feel for Harley Davidson and their satisfaction with, say, a Ford pick-up truck. Satisfied customers still switch brands, often: Seventy per cent of car buyers in the USA claim to be satisfied, yet 35% switch brands when they buy a new vehicle.

Those emotionally committed to an organization may stay with it through difficult times, as **Chart 2.5** and this example show:

Newcastle United is both a well-known English soccer club and a listed company. Its history is long and distinguished, but it has failed to win a major competition for 45 years, and the owners have behaved contemptuously towards loyal supporters. Two senior board members allegedly made insulting remarks about Newcastle women to an undercover journalist and questioned the ability of the club's leading player (idolized by supporters).

They resigned, but were later reinstated. Other Board members resigned, and this further undermined the Club's image with outside investors.

Throughout this saga Newcastle remained one of the best-supported clubs in Europe, and subsequently persuaded a famous manager to join it.

Why are Newcastle supporters so committed, despite mediocre results? Because the club represents the spirit of the community, linked to a great heritage. And because they think things will get better in future.

THE SOURCE

5 Example derived from Rich Teerlink and Lee Ozley, *More than a Motor Cycle* (HBS Press, 2000).

CHART
2.6 Seven key benefits of vision and values

Seven key benefits of vision and values	
Vision	**Vision and values**
1. Perspective	4. Customer focus
2. Future direction	5. Motivation
3. Strategic debate	6. Decentralization
	7. Steering change

THE SOURCE

6 H.A.L. Fisher, *History of Europe* (Edward Arnold, 1949).

This phenomenon is not peculiar to Newcastle. It applies to local and national sports teams everywhere.

Emotional commitment is based on faith and hope, on a vision of better things ahead. That's why excellent employees will sometimes tolerate quite long periods of unsatisfactory management and poor results. This has often been the case in the British National Health Service.

The Roman Empire was one of the most successful organizations in world history. At the time of Julius Caesar, it stood for peace, clemency, order and justice. These values were translated into a professional civil service, a sound legal system, statistical surveys and public accounts. Caesar's able successor, Tiberius, was followed by three disastrous Emperors – a madman (Caligula), a pedant (Claudius) and a monster (Nero).[6] However, they spent most of their time at 'head office' in Rome. People elsewhere in this international organization continued to do a good job, and the Empire's values and systems were so strong that they survived this sustained period of poor leadership for centuries.

How vision and values create Committed Enterprises

The 125 organization leaders interviewed saw seven benefits in pursuing the clear vision and values that create Committed Enterprises, and here they are:

Table 2.1

Seven key benefits of vision and values	
Perspective	Know where you are
Direction	Know where you're going
Strategic debate	Learn on the journey
Customer focus	Eyes down on the top priority
Motivation	Enjoy the journey
Decentralization	People know what to do
Steering change	Keep moving forward

Perspective You can pinpoint your present location by being aware of where you've come from and where you're heading. Otherwise you'll just amble through featureless terrain, muttering, "I'm not sure where I am, so I'll keep on walking until I find out." Unfortunately you're unlikely to arrive.

You can develop a series of objectives and strategies without a long-term direction, but they'll take you on a zigzag path as **Chart 2.7** shows. Eventually the food and water will run out.

CHART 2.7 Vision gives perspective and direction

> If you don't know where you're going, any road will take you there
> **The Koran**

THE SOURCE

7 Interview with Lord Browne, CEO, BP.

8 Interview with Hamish Taylor, CEO, Eurostar.

9 J.Hugh Davidson, *Offensive Marketing* (Penguin, 1987). For details of Tetra-Pak's vision, values and strategies, see pp 174–81.

Vision places objectives and strategies in a larger context.

It "enables you to see them in perspective, and to understand their significance".[7]

"If there is no vision, you just have a long list of commercial objectives and no idea of how they fit together."[8]

Direction   The path to the future is littered with signposts. Developing a vision forces you to look at them, and decide which one(s) to take. This can be done partly by a process of elimination, partly by thinking hard about the final two or three that present themselves as alternatives.

Betting the future on a single signpost may be the right thing to do. It made the Rausings one of the richest families in the world:

Tetra-Pak is the international leader in flexible packaging for milk, juice and other liquids. It was founded by Dr Ruben Rausing in Sweden, and remains family controlled. By 1965 he had six companies, but against the advice of many of his friends, sold five of them. He decided to concentrate all his assets on one company – Tetra-Pak. This decision was based on his philosophy of 'minimizing risk via risk maximization'. His reasoning was that by focusing heavy effort on one major market, and establishing a leadership position there, risk was minimized. As a philosophy, it is the opposite of spreading one's eggs across a number of baskets.[9]

An alternative, but more widely applied approach to future direction, is that of multiple paths, expressed by Lord Browne, CEO of BP:

"Vision alone is not enough since it would create uncoordinated activity. You need to express the unfolding steps which underpin the reality of the vision and these are not linear. Customers, population, society, are always moving, and you must move in response. You need multiple paths to the vision – prediction is a fool's game."[10]

Choosing single or multiple paths to the future trades off risk against focus. The single path involves high risk. Too many paths will diffuse effort. Once a future direction has been chosen, it should be consistently followed, even if the weather is bad, and the way forward isn't clear.

Sun Microsystems's vision of open systems, and computers as easy to operate as a mobile phone, was developed in 1987. "Our consistently followed vision has been the key to our success in the past 10 years. Without it, we would have become diverted and lost direction, like some of our competitors."[11]

And any future action should be checked against the future signpost(s) chosen. If it doesn't follow that direction, don't do it. A senior executive at a leading business school recognized this:

THE SOURCE

10 Interview with Lord Browne, CEO, BP.
11 Interview with Robert Youngjohns, VP, Sun Microsystems.

CHART 2.8 Vision and values must be customer focused – Levi's weren't[12]

 Vision → • Financial success and social commitment

 Values → • Diversity
• Empowerment
• Ethical management
• New behaviours
• Recognition
• Communications

Results → • Massive market share decline in 1990s

THE SOURCE

12 *Source:* Levi Strauss Aspirations Statement, 1987. The response to requests for a current statement of vision and values, in October 2000 and September 2001, was that they were being reviewed.

"Our vision is to be the best school of our kind. This requires avoidance of any activity that does not advance the vision. For instance, we are just reviewing a new program which can make us $3 million extra revenue. But I ask myself, 'Will it help us towards our vision?' I think the answer is 'No', and therefore we shouldn't do it. But what sort of idiot walks away from $3 million? The essence of vision and strategy is to walk away from things which may look sensible in isolation, but don't move you forward."[13]

Strategic debate Many organization leaders said that developing a vision forces everyone to get involved in a strategic debate and to think deeply about the future. "It is not easy to get senior managers who are operationally effective to . . . really think deeply about strategy."[14]

Open and constructive discussion about vision and values is a learning experience for all. People develop their views, face up to issues. They confront future reality rather than pass it by. The debate should involve people at different levels and from diverse backgrounds. The process will give them a better understanding of the questions, force them to consider opposing views, and help create commitment to the route eventually chosen.

Customer focus If your vision is not focused on the customer, it won't work. In the short-term, organizations can keep going or even look good by slashing costs, massaging the accounts, or milking the future. But in the longer-term, where vision operates, failure to satisfy customer needs will drive you into a brick wall.

Most organizations now recognize this, and when thoughts turn to future vision, it becomes more obvious. Questions like: 'Who are our main stakeholders?' and 'How do we serve them better?' quickly lead to the customer, as this school principal relates:

"When I joined the school, it was in decline and obviously run for the benefit of the teachers. I made it very clear to everyone that the school was there for the children and that children would always come first. Eventually the message started to get through. We have doubled the number of children attending the school in the past 5 years and now have a waiting list." [15]

The experience of Levi Strauss in the 1990s demonstrates the dangers of vision and values which are not customer focused:

Levi Strauss is a fine company, but has experienced a torrid decade, with USA market share almost halving, from 48% in 1990 to 25% in 1998. Its values were admirable, but were they relevant? And where was the picture of the customer in the vision? (See **Chart 2.8**).

Robert Haas, the CEO, 'was intent on showing that a company driven by social values could outperform a company hostage to profits alone'.[16] Since 1996, when the company went private, he has been accountable only to three relatives.

┌─ THE SOURCE ───

13 Interview with Eitan Zemel, Vice Dean, Stern Business School, New York University.
14 Interview with Sir Michael Angus, Chairman of Whitbread, former Chairman Unilever.
15 Interview with Principal of a State School in London.
16 Nina Munk, 'How Levi's Trashed a Great American Brand', *Fortune*, 12 April 1999.

Vision and values build motivation

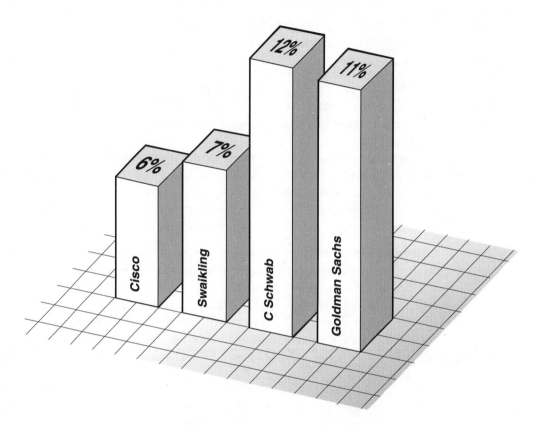

**Annual executive turnover at four companies
with strong vision and values**[17]

┌ THE SOURCE

17 *Fortune*, 8 January 2001.
18 Nina Munk, 'How Levi's Trashed a Great American Brand', *Fortune*, 12 April 1999.
19 Questions derived from interview with CEO of successful global consumer marketer.
20 Interview with Jack Duffy, Senior VP Strategy, United Parcel Service.
21 *Fortune*, 8 January 2001.
22 Interview with Lord Browne, CEO, BP.

Ironically, the Levi Strauss vision and values were implemented effectively. The company pulled out of China – to protest human rights abuses. Compensation plans were changed so that one third of executives' bonuses reflected their ability to manage aspirationally. A global sourcing task force spent 9 months building labour practice guidelines for overseas contractors. Eighty task forces were assigned to make the company more aspirational.

All this got in the way of customer focus. Levi 'stopped innovating ... it ignored or was oblivious to the market place'.[18]

While Robert Haas is clearly a visionary, and still greatly admired, the vision and values were not sufficiently focused on the customer.

Levi Strauss is not the first organization to fall into this trap, and certainly won't be the last. Two questions for Anita Roddick of The Body Shop: 'Are the values relevant to the organization, or are they just the personal beliefs of the owners expressed through a corporate vehicle?' and 'How do the vision and values benefit the customer?'[19]

Motivation   Every organization wants to attract and retain talented people, who ask themselves things like: 'Does it know where it's going?'; 'What are its future prospects?'; 'Is it the sort of place I would enjoy working in?' Through vision and values an organization can help individuals decide whether it's the right place for them, so that, having joined, they will stay. As Napoleon said, in war "the moral is to the physical as three is to one".

"Values are as important as business models, especially in attracting and retaining good people in the E.com world."[20]

As **Chart 2.9** shows, voluntary executive turnover at four companies with strong vision and values is low for their industries, and it's no coincidence that all are in the top 25 at Fortune's 100 Best Companies to Work For.[21]

Effective decentralization   Vision and values provide a framework for everyday behaviour and decision-making. This enables delegation to people on the front line who are close to their customers, and increases job satisfaction for all. As organizations grow in size globally, their senior executives make only a tiny proportion of the daily decisions. Vision and values take much of the risk out of delegation:

"Decentralisation is necessary for people as well as businesses. They need to express themselves at work by doing things and making a difference. As an organization, you provide this opportunity by **creating space** between the core vision, strategies and values on the one hand, and local autonomy on the other. The space is highly motivating and is another aspect of one of our key values – mutuality."[22]

CHART

2.10 Linking individual and organization values

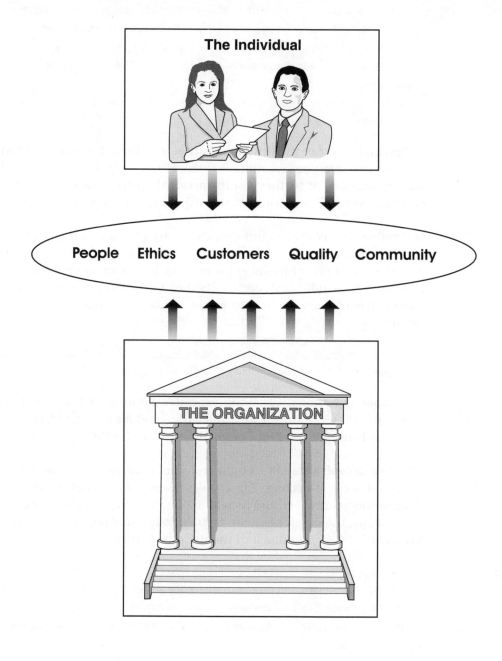

THE SOURCE

23 Interview with Bob Darretta, CFO, Johnson & Johnson.
24 Interview with Hal Burlingame Jr, Executive VP, AT&T Wireless.

If you are CEO of a global company, and new trade terms have to be negotiated with major customers in Thailand, you lack the knowledge to do it. But your local Sales VP, armed with an understanding of your vision and values and local knowledge, would execute in the way you want, better than you could.

Steering change   Vision and values provide a blueprint for consistent change. They are the constant around which strategies and plans revolve, in responding to the turbulent external environment.

"Vision and values are a way to compress the timescale for change, and to accelerate it."[23]

"Values provide both a guidance system for making cuts in appropriate places and ways, and a common platform for change."[24]

Linking the aspirations of individuals and organizations

Vision and values are a medium for linking individuals and organizations. Too often they remain paper-based and fail to soar into hearts and minds.

People work for more than profit or personal gain.[25] **Customers** are loyal to organizations which really understand their needs, build strong relationships and provide superior value.

People don't have to be where they are, for the most part. If the hopes, dreams and values of an organization's leadership differ too much from their own . . . some simply hunker down and become compliant . . . others find someplace else to work, where they're more in synch.[26]

An organization is a collection of individuals dealing with other individuals. To succeed it has to align the vision and values of these individuals with its own. In that way it becomes an Emotional Organization for those people who work for and with it. This applies to both vision and values:

A vision must give people the feeling their lives and work are intertwined.[27]

Visions provide the opportunity for individuals to grow and achieve on a grand scale.[28]

A Living Company will have members . . . who believe the goals of the company allow and help them achieve their own individual goals.[29]

"Managers are not loyal to a particular boss or even a company, but to a set of values they believe in, and find satisfying."[30]

── THE SOURCE ──

25 James C. Collins and Jerry I. Porras, *Built to Last* (Random House Business Books, 2000).

26 Rich Teerlink and Lee Ozley, *More than a Motorcycle* (HBS Press, 2000).

27 Mark Lipton, 'Demystifying the Development of an Organisational Vision'; *Sloan Management Review*, 1996, vol. 37.

28 David Kirk (Captain of All Blacks rugby team), 'World Class Teams', *McKinsey Quarterly*, no.4, 1992.

29 Arie de Geus, *The Living Company* (HBS Press, 1997).

30 Goran Lindahl, Former CEO, Asea Brown Boveri (ABB).

CHART
2.11 What they say isn't what they do

THE SOURCE

31 Interview with Peter Melchett, Former Director, Greenpeace UK.
32 Interview with Robert Youngjohns, Vice President, Sun Microsystems.
33 Interview with Vice President of a global company, identity withheld.

It is easier to link the aspirations of individuals to non-profit organizations, where vision and values may be the primary motivation, and making a living secondary, than in businesses, where the reverse usually applies.

Lord Melchett, former UK Director of Greenpeace, said:

"Unlike commercial organizations, we have to do little to encourage our staff to adopt our vision and values. There's a unity between Greenpeace values and the values of the individuals joining it – most work here to realize and put into practice their own values through an organization. Greenpeace achieves a lot with quite limited resources (only 80 staff in the UK, 1000 world-wide) in part because all of us are driven by strong values and beliefs.

Not that everyone agrees with every detail of our policies and priorities. Internally we are argumentative, but Greenpeace staff are highly motivated by working for an organization whose values they themselves so strongly support."[31]

Vision and values – searching for the truth

How do you know whether an organization's loudly trumpeted vision ever gets implemented? Or if a set of values represents the rose-tinted hopes of senior executives, rather than the grinding reality of everyday behaviour? You can't. Vision is always hard to implement. Real values invariably differ from stated or official ones. And the Board's view will inevitably vary from that of front-line employees discussing the organization in a bar after work:

"There is always a big gap between stating vision and making it happen. The more senior you are, the bigger the problem, since you think by saying things you make them happen, when in practice, nothing happens."[32]

Chart 2.11 illustrates how stated values differ from real ones in a long-established global company, undergoing radical change:

What this company had intended was to graft on to the existing stated values new values of speed and bottom line focus, but as you can see, it's all going badly wrong. A senior VP there said: "I would never have believed it possible to destroy values built up over five decades in less than 5 years."[33]

The company traditionally had a very strong customer commitment, but this was being eroded by cost reductions, and a policy of pushing things to breaking point, then, too late, trying to fix them. The strong service ethic needed to be sharpened, not violated.

Integrity was also sacrificed in pursuit of quick bottom line results. Things said to customers were reinvented, pricing lacked transparency, and trust was declining. The gap between stated and real values kept widening.

2.12 Why tomorrow's society will demand more Committed Enterprises

More customer power	Wider choice, improving information via Internet, drive for value
More employee choice	Greater competition for good people, declining loyalty
More sophisticated finance providers	Looking beyond yesterday's results ...to tomorrow's prospects
Powerful external constituents	NGOs, communities, regulators, making bigger demands

Why tomorrow's society will demand more Committed Enterprises

Customer power   Customers have wide choice, and improving information. Their bargaining power is growing exponentially. Every day they become harder to gain and retain – loyalty is declining in almost every category.

Employee choice   Competition for talented people is greater than ever. They will join and stay with organizations whose vision and values fit their own aspirations. Most build their working life around a series of experiences with different organizations. The concept of company loyalty is fading fast in an environment where 'downsizing' is a regular occurrence. Employees see no reason why they should be loyal to organizations which don't care about them as individuals.

More sophisticated finance providers   Shareholders and analysts are increasingly looking beyond raw financial performance figures to the things that drive them, like customer loyalty, innovation and investment in the future. The concept behind Kaplan and Norton's Balanced Scorecard has struck a nerve, and it is being widely applied by companies.[34] Donors to non-profit organizations, often successful entrepreneurs, are applying hard-nosed business principles and insisting on more rigorous measurements of benefits.

Powerful external constituents   External constituents such as consumer and environmental groups, the media, regulators, local communities, legislators and the general public are constantly probing the conduct of organizations, and questioning their values.

Adopting the principles of the Committed Enterprise will help all types of organization to face these future trends successfully.

THE SOURCE

34 Robert Kaplan and David Norton, *The Balanced Scorecard* (HBS Press, 1996). The authors outline a management system to measure current performance and to target future performance. The Balanced Scorecard takes companies beyond the conventional yardsticks of sales, profit and cash flow. It covers four main categories: financial performance, customer knowledge, internal business processes, learning and growth.

The seven best practices for creating the Committed Enterprise

Overview

Seven Best Practices

1. Building foundations
2. Strong vision
3. Strong values
4. Communication

5. Embedding
6. Branding the organization
7. Measurement

Performance of organizations researched

- 21% met 6–7 of the best practices
- Companies and non-profits got similar results
- Companies better on embedding, measurement
- Non-profits better on strong vision, branding

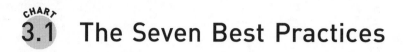

CHART
3.1 The Seven Best Practices

Seven Best Practices (BP) in making vision and values work		
Steps		**Definition**
BP No. 1	**Building foundations**	Needs of key stakeholders understood and linked through vision and values
BP No. 2	**Strong vision**	Vision is memorable, clear, motivating, ambitious, customer-related, translated into measurable strategies
BP No. 3	**Strong values**	Values support the vision, are based on key factors for success, and turned into measurable practices
BP No. 4	**Communication**	Consistent communication by action, signals, words
BP No. 5	**Embedding**	Recruitment, training, appraisal, rewards, promotion and succession, all reflect values
BP No. 6	**Branding**	Organization's branding expresses vision and values
BP No. 7	**Measurement**	Rigorous measurement of how effectively vision and values are implemented

CHART
3.2 Best Practice No. 1 – linking stakeholders

COMMITTED

Committed Customers
+
Motivated Employees
=
Satisfied Resource Providers

ENTERPRISE

THE SOURCE

1 Interview with Douglas Sweeney, VP, Business Strategy, IBM.
2 Interview with Robert Youngjohns, VP, Sun Microsystems.

Best practice defined

Based on research (Chapter 1, p. 14), seven key steps in making vision and values work were identified. They were developed by considering two simple questions for each organization:

- How successful has it been in implementing vision and values, and what are the reasons for success, or failure?
- What practices and processes worked best?

The seven steps in best practice management of vision and values apply to every type of organization. **Chart 3.1** describes and defines them. Each of the seven best practices introduced here is covered individually in later chapters.

The Seven Best Practices

Best Practice No. 1 – building foundations, linking stakeholders

The best practice formula is that of the Committed Enterprise, based on the three legs symbol:

committed customers + motivated employees = satisfied resource providers.

Strong vision and values are the focal point which unites these three main stakeholders. If they are constantly at war, it will be impossible to make vision and values work. If there is friction and politics, much time will be wasted.

At IBM, customers, employees and partners are linked to its vision of the world's premier knowledge management company. So is the key value of customers first. As Lou Gerstner said: "A customer is now running IBM." At all his management meetings, two key charts are always shown – IBM customer satisfaction relative to competition, and market share.[1]

In many companies, such as Microsoft, United Parcel Service (UPS) and Procter & Gamble, the linkages are enhanced by employee ownership of shares.[2] UPS, which adopted a new vision in 1999, is exceptional in this respect – 80% of shares are held by present or former employees.

The best schools are very skilful in linking their stakeholders – children, parents and teachers. Over 75% of schools interviewed achieved best practice. Their task is eased by scale (number of stakeholders is small compared to a global company), and by the ability of principals to meet everyone in a single location, on a frequent basis. By contrast, Oxford and Cambridge Universities have poor linkage between stakeholders, due to lack of clarity in allocation of authority and responsibility.

Best Practice No. 1 is covered in Chapter 4 – Building the Foundations of the Committed Enterprise.

CHART 3.3 Best Practice No. 2 – strong vision

Organization	Vision	Criteria			
		Memorable	Motivating	Customer-based	Turned into strategies
Sun Microsystems	To connect anyone, anywhere anytime – using almost anything – to the resources they need[3]	✓	✓	✓	✓
Mayo Clinic	The *best* care to every patient every day[4]	✓	✓	✓	✓
Priory School (Slough, UK)	Every child to achieve their educational potential, so accessing life's opportunities[5]	✓	✓	✓	✓

CHART 3.4 Best Practice No. 3 – strong values

Good match–Caltech[6]	
Key success factors	**Values**
• Excellent staff • Excellent students • Strong donor base	• Excellence in maths, science and engineering • Integrity • Innovation • Teamwork • Respect for people

THE SOURCE

3 Interview with Robert Youngjohns, VP, Sun Microsystems.
4 Interview with Dr Hugh Smith, President, Mayo Clinic.
5 Interview with Mrs Carole Evans, CBE, Head Teacher, Priory School, Slough, Berks.
6 Interview with Dr Tom Everhart, President Emeritus, Caltech.

Best Practice No. 2 – strong vision

Chart 3.3 shows some strong visions which meet criteria for best practice.

Vision is covered in Chapter 5, Measuring the Strength of the Vision, and Chapter 6, Timing and Building a New Vision.

Best Practice No. 3 – strong values

To qualify as strong, values must be translated into measurable practices. They should also help drive vision and be relevant to those things making the difference between success and failure for the organization – the key success factors (KSF).

KSF will differ by type of organization. For an airline, they might be safety, operational efficiency and customer service, while for an orchestra they could be artistic excellence, teamwork and financial results.

Chart 3.4 gives an example of a good match between KSF and values at Caltech. Caltech has a simple success formula – recruit the best staff to teach the best students. The one attracts the other. Caltech freshmen classes generally have the highest SAT scores in the USA, and over one-third of graduating seniors go on to take doctorates. A key Caltech principle is to stay small and excellent, with a maximum of 2000 students. The average A Caltech graduate has a 1 in 4000 chance of winning a Nobel Prize, based on historical data.

By contrast, here is an example of a poor match between KSF and values, from a significant European company:

Table 3.1

Poor match – European company[7]	
Key success factors	**Values**
• Customer service	• Fair and honest
• Low cost operation	• Community concern
• Innovation	• Innovation

Innovation is the only value that matches the KSF in this organization, and unfortunately it's not being achieved. The other values are worthy, but do not address the KSF. What's missing from the values is single-minded customer focus, and operational efficiency. Worthiness versus relevance in values need not be a choice – both can be achieved. Strong values are covered in Chapter 7, Creating Hard Values for Sustainable Advantage.

THE SOURCE

7 Interview with Chairman of company in the example.

CHART
3.5
Best Practice No. 6 – branding the organization

FBI: Branding the organization[8]	
Values	**Brand**
• Obedience to US Constitution • Respect for dignity of those we protect • Compassion • Fairness • Uncompromising integrity	• Fidelity • Bravery • Integrity

THE SOURCE

8 Interview with Rex Tomb and Philip Edney, FBI.
9 Interview with William Stavropoulos, Chairman, Dow Chemical.
10 Interview with Bob Darretta, Chief Financial Officer, Johnson & Johnson.
11 Interview with Rex Tomb and Philip Edney, FBI. Internal notice by Louis Freeh, Director. The reputation of the FBI was damaged by the tragic events of 11 September 2001.

Best Practice No. 4 – communication of vision and values

Best practice communication is achieved by actions that support the vision and values, illustration and explanation by senior management, and repetition, repetition, repetition:

"There's been a common thread in Dow Chemical values from the time of our founder, H.H. Dow, and in the past decade we've applied more systematic processes to ensure they are lived in action. All our executives talk about vision and values, illustrating their connection with growth and the bottom line. And we communicate the idea of consequences – for living or not living values. For instance, if any senior person was dismissed for breaching our ethical values, we would publish the general reasons for dismissal internally."[9]

As with any form of communication, you need to select a small number of clear ideas, and to repeat them consistently:

"The key is to boil down complexity into simple phrases which people understand."[10]

Communication is covered in Chapter 8, Emotional Activism – Communicating by Action, Signals and Words.

Best Practice No. 5 – embedding

Best practice occurs through implantation in the organization's systems, which are its bloodstream, outlasting any individuals. The most important systems affecting vision and values are recruitment criteria, training, personnel appraisal, promotion and rewards. New joiners therefore, will not only possess the necessary skills but also be attracted by the vision and values. Training will reflect these, and personal appraisal will be based both on what has been achieved (performance) and how (values). Rewards (covering salary, bonus and promotion) will encourage pursuit of the vision and values.

Best Practice No. 5 is covered in Chapter 9, Creating Systems to Embed Vision and Values.

Best Practice No. 6: branding the organization

One of the interview questions was: 'How does your organization differ from your brand?' Many leaders of non-profit organizations said: 'It doesn't, because they are the same thing'. They had branded their organization, so that its external face was similar to its internal one. This is apparent in the way the FBI is branded, as in **Chart 3.5**.

As FBI Director, Louis Freeh stated: "These core values are the fibre which holds together the vitality of our institution."[11]

Tesco, the international grocery retailer, is a very different organization from the FBI, but it sees things similarly:

CHART
3.6

Best Practice No. 7 – measurement

How Home Depot measures its values[12]		
Value	**Measures**	
Customer service	• Store exit interviews • Average purchase	• Market share
Giving back	• Community activities	• Community attitudes
Taking care of our people	• Employee attitude survey • Directors' store visits	• 360° appraisals • Employee turnover
Doing the right thing	• Employee survey • Employee complaints	• Safety record • Environmental initiatives

THE BIG DIY STORE

THE SOURCE

12 Interview with Faye Wilson, Senior VP Values and Director, Home Depot.
13 Interview with Terry Leahy, CEO, Tesco.

"Our corporate brand does not differ from the company. People at Tesco see themselves as part of the brand. Our values are closely aligned with it."[13]

The organization brand is the expression of vision and values, for all stakeholders. It is the flag that unites the efforts of employees and reveals the substance of the organization to customers. It comprises any element which sends out a message – people, behaviour, products, services or performance. The brand in this sense is much broader than advertising, and is not confined to customers.

Every organization is a brand, since people have a mental image of it. The US Supreme Court is an organization brand, so is the Zippy Cleaning Company, and so is General Motors. Best practice occurs when the brand reflects the organization's vision and values.

Best Practice No. 7 – measurement

Best practice rigorously evaluates how well vision and values are executed. Vision is translated into objectives and strategies; values into measurable practices.

Customer and employee satisfaction studies are important measures for companies and the larger non-profits. Others are employee turnover, safety, performance results and direct observation by senior managers.

Chart 3.6 illustrates how Home Depot measures four of its seven values, demonstrating that each value should be individually appraised. The measures are a mixture of the quantitative and anecdotal. Nothing is more important than the feel senior managers can develop for the pulse of an organization, by listening closely to employees and customers.

Best Practice No. 7 is covered in Chapter 11, The Hard-Edged Enterprise – Measurement.

Is each of the Seven Best Practices equally important?

No. All seven of the practices are important, but not equally so. Best Practice No. 2 and Best Practice No. 3 – strong vision turned into strategies, and strong values translated into practices – are the most important. These provide the engine and the steering wheel for all seven practices.

Best Practice No. 1 – aligning all stakeholders through a common vision – is also important, since its absence can cause delay or even gridlock.

Best Practices Nos. 4 to 7 – communication, embedding, branding and measurement – are ways to implement the vision and values efficiently. Of these, embedding and measurement matter most because they tie vision and values to recognition and rewards. Communication can be the least important of the seven, since strong vision and values, embedded in rewards, will spread of their own accord.

If vision and values are flawed, Best Practices Nos. 4 to 7 will make things worse, speeding the journey down the wrong road. This is like advertising an inferior product. The greater the number of people trying it, the faster the news of its inferiority spreads.

CHART 3.7 Percentage of organizations meeting all seven Best Practice standards

CHART 3.8 Percentage of organizations achieving Best Practice standards

No. of Best Practices achieved	Companies (n = 61)	Non-profit organizations (n = 51)
7	8	4
6	15	16
5	27	24
4	13	19
3 or less	37	37
Total	**100%**	**100%**

How organizations performed versus the seven Best Practice standards

The performance of the 125 organizations interviewed was ranked against each of the Best Practice standards. Thirteen were eliminated due to insufficient data, and the final sample size was 112. Evidence for rankings was the interview, which covered each best practice area, and background research about each organization.

As described earlier (Chapter 1, p. 14), the quality of organizations interviewed was way above average. An average sample would therefore achieve much lower rankings on best practice.

Main conclusions from the research were as follows:

- **Only 6% of organizations were ranked Best Practice on all seven criteria**. This is a small percentage, and indicates the big opportunity for managing vision and values better. A further 15% of organizations reached Best Practice on six criteria, but as many as 53% made the grade on only four criteria or less. **Chart 3.8** provides details.

These topline figures disguise important facts. As explained above, not all seven practices are equal. Strong vision and strong values are the most important two. If therefore one takes a score of six or seven, including strong vision and values, as a measure of high performance, only 19 organizations (17% of total) reached this level, as the Table 3.2 shows:

Table 3.2

Breakdown of 19 high performing organizations
• 9 companies
• 4 schools/colleges
• 4 charities/foundations
• 2 hospitals

- **While the calibre of organizations interviewed was high, their management of vision and values was uneven**. Few applied all seven of the Best Practices consistently. Many were strong in some, weak in others. Vision and values were often treated on a stop–start basis. They were rarely seen as a priority for active day-to-day management, like marketing, operations or finance.

Vision and values management is cross-functional, and clear responsibility for implementation needs to be established. In particular, there is often unclear responsibility for managing and measuring the organization brand. It is sometimes micro-managed inconsistently across many departments. Too much senior management effort was put into developing Vision and Values Statements, too little into making them work.

CHART
3.9 # Performance by type of Best Practice

Best Practice type	% Achieving Best Practice	
	Companies	Non-profits
No. 1. Building foundations	52	51
No. 2. Strong vision	34	(63)
No. 3. Strong values	67	71
No. 4. Communication	62	63
No. 5. Embedding through systems	(64)	41
No. 6. Organization branding	52	(81)
No. 7. Measurement	(66)	45
Overall average	**57%**	**59%**

- **Of the Seven Best Practices, the weakest performance area was strong vision, and the highest strong values.** Developing a powerful future vision is not easy, but strong values are easier to establish. Results for each of the Seven Best Practices are shown in **Chart 3.9**.

  Only 34% of companies were judged Best Practice on 'strong vision', compared with 63% of non-profit organizations (see Chart 3.9). This is not surprising, since the purpose of many non-profits is to realize a vision.

  Best Practice on 'strong vision' was judged on six criteria – memorable, clear, motivating, ambitious, customer-related and translated into strategies. Some organizations failed to reach the starting line because they had no vision. Of those with visions (in the sense of a strong sense of future direction), most fell short on two criteria – memorable and motivating.

  A vision was considered **memorable** if its rough sense could be repeated after two readings. It was judged **motivating** if likely to enthuse a bright graduate.

  Anyone reading a few dozen random Vision Statements by companies will be struck by their consistent dullness. Most are solid and uninspiring. Perhaps they have been written by committee, or are full of compromises designed to satisfy all stakeholders. If a vision doesn't move people, it's unlikely to work.

  Here are some of the best visions encountered in the research – though few set the blood racing:

  To make London the safest city in the world

  SCOTLAND YARD

  To halt environmental abuse and promote environmental solutions

  GREENPEACE

  To be the best in research, education and patient care, and to support the community

  UCLA MEDICAL CENTER

  Most organizations scored well on the criteria 'customer-related', and 'translated into strategies'.

- **The research confirms that companies have much to learn from non-profits about vision and values management, and vice versa.**

  One of the hypotheses behind this book was the opportunity for cross-learning between companies and non-profits. The size of this opportunity is evident from the research.

  Many business leaders work with non-profits on a voluntary basis, and it is clear that they have much to contribute. US companies often have non-profit leaders on their Boards (though European companies generally don't), and the research demonstrates why this is a good thing.

  As **Chart 3.9** shows, companies (57%) and non-profits (59%) were ranked similarly overall on achieving the Best Practice standards. However, as already noted, non-profits were better at developing strong vision, and at managing their organization brand.

3.10 Percentage ranking of organizations by the Seven Best Practices for UK, USA and overall

Best Practice type	Business			Non-profit			Total		Grand total (112)
	USA (27)	UK (34)	Total (61)	USA (31)	UK (20)	Total (51)	USA (58)	UK (54)	
No. 1. Foundations	**70**	38	52	45	60	51	57	46	52
No. 2. Vision	37	32	34	61	65	63	50	44	47
No. 3. Values	**78**	59	67	**77**	60	**71**	78	59	69
No. 4. Communication	67	59	62	61	65	63	64	61	63
No. 5. Embedding	**74**	56	64	35	50	41	53	54	53
No. 6. Brand	56	50	52	**81**	**80**	**81**	69	61	65
No. 7. Measures	67	65	66	42	50	45	53	59	56
TOTAL	**64**	**51**	**57**	**57**	**61**	**59**	**61**	**55**	**58**

No. of Best Practices achieved									
Seven	7	9	8	3	5	4	5	7	6
Six	22	9	15	13	20	16	17	13	15
Five	26	29	27	23	25	24	24	28	26
Four	22	6	13	19	20	19	21	11	16
Three	8	18	13	29	10	21	19	15	17
Two	7	12	10	13	20	16	11	15	13
One	8	14	11	-	-	-	3	9	6
None	-	3	3	-	-	-	-	2	1
TOTAL	**100**	**100**	**100**	**100**	**100**	**100**	**100**	**100**	**100**

One surprise result was the clear superiority of non-profits in organization branding, an area in which companies might be expected to excel. There were two reasons for this. First, for most non-profits the name of the organization was the same as the brand. In many companies the situation was more complex, with different brand names for different business units, or hundreds of individual consumer brands. Secondly, non-profits tended to market their brand to all stakeholders, whereas many companies focused branding on customers, and marketed their organization brand less effectively to other stakeholders.

It is not surprising that companies were stronger on embedding and metrics. For many non-profits, performance appraisal, rewards systems, selection of measures, and market research among stakeholders were big opportunities for improvement.

- **US organizations outperformed UK and international organizations, due to the superior ranking of US companies.**

  While US companies scored best overall, their performance on strong vision (only 37% judged Best Practice) and managing the organization brand (56% Best Practice) was relatively weak. See **Chart 3.10**.

  UK companies lagged behind the USA on all of the Seven Best Practices, although they included three of only seven organizations judged to have successfully met all criteria.

  UK and US non-profits had similar overall scores. However, US non-profits scored relatively higher on strong values, and UK non-profits did better on building foundations, embedding and measures.

- **A range of tools were used by organizations to measure vision and values, but these were not always integrated.** Qualitative measures like the personal observation of senior managers, and quantitative ones like customer or employee surveys, quality, safety, market share, customer and employee retention, were the main measures. However, they tended to be run by different functions, and need to be integrated.

- **It is a good discipline to review progress towards vision, and performance on values prior to the annual business planning cycle. In this way, they will receive a formal review, using integrated measurement, and the new 3-Year and 1-Year Plan will be developed in the right context.**

Best Practice **1**

Building the foundations of the Committed Enterprise

Overview

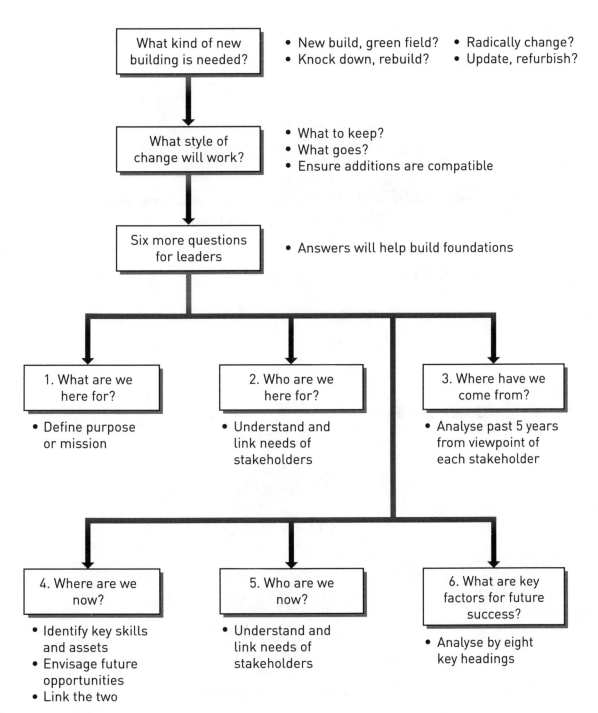

What kind of new building is needed?

- New build, green field?
- Knock down, rebuild?
- Radically change?
- Update, refurbish?

What style of change will work?

- What to keep?
- What goes?
- Ensure additions are compatible

Six more questions for leaders

- Answers will help build foundations

1. What are we here for?

- Define purpose or mission

2. Who are we here for?

- Understand and link needs of stakeholders

3. Where have we come from?

- Analyse past 5 years from viewpoint of each stakeholder

4. Where are we now?

- Identify key skills and assets
- Envisage future opportunities
- Link the two

5. Who are we now?

- Understand and link needs of stakeholders

6. What are key factors for future success?

- Analyse by eight key headings

4.1 What kind of building is needed?

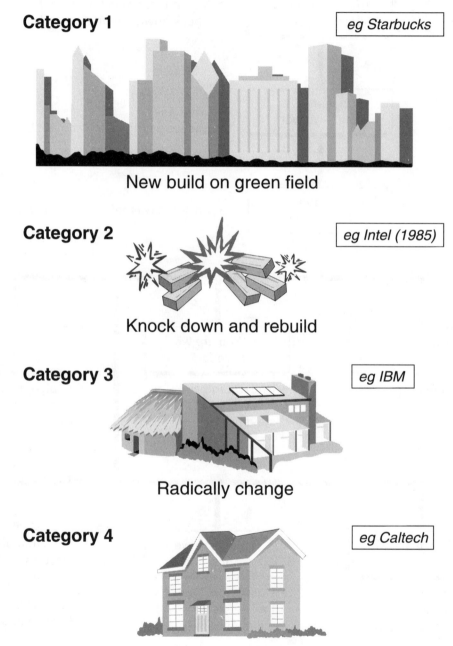

Category 1   *eg Starbucks*

New build on green field

Category 2   *eg Intel (1985)*

Knock down and rebuild

Category 3   *eg IBM*

Radically change

Category 4   *eg Caltech*

Update and refurbish

Your first hundred days as leader

It's your first day as the new leader. The organization may be a global company, a small business, a school, hospital or police force. Successful or in trouble. Yours may be a familiar face or a new one from outside. Whatever the circumstances, people will be watching you closely, and wondering what impact your promotion will have on them. What changes are you likely to make? How will they fit in, if at all? Will they like the changes? During this time you may be thinking: 'What are we best at?', 'What are the big opportunities?', 'How do we become a Committed Enterprise?'

Most new leaders begin by looking at the key numbers, talking to colleagues at all levels, walking around, meeting customers/parents/alumni, observing listening and thinking. Before considering the future, they know they must first secure the present.

Here's the view of a Chairman and CEO[1] who has successfully led a number of organizations:

"When you first come in, people see a vacuum, and worry. You have to keep things very simple, otherwise you add to the confusion. I start by asking three things:

- Tell me about the money. Are we on budget? If not, how do we hit budget?

- What's going on? What are the key issues and who is responsible for them? How well are they being handled?

- Where are we going, and have we got the right people in key positions?

Once these immediate things are fixed, you can start to develop a future vision."

And here's the approach of a Head Teacher who has succeeded at three different private schools, including Eton College:

"When I went to a new school I always liked to talk to the staff individually early on. If a school is in trouble you have to act quickly. If it's going well you should leave well alone and err on the side of caution.

None the less, some little things will strike you right away and you should change them right away. Other things – however important – can wait. Schools have their particular ethos and people have to trust you to understand that before they co-operate with change.

My advice is never say you'll change nothing (because you will,); never say you won't make changes for the first six months or year (because you will find some things you simply can't live with); and never spell out major changes until you have had time to begin to know the school and to be known."[2]

Chart 4.1 uses a building analogy to cover the four categories of organization a leader may encounter. The first is a start-up – vision and values need to be built from scratch.

THE SOURCE

1 Sir Brian Smith, who has been Chairman or CEO of Cable & Wireless, British Airports Authority, Metal Box and Heatherwood & Wexham Park Hospitals Trust.

2 Dr Eric Anderson, Provost of Eton College. He was previously Rector of Lincoln College, Oxford University; and Headmaster of Eton College, Shrewsbury School and Abingdon School.

CHART
4.2 What style of change is most likely to
work?

This?

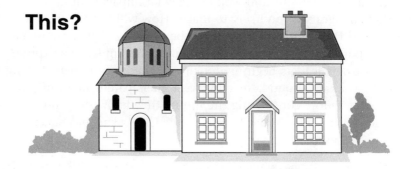

Or this?

The next three categories are operational and already have values, perhaps vision too. The issue for the new leader is how much to keep of the old, how much to knock down and what to add on. A failing organization with the wrong people moving in the wrong direction may need to be metaphorically knocked down and rebuilt: whereas another which has enjoyed lasting success may just require refurbishment.

By the end of 100 days, the leader should know which category his/her organization fits into. Most on-going organizations fit into Categories 3 or 4. One of the biggest mistakes is to diagnose your organization as Category 4 when in reality it needs Category 3 treatment. A rare example of Category 2 was Intel's withdrawal from the memory-chip market in the mid 1980s, to concentrate on microprocessors.[3,4]

Intel was founded to make memory chips. Leaving the business would be like a car maker deciding not to make cars . . . nearly 30% of Intel's workforce was let go.[4]

What style of change is most likely to work?

Once you've broadly decided what you'd prefer to keep in the organization, and what has to go, you need to consider whether the things you wish to add are compatible, and will 'take' (see **Chart 4.2**).

For instance, you may have joined a pharmaceutical company which is very strong on R&D, but weak at marketing. Excellent scientific ideas are not fulfilling their commercial potential. How do you make the organization more customer-driven without eroding its scientific excellence?

Or you may be the new head of a university with excellent academic standing, but a 'nerdy' reputation. How do you broaden the educational curriculum, and focus more on developing the students as people without compromising academic results?

Returning to the building analogy, which bits of the existing building do you change, and what is the style of the pieces to be added on? Do you want to transform the building, or do you wish to extend it while retaining its present character?

Every organization is a living entity with its own distinctive history and DNA. To achieve radical change, you will also need the right new people otherwise they will not 'take'.

"It's almost impossible to change vision and values without changing people at the top."[5]

Here is an example of a state school needing radical change when the new Head Teacher arrived in end 1994:

THE SOURCE

3 Tim Jackson, *Inside Intel* (HarperCollins, 1997; see ch. 27).
4 A. Slywotzky and D. Morrison, *The Profit Zone* (Wiley, 1997).
5 Interview with Dr Holger Hätty, Senior VP, Lufthansa.

CHART
4.3 Six questions for building foundations

1. WHAT ARE WE HERE FOR?

2. WHO ARE WE HERE FOR?

3. WHERE HAVE WE COME FROM?

4. WHERE ARE WE NOW?

5. WHO ARE WE NOW?

6. WHAT ARE THE KEY FACTORS FOR FUTURE SUCCESS?

Hurlingham and Chelsea school serves a disadvantaged client base in London. Eighty per cent of children are from single parent families; 30% have special educational needs. In May 1994 there was a damning report by the Schools Inspectorate, and the school risked closure. A new head was appointed, starting in September. He did a lot of preparation during the summer vacation, and from Week 1 immediately changed stakeholder priorities.

Previously the culture was 'keep teachers happy and the children will achieve'. This hadn't worked. The Head made it clear that children would be No. 1, parents No. 2 and staff No. 3.

A new vision, stressing academic achievement, was established. All local children were to be provided with an effective education, so they would either get a job at 16 or move up educationally. Staff were set targets in four areas: pupil performance, professional development, planning and assessment, and use of knowledge.

By the end of Year 1, 75% of staff had been replaced. January/February 1995 was the worst time, when children, parents and staff were all screaming at the pain of change, before any results had shown through. The Head kept emphasizing the vision, built the right strategies and retained his sense of humour.

Five years later, in 2000, student numbers have grown from 400 to 1000, and the school was ranked by the Schools Inspectorate as one of the most improved in England and Wales. It is now planning to open an Adult Education and Visual Arts Centre.[6]

Six more questions for new organization leaders

The two questions just considered – 'What kind of building is needed for the future?' and 'What style of change is most likely to work?' – are difficult ones. They haven't yet been answered. To find answers, leaders need to address six other questions. These are listed in **Chart 4.3**, and will be probed individually in this chapter.

Here are the answers to the six questions which General McCaffrey might have given, when he was made Director of the Office of National Drug Control Policy (ONDCP) in 1996:[7]

- **What are we here for?** To reduce drug use through prevention and education.

- **Who are we here for?** The general public (prevention), existing and potential drug users, their parents, relatives and mentors (education).

- **Where have we come from?** The ONDCP was set up in 1988 and had three Directors in its first eight years. It is now down to 25 staff. Many influential people consider it a failure and want to close it.

THE SOURCE

6 Interview with Michael Murphy, Head of Hurlingham and Chelsea School.
7 Interview with General Barry McCaffrey, Director of ONDCP, and Pancho Kinney, Director of Strategy, plus perusal of ONDCP publications. The answers to the six questions represent the author's view of Director McCaffrey's likely responses, based on actions he took.

CHART
4.4 First question – 'What are we here for?'

Goldman Sachs: Purpose and Vision	
Purpose	To provide excellent investment and development advice to major companies
Vision	To be the world's premier investment bank in every sector[8]

THE SOURCE

8 Interview with John Powers, Managing Director, Goldman Sachs.
9 Interviews with Sir John Stevens, QPM, Commissioner; David Veness, QPM, Assistant Commissioner, Specialist Operations; Superintendent Simon Corkill.
10 Interview with Dr Hölger Hatty, Senior VP, Lufthansa.

- **Where are we now?** The President wants to reinvigorate the ONDCP. Drug issues are highly controversial, and there is no broad agreement on policy. ONDCP past plans were for 1 year only, and lacked consistency. It also lacked leverage over other agencies.

- **Who are we now?** An organization at the crossroads.

- **What are the key factors for future success?**

  - A 5-year plan accepted by both political parties

  - 5-year budgets, reviewed annually

  - International cooperation within the Americas

  - Ability to 'work the system' to get other agencies to implement

  - 150–200 top-quality staff in ONDCP.

First question – 'What are we here for?'

Separating Purpose from Vision

Purpose ('What are we here for?') is different from Vision ('Where are we going?'). Once purpose has been established, vision is easier to develop. The two sometimes overlap, and are often confused. It is best practice to separate them, so that each can be considered separately. Goldman Sachs demonstrates this in **Chart 4.4**, and the Metropolitan Police, London, make a similar distinction (Figure 4.1).

Figure 4.1

Metropolitan Police: Purpose and Vision[9]	
Purpose	Making London safe for all the people we serve
Vision	To make London the safest major city in the world

Second question – 'Who are we here for?'

Understanding and linking needs of stakeholders

Having established **why** they exist, organizations need to decide for **whom** they exist, and this is where their stakeholders (sometimes called constituents) come in.

It is obvious that the interests and needs of different stakeholders often conflict. Leading physicians may give priority to advancing their career through research rather than servicing patients. Employees may regard customers as unwelcome intrusions into their well-ordered regimes. *How are these conflicts resolved?* By really understanding the needs of each type of constituent, and uniting them under a commonly accepted set of vision and values.

"All constituents are important and need to be kept in balance – this requires constant adjustment and rebalancing."[10]

CHART
4.5 Second question – 'Who are we here for?'

How Coca Cola alienated constituents in 1999/2000	
Stakeholder	**Adverse event**
Consumers	• Sick children in Belgium and France after drinking Coca Cola – temporary ban in these countries
Bottlers	• Large increase in cost of concentrate supplied by Coca Cola
Regulators	• European Commission incensed at attempt to acquire Cadbury Schweppes drinks brands without regulatory clearance • Investigation by Europe's competition commission
Shareholders	• Earnings estimates not met, share price performance poor
Employees	• Major legal suit for racial discrimination in USA • Many stock options worthless

Lufthansa's main constituents are united around its vision of becoming an aviation services group (rather than just an airline), and its values of safety, reliability, operational efficiency and teamwork.

It is possible to offend one key constituent for limited periods of time, but more spells trouble for any organization, as Coca Cola discovered in 1999 (see **Chart 4.5**). Its CEO departed, because 'he knew the maths, but not the music'.[11] He did not fully understand and integrate the needs of his stakeholders.

This example demonstrates the linkage between stakeholders in reverse, where a negative momentum is generated. That such misfortune so quickly affected a well-run organization with strong values, is a warning to all.

"The folks didn't think there was someone there who was the keeper of the flame, who understood the torch."[12]

Whilst it is remarkable that so many unfavourable incidents should have affected Coca Cola on so many fronts in such a short space of time, it seems that once you chalk up a couple of adverse headlines, the media tends to actively seek others and these are rapidly linked together into stories.

Third question – 'Where have we come from?'

Lessons from digging into the past

Any organization is shaped by its past experiences, just like a person, and history is full of lessons. Visions, and especially values, may date back decades. Many of Procter & Gamble's core values stem from William Cooper Procter (1862–1934).[13] Strong vision and values, however, are often overlain, misapplied or just forgotten.

A deep understanding of the past, and what it means for the present is crucial to deciding what to retain and what to change. Unfortunately, succinct and penetrating analysis is becoming something of a lost art, a victim of overworked people and rapid change. However, the faster the rate of change, the more important analysis becomes.

Before starting your dig into the past, develop a single-page Critical Incidents Summary covering the past 10 years. This will include anything that people still talk about. Events likely to feature include changes in personnel, major successes or failures, reorganizations, acquisitions or disposals, downsizing, strikes, glitches, promotions and dismissals. For global companies, you could draw a chart for the total organization, your area, your department. Table 4.1 is a 10-year Critical Incidents Chart for Sony world-wide:

THE SOURCE

11 'Is Douglas Daft the Real Thing?', *Business Week*, 20 December 1999.
12 *Wall Street Journal Europe*, 6 December 1999. Comment by Robert Hope, a former Coca Cola executive, about the former CEO.
13 Speech by Richard Deupree, former Chairman of Procter & Gamble, to Newcomen Society, Cincinnati, 1951.

CHART
4.6 Third question – 'Where have we come from?'

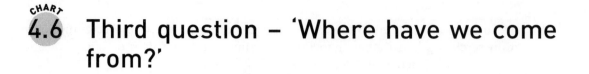

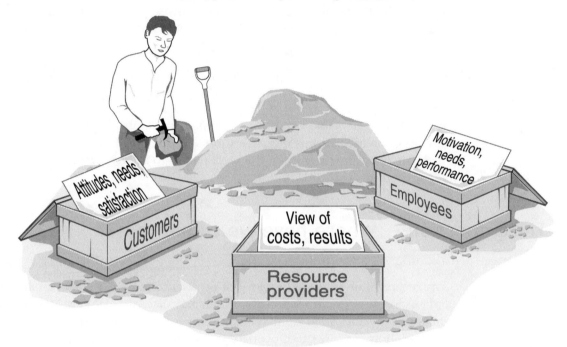

Analyse the past by stakeholder

Attitudes, needs, satisfaction
Customers

View of costs, results
Resource providers

Motivation, needs, performance
Employees

THE SOURCE

14 Derived from John Nathan, *Sony – the Private Life* (HarperCollins, 1999).
15 Interview with Terry Leahy, CEO Tesco.
16 Conversation with Andrew Glover, J. Sainsbury.

Table 4.1

Sony Critical Incident Chart, 1990–2000[14]	
Date	**Critical incident**
1993	Akio Morita, Co-founder, suffers stroke Launch of Playstation 1
1994	$2.7 billion write-off on Columbia Pictures
1995	Nobuyuki Idei appointed CEO Micky Schulhof, Head of USA, goes
1997	Masuru Ibuka, Co-founder, dies Launch of new laptop computer – VA10 Superslim 505
1999	10 electronic divisions grouped into 3 business units
2000	Launch of Playstation 2. Supply problems

New organization leaders digging into the past will be overwhelmed by data unless they focus their spades on productive areas. This can be done taking the viewpoint of each individual stakeholder and their needs as **Chart 4.6** shows.

A brief balance sheet can be compiled for each major stakeholder, covering positive and negative points through listening, and examining facts. Scores on customer satisfaction studies and employee attitude surveys, sales and market share trends and cost comparisons versus competitors are useful pointers. This analysis will enable you to learn lessons from the past, check the needs of each stakeholder and how they are linked, and start to draw conclusions on whether the vision and values are working.

Fourth question – 'Where are we now?'

Skills and assets to build on

You may find that the organization has lost touch with its original values and needs to return to them:

"Vision and values are the mirror of the business – they exist already and you have to uncover and express them. Tesco stands for getting things done – it executes well. It's always been a large scale discount retailer, but in the late 1980s lost sight of its discounting heritage by moving up market."[15]

Previously strong vision and values may have become distorted or disappear below the waterline. Sometimes it's just necessary to rediscover and clarify what has been lost:

"...they are often uncovered... things are scraped away, and there they are."[16]

CHART
4.7 Fourth question – 'Where are we now?'

Examples of key skills and assets to build on

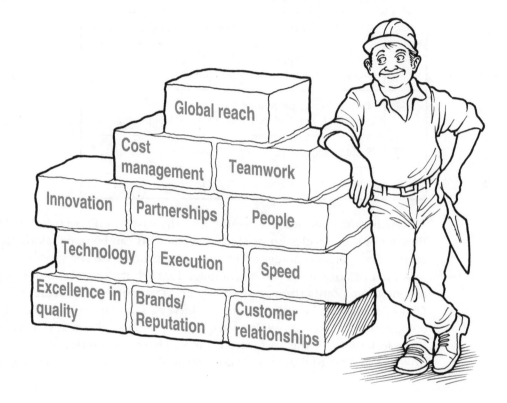

THE SOURCE

17 Interview with Headmaster, identity withheld.
18 Interview with Rex Tomb; Director of Fugitive Publicity and Internet Strategy, FBI.

The Head Teacher of a well-known private school illustrated this point:

"The School's founder created a distinctive culture, but this got rather lost among his successors. The school drifted for some years, living on its reputation, with little forward direction. Quality of staff remained good, but there was little co-ordination, and some poor relationships among staff, and between staff and parents. We returned to and enhanced the original vision and values, developed a long-term strategic plan, and took some tough decisions on co-ordination. This has worked well."[17]

A number of the organizations researched had also returned to an earlier set of vision and values. The digging which enables this is essential, because organization memories are often weak, inaccurate or highly coloured. Individuals can recall their own past on a lifelong basis, but organizations are a changing collection of individuals who only spent part of life there, and for a limited term. "Organizations don't reciprocate loyalty like individuals."[18]

As well as searching for remains of vision and values which can be used as a new foundation, you should list your organization's key skills and assets. Linking these to future opportunities is the stepping-stone to building the vision.

Every organization will have a range of assets and skills to draw on, and **Chart 4.7** gives some examples. There is overlap between the two. For instance, excellent people are an **asset**, and their capabilities are a source of **skills**. Understanding your skills and assets, and concentrating on those which can give you competitive advantage is crucial to building firm foundations. If you can then link your skills and assets to future opportunities, your organization will really take off. Figure 4.2 summarizes this approach.

Figure 4.2

Here are some examples of assets and skills which have built future competitive advantage (Table 4.2).

CHART
4.8

Fifth question – 'Who are we now?'

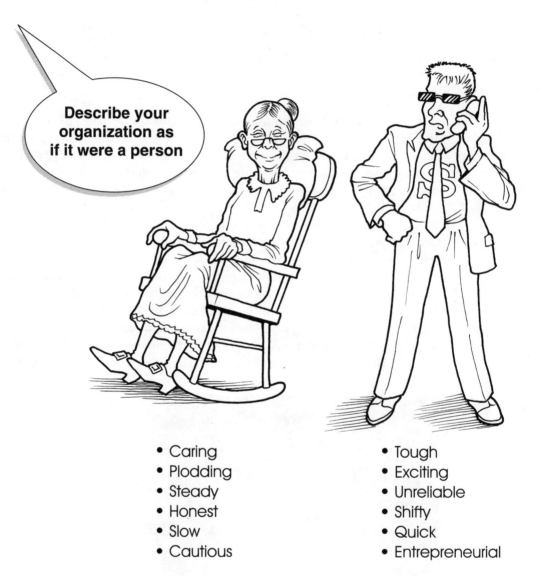

Describe your organization as if it were a person

- Caring
- Plodding
- Steady
- Honest
- Slow
- Cautious

- Tough
- Exciting
- Unreliable
- Shifty
- Quick
- Entrepreneurial

THE SOURCE

19 Interview with Paul Guenther, Chairman, New York Philharmonic Orchestra.

20 Interview with Dick Brown, Chairman and CEO, EDS.

21 Interview with Lew Platt, Chairman and CEO, Hewlett Packard, 1992–9; CEO, Kendall Jackson. Lew worked for both Bill Hewlett and David Packard.

Table 4.2

Organization	Asset or skill
New York Central Park	Unique location
Johns Hopkins Hospitals	Teamwork across disciplines/functions
Disney	Creative content, and brands
New York Philharmonic	Artistic excellence[19]

Fifth question – 'Who are we now?'

Define the real vision and values

Write down what you think the organization's real vision and values are, as opposed to the stated ones. There may be no vision at all. And the values will contain good and bad:

"The values system is the foundation upon which this company is built. There is a need to understand and challenge an organization's beliefs and to kill negative ones, like doubt about the ability to grow as fast as the market."[20]

Describing your organization as a person often produces useful insights, as **Chart 4.8** illustrates. The question 'Who are we now' also gets people to think hard about what business their organization is in.

Sixth question – 'What are the future trends and opportunities?'

Identify the key factors for future success

A deep look into the future is necessary to chart a vision that will stand the test of time, and to adjust the values. Values should not only support the vision, but also reflect the future success factors in your category. In this way, they will be more than a passive set of 'nice things to be', and will actively build future competitive advantage for your organization. Visions can last for centuries, but in the present context of accelerating change, they are more likely to require modification every 5 or 10 years. Values by contrast, should be enduring, but the detailed practices into which they are translated need to be regularly reviewed:

"Values are the core and they are timeless. But the practices and policies, which transform them into everyday behaviour, change at an accelerating rate, often influenced by external factors not under your control, such as competition and markets."[21]

CHART 4.9 Sixth question – 'What are the future trends and opportunities?'

Key factors driving future change

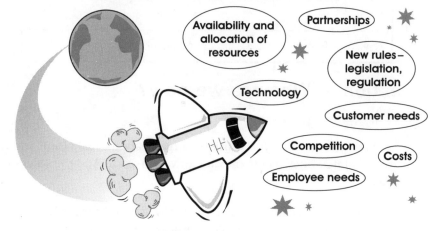

- Availability and allocation of resources
- Partnerships
- New rules – legislation, regulation
- Technology
- Customer needs
- Competition
- Costs
- Employee needs

CHART 4.10 Changes in customer needs

Increasingly sophisticated customer needs for hair care[22]

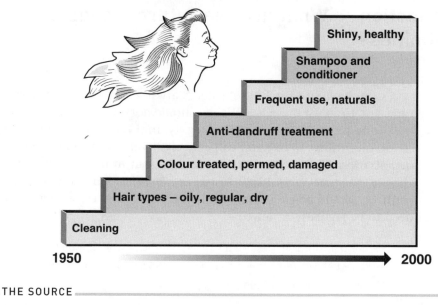

- Shiny, healthy
- Shampoo and conditioner
- Frequent use, naturals
- Anti-dandruff treatment
- Colour treated, permed, damaged
- Hair types – oily, regular, dry
- Cleaning

1950   2000

THE SOURCE

22 J.H. Davidson, *Even More Offensive Marketing* (Penguin, 1997).

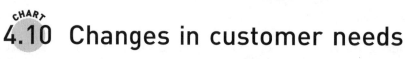

You are charting a map of the future environment in which your vision and values must work. The map will never be perfect, but the process of drawing it, and the questions it forces you to confront, make the process worthwhile.

Vast amounts of time can be spent gazing into a crystal ball. For most organizations, there are eight key factors driving future change, shown in **Chart 4.9**. These need to be considered imaginatively. You are not predicting the future (since this 'is a sure route to humility'[23]). Instead you are considering future possibilities, and how they can be translated into opportunities.

Here are some comments on the key factors driving future change, focusing on customers:

Customer needs   These are changing all the time. They can be broken down into basic needs, demographics, usage and attitudes. As each need is successfully met, another emerges. **Chart 4.10** illustrates changing needs in the hair care market in the past 50 years.

Here is an example of a new vision based on a school's better understanding of future pupil needs:

North Campus Continuation School is a 'last chance' place for 15–18 year olds in San Francisco. Many are expellees, on probation, or with guardians based on court orders. The new head discussed barriers to success with staff, and identified a lack of pupil motivation as the main one. A new vision was developed, linking schoolwork to career, stressing high expectations, and focusing on technology.

School is from 8.30 to 12.30 am, very practical, and connected to part time afternoon/evening jobs in carpentry, electrics, urban gardening. Based on a Panasonic grant, there is now a film and video business run by students, filming marriages for example. There are close school links with parents and guardians. Success stories are now numerous, and the vision is being achieved.[24]

Employee needs   Changing expectations, such as flexibility, childcare, lifelong learning, respectful treatment and personal development plans, are well documented elsewhere.

Technology   The most important future technologies are those that help meet customer needs better, or enable employees to work more effectively. e-Commerce affects everyone, and there are specific technologies relevant to each organization.

Partnerships   Few organizations can do everything. Partnerships enable them to extend their future reach, and focus on what they do best.

Competition   This extends beyond markets and customers. In future, the most intense competition will be for the most talented people, who can develop new intellectual capital, lead people and make the right things happen.

THE SOURCE

23 Michael Eisner, Chairman and CEO, Disney, taken from *Work in Progress* with Tony Schwartz (Penguin Books, 1997).
24 Based on interview with Doris Avalos, Principal, North Campus Continuation School.

CHART
4.11 Key factors driving future change in US universities

US universities – looking at the future	
Key factors	**Future issues**
1. Customer needs	• Meeting needs of changing demographics in USA • Demand for lifetime learning
2. Employee needs	• Mastering accelerating knowledge base • Building interdisciplinary skills
3. Technology	• Capitalizing on IT developments
4. Partnerships	• With businesses, government and overseas
5. Competition	• From traditional sources and new providers • From distance learning
6. Costs	• Increasing cost of best staff • Need to improve all facilities
7. New rules	• Growing privatization of education world-wide
8. Resources	• Changing donor attitudes • Unpredictable government and state resourcing

THE SOURCE

25 Interview with Dr Frank Rhodes, President Emeritus of Cornell University. Chart 4.11 and list of future trends are largely based on Dr Rhodes's comments at interview.
26 Michael Eisner, Chairman and CEO, Disney, taken from *Work in Progress*, with Tony Schwartz, Penguin Books, 1997.
27 Watts Wacker and Tim Taylor, *The Visionary's Handbook* (HarperBusiness, 2000).

Costs Customers will demand higher quality at lower cost in future. Continuous increases in future productivity are therefore necessary.

New rules – legislation, regulation Organizations that anticipate future changes create new opportunities.

Availability and allocation of resources Ability to allocate resources to the best future opportunities is a key success factor.

Chart 4.11 applies the key factors driving future change to a leading US university in an interesting way.[25]

The key future insights in Chart 4.11 are:

- Strong need for lifelong learning, with knowledge the new economic currency.
- Traditional concept of universities linked to residence, and face to face teaching will change, and distance learning will grow.
- Government monopoly of higher education will decline and private funding will increase.
- No one institution can do it all in future – partnerships will flourish in USA and globally.

With a clear view of possible future trends in your category, you can then ask some key questions:

- What will the key future success factors be?
- Will our existing vision sweep us into the future or should it be changed?
- Are our present values relevant to exploiting the key future success factors?
- Should the practices into which they are translated be strengthened or modified?

Michael Eisner summed up the link between past and future in building Committed Enterprises:

Our job is to keep Disney young by forever looking ahead and anticipating what's next, without sacrificing the wisdom and stability of our past.[26]

With a deep understanding of your skills and assets, and a clear view to the future, you can now evaluate the strength of your vision (Chapter 5), and if necessary build a new one (Chapter 6).

The key to a true vision is that, in the face of knowing for sure that the world is going to change, an organization... or an individual aspires to change with it and stay the same simultaneously.[27]

Best Practice (2)

Measuring the strength of the vision... If there is one

Overview

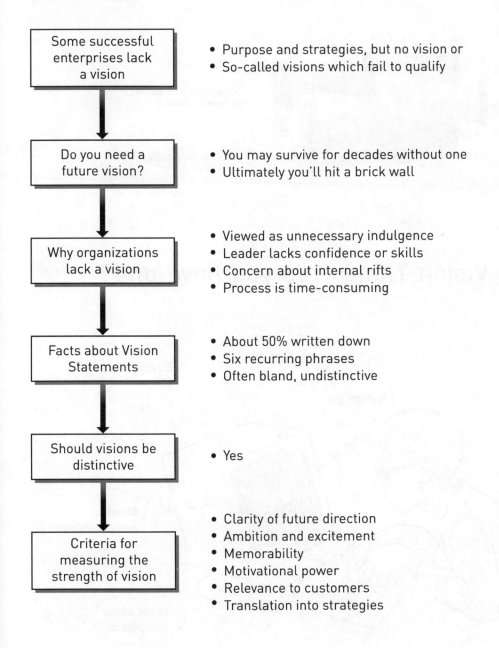

Some successful enterprises lack a vision	• Purpose and strategies, but no vision or • So-called visions which fail to qualify
Do you need a future vision?	• You may survive for decades without one • Ultimately you'll hit a brick wall
Why organizations lack a vision	• Viewed as unnecessary indulgence • Leader lacks confidence or skills • Concern about internal rifts • Process is time-consuming
Facts about Vision Statements	• About 50% written down • Six recurring phrases • Often bland, undistinctive
Should visions be distinctive	• Yes
Criteria for measuring the strength of vision	• Clarity of future direction • Ambition and excitement • Memorability • Motivational power • Relevance to customers • Translation into strategies

CHART 5.1 Watch out for the Vision Pretenders

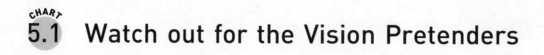

Objectives and strategies are not a vision

Purpose or mission is not a vision

CHART 5.2 The Vision Thing – do you have one?

This chapter will explore the kind of visions organizations have, if any, whether visions need to be distinctive, and how to measure their strength.

The Vision Thing – do you have one?

This is a strange question to have to ask. You wouldn't ask an organization whether it had objectives, budgets or job descriptions because the answer would almost certainly be "Yes". When you enquire whether leaders have a vision (having already underlined that it is a picture of a future destination) they may quite genuinely say "Yes", when the real answer is "No".

Objectives, budgets, or job descriptions are instantly recognisable. You look at a budget and say, "Yes, this is a budget". It may not be a very good one, the numbers may look impossible, but it's still a budget. The same ease of recognition does not apply to Vision. What is presented as a vision may be nothing of the sort (see **Chart 5.1**), but rather a strategy, a statement of purpose (What are we here for?) or a collection of platitudes. Just as a budget without target numbers is not a budget, a vision that doesn't create a picture of a future destination isn't a vision.

On this measure, many famous organizations don't have a vision. Let's look at some of those shown in **Chart 5.2**:

Coca Cola has a purpose, which is to build shareholder value on a long-term basis. It also has a global franchise, powerful strategies and excellent execution skills. But it doesn't have a vision.

ExxonMobil has clear objectives and strategies, and first-rate people who implement very well. But where's the vision? Will oil and the internal combustion engine last forever? For how long can the environmentalists be kept at bay?

Public hospitals would like to have a vision, but usually lack the resources to turn it into reality. So they don't bother.

Governments everywhere do – propounding impractical pseudo-visions in order to get elected, which is their primary objective.

These points are summarized in Table 5.1:

Table 5.1

Organizations without a vision					
Organization	Vision	Clear objectives	Clear strategies	Strong values	Good execution
Coca Cola	✘	✔	✔	✔	✔
Exxon	✘	✔	✔	✔	✔
Most state hospitals	✘	✘	✘	✔	✔
Most governments	✘	✔	✘	✘	✘

CHART
5.3 **Many so-called visions fail to qualify**

Blurred

Rear view mirror

Too complex

Irrelevant

CHART
5.4 **So-called visions**

Blurred

Becoming a knowledge-emergent enterprise in the broadband era

Sony, 2001

Rear view mirror

We will achieve and sustain our place as the world's premier research-based health care company

Pfizer, 1997

Too complex

AOL Time Warner... a media savvy, internet-intelligent, customer focused company with multiple revenue streams for branded subscriptions, advertising and commerce and content.

AOL Time Warner, 2001

Irrelevant

To dedicate our business to the pursuit of social and environmental change

Body Shop, 2001

Many so-called visions fail to qualify

It's one thing to lack a vision and to recognize this, another to think you have one when you don't.

So-called visions that fail to meet the qualifying test fall into four categories – blurred, rear view mirror, too complex, or irrelevant (**Charts 5.3 and 5.4**):

1 **Blurred.** It doesn't matter how many times you re-read these vision statements. No clear picture of a future destination will emerge. There's just a blur.
The Sony statement in Chart 5.4 is part of its concept of creating dreams for all its constituents. The company has a deep-rooted commitment to improving quality of life, creating new markets with its products and innovating rather than copying. However, this instinctive feeling is not communicated in the words in Chart 5.4.

2 **Rear view mirror.** This so-called vision provides a picture of the past, and assumes it can be extrapolated into the future. It looks backwards not forwards. The Pfizer statement provides no picture of the future, and implies that Pfizer will continue to succeed through superior R&D and marketing.

3 **Too complex.** This statement is like a jigsaw with the pieces forced into place. AOL Time Warner's complex statement may have meaning, but it's difficult to grasp. Its Annual Report is full of long words and cumbersome sentences. The world is still waiting for a succinct two-liner which captures future vision for this exciting company.

4 **Irrelevant.** The picture is clear, but sadly irrelevant to the purpose of a business organization.
Anita Roddick would certainly argue that hers is a relevant vision, and Body Shop does link its business and social objective: 'to creatively balance the financial and human needs of our stakeholders'. She is a courageous trailblazer, who forces business to re-examine its assumptions. Body Shop's approach is clear, consistent and motivating to some. However, it is owned by its shareholders, and most CEOs would say that the fundamental purpose of any company is to produce long-term wealth for shareholders.

Do you need a future vision?

Is clear vision an essential, or just an optional extra? On the one hand, the ability of famous companies like Exxon, Wal-Mart and Coca Cola to flourish without a vision raises doubts. On the other hand, vision can bestow important benefits, as we saw in Chapter 2. It can unite diverse stakeholders, provide strategic direction, place short-term strategies in a longer-term perspective and stimulate useful debate.[1]

THE SOURCE

1 See Chapter 2, pp. 27–36.

CHART 5.5 Ways to survive without a future vision but for how long?

- Pursue series of short-term objectives
- Keep on exploiting a dominant market position
- Build great values like delighting customers
- Really control costs
- Hire the very best people

CHART 5.6 Why many organizations don't have a vision

- CEO or Board thinks it's an unnecessary indulgence
- Leader lacks skills or confidence to initiate
- New vision might limit leader's room for manoeuvre
- Process could open up internal rifts

Let's test the need for a vision. What would happen if you became leader of a new organization, and were told to run without a vision? Table 5.2 considers some of the initiatives you might take, and the effect of having no vision.

Table 5.2

Possible ways to survive without a vision	
Key initiative	**Effect of no vision**
Pursue series of 3-year goals and objectives	No long-term perspective in which to place these
Keep on exploiting a dominant market position	Market may deteriorate, so you dominate decline
Build great values like delighting consumers	You may delight the wrong consumers
Really control costs	Low cost will not save you if category becomes unattractive
Hire the very best people	They may not join if they can't picture your vision

Conclusion? You will probably survive for some time with clear objectives, strong values and good executional skills. But you risk driving your beautifully engineered profit machine to the wrong destination. With change accelerating rapidly, and people's desire to know where they are heading, lack of vision will eventually drive your organization into a cul-de-sac or brick wall. The only question is how long it will take.

Even if it were possible to operate long-term without a future vision, what is the benefit of doing so, when it carries such obvious advantages?

Why many organizations don't have a vision

If there are such compelling reasons for having a vision, why doesn't everyone have one? Keeping fit is an apt analogy. Most people agree that healthy exercise is a good thing, yet many are overweight. Food is liked more than exercise. Jogging is boring. The excuses, like the fat, roll out and build up.

The reasons for not having a vision are less obvious. The main ones are listed in **Chart 5.6**:

An unnecessary indulgence For some CEOs and Boards, visions have an image of being soft, woolly and theoretical. Not the kind of thing a results-driven CEO wants to be associated with. As one said: "If anyone came up to me and said he was a visionary, my reaction would be, 'Hey, watch this guy carefully'."[2]

THE SOURCE
2 Interview with Chairman, CEO of major global company.

CHART
5.7

Real visions

Real visions involve heated debate, big ideas, fights, emotion, discomfort... and some leaders don't relish this

" Vision must excite, engage, frighten ... and be so big that even the most confident member cannot feel sure of achieving it"

David Kirk
Captain of legendary All Blacks rugby team
(World Cup winners, 1987)

THE SOURCE

3 Mark Lipton, 'Demystifying the Development of an Organizational Vision', *Sloan Management Review*, Summer 1996, vol. 37, no.4 (1985 survey was by Posner, Kouzes and Schmidt).

4 Author's interviews with 125 organization leaders, 1999–2000.

Leader lacks confidence or skills Organization leaders often initiate a new or changed vision. Their leadership is essential for success. Necessary skills include an ability to listen, to stimulate others to contribute, to face up to difficult issues, to debate future scenarios. This leadership list is different from managing cost, restructuring or executing excellently. The leader does not have to develop the vision personally, but must have the insight to use the imaginative contributions of others.

In 1985, 1500 senior leaders from 20 countries were asked to list the most important traits for a CEO in the year 2000. Ninety-eight per cent said a sense of vision was most important, but 90% lacked confidence in their ability to develop a vision.[3]

While the skills of organization leaders have advanced greatly since 1985, some of those interviewed in 2000[4] were not comfortable discussing the intangibles of vision. They may expect too much of themselves with the lingering image of Moses before them as a visionary leader.

Leader concerned that a new vision would be 'hand-tying' In one sense, this concern is justified. A new vision should chart a clear future direction, and prevent the leader from straying off the road. This would be unattractive to a highly tactical leader, who prefers unlimited room for personal manoeuvre. Equally, it should result in significant change, like exiting certain markets, entering others, and making acquisitions and disposals. In practice, a vision will be clear, while offering many routes to the long-term destination.

Process could open up internal rifts It will and it should (see **Chart 5.7**). Rifts between members of senior management, across divisions and departments, whose present interests and future views differ. There are opportunities for lively debate and open disagreement. There may be emotion and disappointment. That's fine. The objective is to build up a strong vision, not to achieve 100% consensus. The process will sometimes be uncomfortable, and this is where the CEO's leadership skills are needed.

Developing a new vision will be time-consuming Yes, it will. Allow at least a year, lots of senior management time, and plenty of debate throughout the organization. It provides a great opportunity to build a team.

The benefits are uncertain. You may end up with a bland vision that gets ignored or with an exciting one which polarizes people. As a CEO, you're unlikely to be in the job for more than 5 years and perhaps you wish to invest this time in shorter-term initiatives. That's tough on your successor.

Visions have similarities to new products and acquisitions. They all involve risk, the failure rate is high, but they need to be done. And a well-managed vision programme has a much higher chance of success than an acquisition or merger.

It is no coincidence that many of the best visions are either 50–100 years old, developed by confident founders or leaders in the days before empowerment, or recently initiated by entrepreneurs like Bill Gates of Microsoft, or Scott McNealy of Sun Microsystems, whose visions became organizations.

5.8 Should visions be written down?[5]

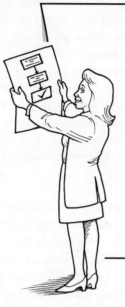

- Around 50% of visions are written
- Advantages of written visions are:
  - Certainty
  - Clarity
  - Basis for scrutiny, debate, communication
- Better to have a strong vision written in people's minds than a weak one on paper

5.9 Six recurring words or phrases in Vision Statements[6]

	Companies	Non-profits
International/global/world-wide	(48)	24
Favourite/best/top/first choice	39	31
Customer/consumer/client	21	(59)
Lead/leader	(30)	7
Selective/specialize	(15)	-
Most successful	(12)	-
Any one of the six used (%)	88	76
Average number used per organization	1.9	1.6

THE SOURCE

5 Author's interviews.
6 Author's interviews.
7 Author's interviews.

Should visions be written down?

The research survey indicated that about 50% of organizations had written Vision Statements. Their drawback is that the instigators think their task is complete, when it's only just begun. The reality of visions is in hearts and minds, not in words on paper or even tablets of stone. However, if a vision is written, it can be scrutinized, debated and communicated. There can be no doubt as to what the vision is.

What Vision Statements contain

An analysis of Vision Statements[7] revealed that six phrases recurred frequently, and 1.8 of these were used by the average organization. The three most frequent related to globalization, use of superlatives and 'customer or client' (Table 5.3).

Table 5.3

Six recurring words or phrases in Vision Statements	
International/global/world-wide	35%
Favourite/best/top/first choice	35%
Customer/consumer/client	40%
Lead/leader	19%
Selective/specialize	8%
Most successful	6%
Any one of the six used	82%
Average number per organization	1.8

There were major differences between companies and non-profits (see **Chart 5.9**). Companies were more inclined to have a global vision, or to seek market leadership. Non-profits pursued quality rather than worldly success, and, perhaps surprisingly, gave customers (such as patients or children) more priority in their visions.

Table 5.3 does suggest a lack of distinctiveness and a certain poverty of imagination in the typical Vision Statement. Indeed it would be easy to get approval to formulaic Vision Statements for companies such as:

We will become global leader and first choice for customers in those selected markets in which we choose to compete.

You do not have to search long to discover companies with vision statements almost identical to this one.

5.10 Strong visions are distinctive

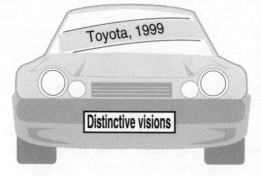

We want to set the tone for the era...
green and affordable...that means
establishing a new paradigm for
harmonizing personal transport
with the environment.
It means revolutionary cost savings
in products and production processes

'Me-too' visions

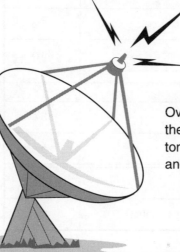

Overall goal is to be
the leading company in
tomorrow's converged data
and telecommunications market

Ericsson, late 1990s

Should visions be distinctive?

Strong visions are usually distinctive (see **Chart 5.10**). If they're not, and resemble the one above, they probably haven't been imaginatively thought about. A vision that could apply to scores of other organizations is unlikely to excite. General Electric's does:

We will become number one or number two in every market we serve, and revolutionize this company to have the speed and agility of a small enterprise.

And here is a comment by the Chairman of a successful new software company:

"A vision must be distinctive and specific to your company. A key test is that you can't substitute the name of another organization for your vision. We market human resource and marketing management software to companies and our vision is to use software to help people run businesses with unmatched simplicity and for outstanding value."[8]

Like individuals, every organization is different. While it may be marketing 'Me-Too' or 'Me-Three' products and services, its history and personality are both unique. A distinctive vision will reflect this uniqueness. It's often proof that the organization really understands its foundations, has faced up to difficult issues, and had the courage to develop an independent view of the future.

The easy option with visions is to project forward a continuation of the present, tempered by clichés such as 'increased competition', 'globalization', 'concentration' and as many other long words ending in 'ion' as you can drum up. Companies in certain industries, like pharmaceuticals, have very similar visions of the future.

Look at the two views of the future in **Chart 5.10**. The Toyota one could be written more simply, but it is certainly bold and distinctive.[9] Toyota has delved deeply into the future and decided how to tackle it. The first fruit of the 'green and affordable' vision was the Prius hybrid car, running on gas and electric power – it starts with battery power, gas takes over for ordinary driving, and the batteries supplement acceleration and braking. The second fruit is the successful new small car, the Yaris, with a powerful yet very light engine.

Contrast the 'Me-too' vision of Ericsson. This vision could equally well apply to two or three other telecom companies. While Ericsson does separately define what it means by 'data and telecommunications', and lists its strategies, the picture which emerges is neither clear nor distinctive.

THE SOURCE

8 Interview with Keith Holloway, Chairman, OneClick HR.

9 Toyota does not seem to have an official vision statement. The words in Chart 5.10 are derived from the Chairman and CEO's statement in the 1999 Annual Report.

CHART
5.11 How to measure the strength of your
vision

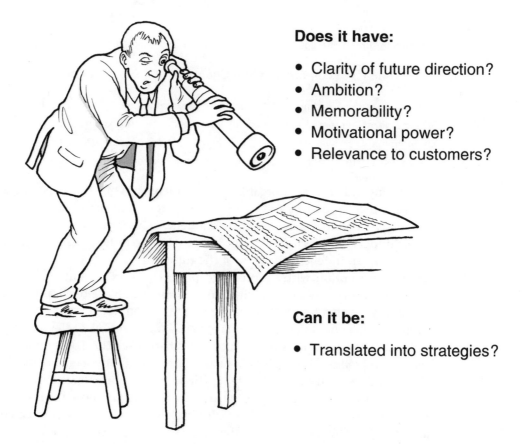

Does it have:

- Clarity of future direction?
- Ambition?
- Memorability?
- Motivational power?
- Relevance to customers?

Can it be:

- Translated into strategies?

How to measure the strength of your vision

Clarity of direction   The vision statement must take the reader somewhere, otherwise it fails to qualify. And the direction should be clear, not circuitous or ambiguous.

It should articulate a picture of what might be, so compellingly that people begin to say, 'This is interesting. What will it take to make this real?'[10]

Ambition and excitement   Does it involve courage and risk? Does it sound like an exciting journey to a worthwhile destination? Will it drive innovation and change?

Memorable   When you have read the vision twice, can you play back its key elements? If not, your vision fails the test. Only a minority of companies pass it. Microsoft's original vision (which has now changed) was highly memorable:

A computer on every desk, and in every home.

Motivational power   Visions should excite and enthuse. That is why they should be ambitious and challenging, 'falling well outside the comfort zone'.[11] The key test of vision is whether it can win hearts and minds. As the captain of the legendary 1987 All Blacks (New Zealand) rugby team wrote:

Visions must be rational, but they must also be emotional. They are often distant. The world-class teams I played with had a vision of pushing back the boundaries of the game, of moving the playing [of rugby] onto a higher plane. We were simply trying to play the game better than any other team had ever played it before. The opposition was no longer the other teams we played against, but ourselves and the game itself. Opponents were the medium through which we attempted to realize our vision.[12]

Relevance to customers and employees   Successful visions are built around customers and employees, not profits and cash flow. By understanding and meeting customer needs in a visionary way, you will also satisfy employees and resource providers. However, the vision should be highly motivating to employees in its own right, by picturing a future which moves and excites them.

Translation into measurable strategies   Convert high-flying visions into hard-edged objectives and strategies that can be regularly measured. Every leading American Football team has a vision of winning the Super Bowl, but each will pursue this with different strategies, resource levels and commitment... and with very different results.

THE SOURCE

10 Peter M Senge, *The Fifth Discipline* (Century Business, 1997).
11 James C. Collins and Jerry I. Porras, *Built to Last* (Random House Business Books, 2000).
12 David Kirk (Captain of All Blacks rugby team), 'World Class Teams', *McKinsey Quarterly*, no.4, 1992.

5.12 Some visions measured

Measurement	Johns Hopkins	Hitachi	McDonalds	Microsoft
Clarity	✓	✗	✗	✓
Ambition	✓	✓	✓	✓
Memorability	✓	✗	✓	✓
Motivation	✓	✓	✓	✓
Relevance	✓	?	✓	✓
Strategies	✓	✓	✗	✓

Some visions measured

Chart 5.12 applies the six measures to four different visions:

The vision of **Johns Hopkins Hospital, Baltimore** was clearly set out by Johns Hopkins in his founding trust statement in 1873. The modern version is too long (17 lines) and has lost some of the flavour of the original. Its essence is for Johns Hopkins Hospital *to be the world's pre-eminent health care institution and leader in medical education, discovery and innovation.* This includes:

fostering a revitalized and redeveloped East Baltimore [an area of high crime and unemployment in which the hospital is located].

The vision statement scores well. It is reasonably clear, and the hospital has well designed strategies to implement the vision. Since Johns Hopkins is consistently ranked No. 1 in the USA, it could be argued that the vision is not sufficiently ambitious, but you can't beat being the world's best.

Hitachi's vision is to transform society:

Our vision is to create richer lives and a better society by providing products, systems, and services with a new level of value and potential, based on the latest advances in technology, especially knowledge and information technology.

This statement is somewhat soporific but may be motivating to employees.

McDonald's vision is:

to be the world's best quick-service restaurant experience.

This is simple and memorable, but lacks clarity because the words are open to interpretation. In the Annual Report strategies for delivering the vision do not sound convincing and there is a whiff of complacency.

Microsoft has changed its vision, and now aims to:

empower people through great software – any time, any place, and on any device.

This is clear and memorable, but does not sound ambitious; perhaps a deliberate move in view of the company's past anti-trust brushes. Strategies include making PCs simpler and more reliable, helping consumers to develop their own personal internet, and enabling companies to manage their knowledge bases. The Microsoft vision scores well, while lacking the riveting simplicity of its original one.

This chapter has reviewed the role of visions, and how to measure their strength. The next will provide guidance on **when** to introduce a new vision, and how to build it.

Chapter

Best Practice ②

Timing and building a new vision

Overview

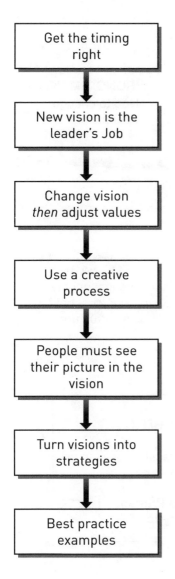

Get the timing right
- Wrong timing can kill great visions
- Get people, structure and costs right first

New vision is the leader's Job
- Leader should initiate and establish vision process
- He should decide who to involve and manage the process ambitiously

Change vision *then* adjust values
- Values should support the vision
- But there are exceptions

Use a creative process
- Agree objectives and responsibilities
- Establish criteria for measuring strength of vision
- Develop and test trial vision statements
- Re-discuss, revise and complete

People must see their picture in the vision
- Central vision translated into working visions for each part of organization
- Then included in personal objectives

Turn visions into strategies
- Visions are long-term (eg 10 years+)
- 3 Year objectives/strategies convert them into action

Best practice examples
- ER Taylor School, San Francisco
- Estée Lauder
- Baylor Health Care System, Dallas
- HM Inspectorate of Prisons, UK

CHART
6.1 # Getting the timing right

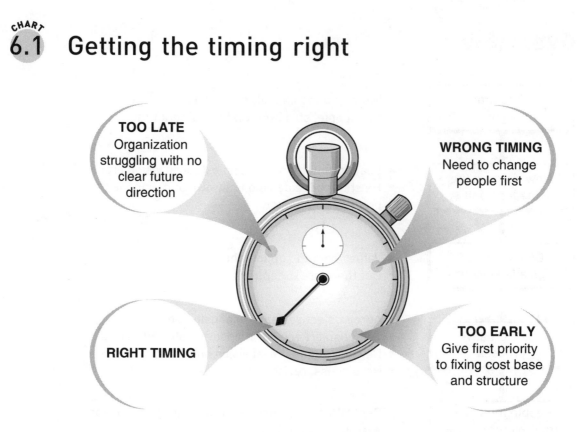

TOO LATE
Organization struggling with no clear future direction

WRONG TIMING
Need to change people first

RIGHT TIMING

TOO EARLY
Give first priority to fixing cost base and structure

SPEED AND TIMING OF CHANGE IS CRITICAL

" If you want very rapid change, you can expect massive resistance. Yet if change takes too long, it won't work"

**Sir Brian Pitman,
former Chairman, Lloyds TSB**

How to get the timing right

A new vision can absorb a vast amount of energy in the short term, and payout is longer term. For a company struggling with immediate problems, like incompetent managers or unnecessary costs, a new vision is probably the last thing needed. That's why on taking over the leadership of IBM in 1993, after record-breaking losses of $8 billion, new chairman Lou Gerstner said:

"There's been a lot of speculation on when I will deliver a vision. The last thing IBM needs right now is a vision."[1]

Gerstner wasn't denigrating visions. Other things had to be put right first, before a vision could work. Things like costs, productivity, structure and dedication to serving customers. Three years later, Gerstner unveiled a new vision:

"So it's with an enormous sense of irony, I say this: What IBM needs right now is a vision."[1]

He understood the importance of timing. 'Do it now' is often a recipe for failure in developing a new vision.[2] **Chart 6.1** illustrates right and wrong timing.

Another reason for not rushing into a new vision is that it is a creative process. The answers are not obvious, and take time to work out.

"You can't impose and have to be inclusive. It's dangerous to go into a darkened room – it's best to go and wander about until your eyes become accustomed to it and you begin to see things. You can only **say** what you are when you **know** what you are. It's all about respect for the views of others, listening, motivating, becoming involved and asking people for their help. This is 'inclusive'."[3]

Leaders are often under pressure to provide a new vision, and must be prepared to resist, if necessary.

"Give us a Vision, Boss." I was expected to order a vision de jour from some talismanic menu.[4]

The new head of a world-class private school was surprised when people began asking him soon after arrival, "What's the vision?" His answer was: "Why are you asking me this question? I only arrived last week. Surely you know – after all, the school's been in existence for over 100 years."

THE SOURCE

1 Quoted in Robert Slater, *Saving Big Blue* (McGraw Hill, 1999).
2 Interview with Barry Clarke, OBE, Chairman of Save the Children Fund UK.
3 Interview with Lord Browne, CEO, BP.
4 Gerald Langeler, 'The Vision Trap', *Harvard Business Review*, March/April 1992.

CHART
6.2 How to get the timing right

Questions to ask	Best timing for new vision	
	Now	**Later**
1. Are the people, structure, cost base and customer focus right?	✓	
2. Is there broad consensus on future direction?	✓	
3. Are there short-term performance problems?		✓
4. Are the values strong and relevant?	✓	

CHART
6.3 Vision should be initiated and completed from the top

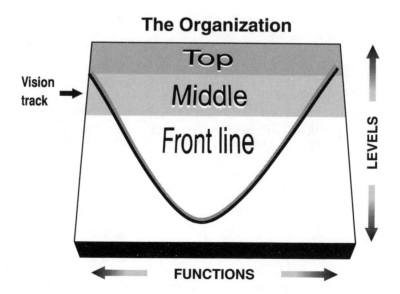

Leaders should therefore carefully consider the timing of any new or changed vision. The right time may be now, especially in non-profits, where future vision is the main reason for working there, or in smaller companies, where it can be used as the blueprint for other changes. Or the right time may be 2 years hence. **Chart 6.2** provides guidelines on getting the timing right.

If there are fundamental weaknesses in people, structure, values or short-term performance, fix them first, before addressing future vision. A great vision, introduced at the wrong time, will fail.

Should vision be decided on a top-down basis?

Vision should start at the top, travel through the organization, and continue to be driven from the top (**Chart 6.3**). A starting point is needed, to get discussion going with all stakeholders at all levels. The role of the leader is to decide when to initiate the process, to ensure that the process is inclusive, and to personally lead it, listening to a wide range of people, not just senior managers. He or she should be completely committed to the importance of developing the right vision.

"Vision consists of thinking ahead and ensuring that colleagues address the right issues."[5]

Some leaders get things wrong right from the start. They think their job is to find a vision everyone feels comfortable with. That's why most visions consist of easy options like 'market leadership', 'leader in quality', or 'the No. 1 choice of customers'. They make people feel good, require little imaginative effort, and attract consensus.

Strong visions are different. They excite strong emotions. They are challenging, uncomfortable, nail biting and polarizing. Some people will be so opposed that they will wish to leave. Consensus may be impossible to achieve, but the critical mass of people who believe strongly in the vision will then turn it into reality.

Strong visions only emerge from organizations with demanding and determined leaders. In their absence, the easy option route to bland consensus is likely. The leader may well have a personal vision, but this is not essential at the outset. It's perfectly reasonable to say to the Board, "We need a new vision, and right now, I'm not sure what it should be. But I know it must excite and engage people. We'll develop a process for building a vision, I'll personally lead it, and ensure that it works in practice." Note that in this case, the leader is not going to personally craft the words.

Who needs to be involved? Senior managers obviously, because as future evangelists and implementers, they have to be convinced. It can also be useful to put bright 30–35-year-old managers on the case, in cross-departmental teams, led by the CEO or a senior manager, and drawing on views throughout the organization. It's essential to listen to people on the front line – service engineers, telesales operators and customer service people, because they really know what's going on, and to involve customers themselves, either informally or through research.

THE SOURCE

5 Interview with Sir Peter North, Master of Jesus College, Oxford University, formerly Vice Chancellor.

CHART
6.4
Change vision first, then adjust values

OLD VISION

Dominate highly regulated market

OLD VALUES

• Safety
• Reliability
• Service

NEW VISION

Best in quality and innovation in highly competitive market

NEW VALUES

• Safety
• Customer focus
• Innovation
• Quality
• Speed

Change vision first, then adjust values

Should new values be developed concurrently with a new vision? Or is it best to decide on a new vision first, and then change the values later? There are good reasons for changing the vision first, because:

- Vision charts future direction, values provide the motor to get there. You can't sensibly choose the engine you need without some idea of the terrain ahead. If it's mountainous, you'll need four-wheel drive and a gutsy engine. If it's high-speed track with lots of corners, you'll want fast acceleration and sophisticated steering.

- The new vision may radically change your future markets and competitors. For instance, you may be planning to expand into services and to run down manufacturing; or to develop from schooling only to a broader offer, including adult education.

- Since values should be based on the key success factors, they might have to change as well, influenced by the new vision.

Chart 6.4 illustrates these points. The company in question is a recently privatized gas utility, with a new vision of broadening its range of services from gas only, to electricity, credit cards and telecom. To support the new vision and to meet tomorrow's key success factors – speed, innovation and excellent customer service – the values have to change. They could not have been developed in ignorance of the new vision.

In practice, because new visions take much longer to develop than new values, considering values second loses little time. The two areas are linked. Values are likely to crop up in discussions about vision. Those adopting the 'vision first, then values' approach can complete the whole process, then communicate the new vision and values together.

While 'vision first, then values' seems the best approach, the reverse can work if the vision subsequently agreed does not represent radical change. There may be good reasons for delaying the vision. Diageo, which was a result of the merger of Grand Metropolitan and Guinness, illustrates this:

The merger took place in November 1997. The purpose of the new company was 'creating value for shareholders through consumer enjoyment'. At that stage, there was not a clearly articulated vision.

A new set of values was agreed soon after the merger. The CEO was determined to have a common set of values for the total organization, but there was strong opposition from the CEOs of the four operating companies. Values statements were collected from all operating companies, common ground identified, and trial descriptors developed. After some weeks' discussion, the CEO got the four operating heads into a room away from the office, and said they'd stay there until the values were agreed.

This was done, and the agreed values were:

CHART
6.5 # Use a creative process to develop vision

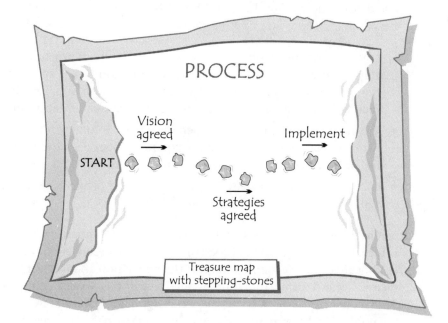

PROCESS

Vision agreed

Implement

START

Strategies agreed

Treasure map with stepping-stones

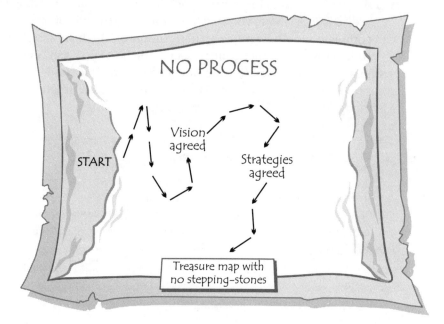

NO PROCESS

START

Vision agreed

Strategies agreed

Treasure map with no stepping-stones

THE SOURCE

6 Interviews with John McGrath, CEO, Diageo 1997–2000, and Paul Walsh, the present CEO.

- Be the best (e.g. beating competition, delivering results)

- Passionate about consumers (e.g. innovative, caring about brands)

- Freedom to succeed (e.g. openness and risk-taking)

- Proud of what we do (e.g. integrity, social responsibility)

Heads of operating companies were able to add their own specific practices to these values.

At merger, Diageo was a food and drinks company, but exited food. As a specialised drinks business, Diageo was better able to construct a new vision, which was to 'capture the winning share of high value adult drinking occasions'.[6]

Another organization which successfully established values first, then vision, is the Rockefeller Foundation (see next page).

Use a creative process to develop vision

A process gets you from A to B in a number of pre-planned steps. You analyse what needs to be done, set up a number of tasks, connect them, and then explain to everyone involved what's expected. The process gets things done quickly and systematically, avoiding wasted effort. **Chart 6.5** illustrates the advantage of using a creative process for developing vision.

Process is widely applied in planning, budgeting and production by many of the organizations researched. Yet few used it in developing vision. The typical approach was to get some background papers written; discuss them at a meeting of anything from 5 to 200 senior managers; have a follow-up session where the words were agreed; and then to present to the troops, with supporting videos, brochures and manuals.

This ad hoc approach is unlikely to create a sustainable vision, because:

- Clear objectives and responsibilities for developing the vision are not established.

- Criteria for measuring the strength of the vision are not agreed at the outset.

- There is too much emphasis on agreeing a vision statement rather than developing a vision that works.

- Based on organizations researched, quality of analysis of the past, and of insights into the future, was mediocre.

While the process is important, there is no perfect method, and one size certainly doesn't fit all. Much will depend on whether you are modifying an existing vision or developing a new one from scratch. The process will also be influenced by the organization's attitude to change, past experience of vision and values, and need for speed.

Large global companies have much greater need of process than small start-ups, where people know each other and their customers well. So do Hospital Groups, since they need to involve and unite people from different locations and departments, from clinical care and research centres. The quality of process in the leading American hospitals visited was very good.

CHART
6.6 Creative vision process in action

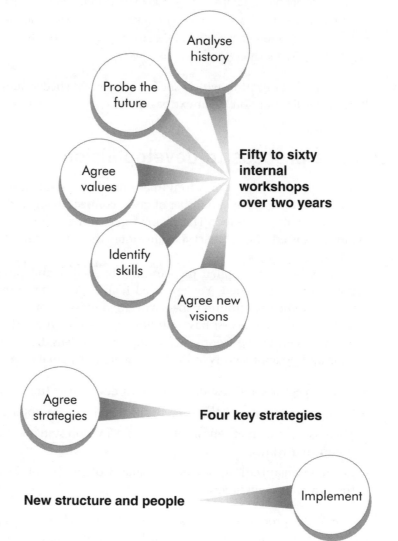

The Rockefeller Foundation

Fifty to sixty internal workshops over two years

Four key strategies

New structure and people

A vision should relate the views of employees about the organization's skills to future customer needs, in an exciting way. The process for doing this should be managed with all the excitement and sophistication of developing a new brand. A new vision relaunches an organization internally and externally, and is therefore infinitely more important than any individual new brand introduction. Unfortunately, because they underestimate the size and importance of the challenge, many organizations manage vision in an amateur way, with unclear responsibilities, and weak skills. Unqualified senior people flit in and out of the process, and internal politics can creep in. When launching a major new brand it is always clear who is responsible and what the budget is. Not so with new visions.

Creative vision process in action

The Rockefeller Foundation[7]

The Rockefeller Foundation was started in 1913 by John D Rockefeller. The original vision was 'to promote the well-being of mankind throughout the world'.

A new President of the Foundation was appointed in 1998, and it was decided to develop a new vision which extended the original one.

The Foundation, led by the President, covered the first four processes illustrated in Chart 6.6, in developing the new vision. The original vision was examined in detail, changes were tracked, and the Foundation's achievements were evaluated. Thought was then given to desired changes for the poor of the world in the next 20 years, such as enough food for Africa, and successful medicines for HIV and TB.

The next key step was to agree values as a Foundation. They were equity and fairness, diversity, knowledge and creativity, participation, humility and respect.

The comparative advantages of the Foundation and its key competencies were defined as a basis for building the future. Fifty to sixty internal workshops of 2 hours' duration were organized to cover these topics over 2 years.

The agreed new vision was to be a 'knowledge-based, global foundation with a commitment to enrich and sustain the lives and livelihoods of the poor and excluded people throughout the world'.

Four key strategies were agreed to implement this vision:

- **Knowledge-based** approaches require the best skills in science, technology, research and analysis.

- **Global** means applying global processes to local realities.

- **People's lives and livelihoods:** themes include food, health, jobs, and culture linked in an integrated way.

- **Poor and excluded people** need to be included, and this means listening to them, and encouraging them to articulate their own priorities.

THE SOURCE

7 Interview with Prof. Gordon Conway, President, The Rockefeller Foundation.

CHART
6.7

Designing and testing the new vision

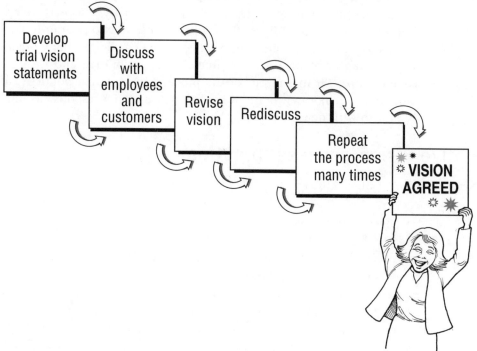

Develop trial vision statements

Discuss with employees and customers

Revise vision

Rediscuss

Repeat the process many times

✳ VISION AGREED ✳

CHART
6.8

Revising a vision

DECLARATION
OF INDEPENDENCE

We hold these truths to be self-evident, ~~sacred and undeniable;~~ that all men are created equal, that they are endowed by their Creator with certain inalienable rights, that among these are life, liberty and the pursuit of happiness.

- Original version
  – Thomas Jefferson

- Revision
  – Benjamin Franklin

The new vision and strategies were implemented by moving to a single structure which stressed globalization (USA and International were previously separate), building up new knowledge-based skills, changing people, and revising the guidelines for making grants.

Designing and testing the new vision

Armed with a clear analysis of where the organization is, how it's got there, what it's best at, and how the future might look, you've got all the ingredients you need to write a draft vision statement. This is likely to be one of many. Each successive draft will stimulate debate and increase understanding among those included. Initially the vision may be seen through a glass darkly, but over many versions, it will become clearer and gain commitment, as **Chart 6.7** illustrates.

Highly charismatic leaders with strong future visions and compelling communication skills can make vision work, while breaking rules about consulting others. This approach often worked for founders. Indeed, it worked for one of the greatest of all visions – the American Declaration of Independence – drafted first by the 31-year-old Thomas Jefferson, changed once following discussion with four senior colleagues, then approved by Congress, after three days of debate. The change highlighted in **Chart 6.8** from 'sacred and undeniable' to 'self-evident' was made by Benjamin Franklin before the text went to Congress. For those of us lacking Thomas Jefferson's insight and superb drafting skills, wider consultation with employees and customers is advisable.

Grand Met, which merged with Guinness in 1997 to form Diageo, had a new CEO in 1986 and a need for a new vision. This was written and re-written many times over a 12 month period:[8]

In 1986, Grand Met was a conglomerate, involved in 28 different sectors including spirits (Smirnoff, Malibu, Baileys); hotels (Intercontinental); tobacco (Liggett & Myers) as well as public houses, milk, contract catering, dancehalls and bingo, among others.

In the previous 20 years the company had been property-based. The company nearly went bust in 1973 (oil crisis) and probably would have blown up in 1990 if its vision and strategy had not been changed.

The new CEO insisted that four questions were confronted and answered:

- **What is Grand Met?** Trial statements were developed for people to react to. Was it a hotel company with other businesses? Was it a drinks company? Was it a property business?

- **What are Grand Met's core skills?** These were agreed as ability to turn round acquired businesses, skills in brand development, good financial disciplines, and an entrepreneurial culture.

THE SOURCE

8 Interview with Lord Sheppard, former Chairman, Grand Metropolitan 1987–96, and Keith Holloway, former Director of Strategy.

CHART 6.9 People must see their own picture in the vision

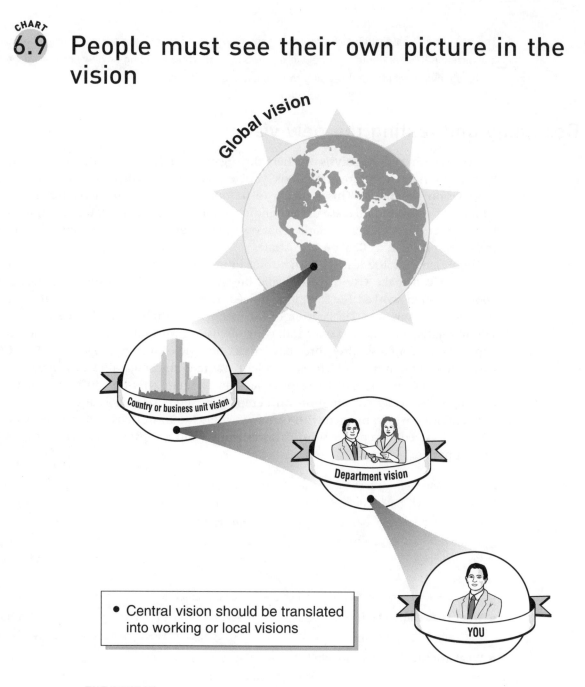

Global vision

Country or business unit vision

Department vision

YOU

- Central vision should be translated into working or local visions

THE SOURCE

9 Interview with Charles Holliday Jr, Chairman and CEO, DuPont.
10 Interview with Nigel Worne, Managing Director, Denby Pottery.
11 Korea was ranked No. 2 in Mathematics achievement and No. 5 in Science in the IEA Third International Mathematics and Science Study (TIMSS). This involves a standard test for 14 year olds. Singapore was top in Maths, second in Science.
12 John Katzenback, *Real Change Leaders* (Nicholas Brealey, 1997; see Chapter 2, 'Working Vision').

- **What are the big future trends affecting Grand Met?** Grand Met's strategy group developed a view of the future which highlighted three key themes – globalization of business, liberalization of women, and importance of Islam. It was also felt that brands and people would matter more in future than property.
- **What does Grand Met want to be?** Many trial vision statements were developed and discussed.

Argument raged for months on these questions, and in 1987 a new vision was agreed: 'Grand Met will specialize in highly branded consumer businesses, where its marketing and operations skills ensure it is a leading contender in every market where it operates.'

It was decided to exit beer because Watney's brands were too weak, and to sell Intercontinental Hotels, since too much cash would be needed to build a global hotel brand. Focus would be on globally branded food and drinks. Grand Met already had strong drinks brands, and acquired Pillsbury.

Grand Met's new vision led it to rationalize from 28 to two sectors, to change from a mainly UK property-based company, to a global food and drinks brander.

People must see their own picture in the vision

The central vision needs to be translated into working visions, which have meaning for individual countries, plants, operations centres and departments. "If people can't see their own picture in the vision, it won't work."[9]

For most people, the 'organization' will be the place where they work, or do business, not the collection of perhaps 300 locations and 200000 people comprising the entire company. On trips away from Head Office, CEOs asking employees or customers about the future almost always get answers relating to the nearest place of work or market.

"Everyone should understand their contribution to the vision. Every objective should be traceable back to the vision. If it can't be, it shouldn't be there."[10]

A country like South Korea, for instance, may have a national vision for education, like 'Being No. 1 in the world for Maths and Science, as measured by international surveys'.[11] The translation of this into working visions will differ between primary and secondary schools, between inner city and rural schools. The working vision should be consistent with the central vision, yet provide meaning and vitality at a local and individual level.

A really good working vision tends to spread on its own ... it not only aligns those already in the organization, it also draws in those who pass, like a magnet.[12]

CHART
6.10 Turning visions into hard-edged strategies

United Parcel Service

We enable global commerce

Key strategies*

- Grow core business of world-wide distribution and logistics

- Build new skills to integrate global flows of goods, funds and information

- Use technology to create new services

- Attract and develop the most talented people

- Exceed customers' expectations

*shortened version of original**

THE SOURCE

13 Ibid.

14 Interview with Lord Browne, Chairman and CEO, BP.

15 Interview with Jack Duffy, Senior VP Strategy, United Parcel Service. UPS uses the word 'purpose' where we use 'vision'. The UPS charter integrates its purpose, mission, values and strategy.

16 *Inside UPS*, July 1999 (internal UPS publication).

Like central visions, working visions require time, effort and re-iteration:

Forming a working vision inevitably requires one or more periods of intense discussion without a clear resolution as the result. Several people consider a wealth of ideas, facts and opinions and forge them into early-vision phrases and alternatives, one of which eventually catches on, or gets pieced together over time.[13]

Turning visions into hard-edged strategies

Strong visions are uplifting and motivating, but unlikely to work unless translated into measurable objectives and strategies. Visions must be more than slogans and contain real substance.

"Vision must be practical. 'I have a dream' is a step too far in business – it's politics. You need to express the unfolding steps which underpin reality, and these are not linear."[14]

If you saw the new vision of UPS (United Parcel Service)[15] in isolation ('We enable global commerce'), you might say: "It sounds interesting, especially for a parcel company, but what does it mean in practice?" The strategies – see **Chart 6.10** – provide the meaning and the action:

UPS is 93 years old and one of the world's leading package delivery companies, with 359 000 employees. Eighty per cent of its shares are held by present or former employees. Its first vision was developed in 1991. This involved becoming more customer focused, and a global leader in package distribution.

In 1997, senior management recognized the massive changes in access to information, and the need to build the physical package business, yet move beyond it. In October 1998, it was decided to develop a new vision – 'We enable global commerce'.

The new vision (1999) will help UPS to manage the customer's entire supply chain from distribution services and electronic commerce to financial services, inventory management and more.[16]

The Baylor Health Care System in Dallas, provides another good example of clear and measurable strategies to implement the vision:

Baylor Health Care System is a non-profit organization, founded in 1903, with 13 000 employees working in 72 different health centres or hospitals in Texas. In 2000, the vision and values were updated after 20 years, and new structure and strategies developed to apply them. The new vision was, 'Before the end of this decade, to become the most trusted source of comprehensive health services'.

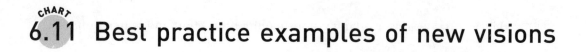

6.11 Best practice examples of new visions

CHART

- ☀ **ER Taylor School**
- ☀ **Estée Lauder**
- ☀ **Baylor Health Care**
- ☀ **UK Prisons Inspectorate**

A number of objectives and strategies were developed to support this vision, and a senior executive made responsible for each one. They included:

- Create and enhance physician relationships.

- Grow the system (growth areas were pinpointed geographically).

- Connect consumers, clinicians, and other stakeholders.

- Strive to deliver the best care available anywhere.

- Deliver superb customer service.

- Develop people at Baylor.

- Produce optimal cash flow.[17]

Best practice examples of new visions

This section illustrates best practice in building new visions, using examples from four different kinds of organization – a school, a global company, the only independent prisons inspectorate in the world, and a leading hospital group. Each example highlights a different aspect of how to successfully build a new vision.

ER Taylor Elementary School, San Francisco   ERT has 750 students aged 4 to 11. Half live with single parents and fewer than 5% are white. The largest racial groups are Chinese American (41%) and Hispanic (26%). Children and parents are seen as the No. 1 stakeholders, then staff. This example shows the importance of talking to customers in building vision.

The vision originated from ERT parents. Parents were informally asked how they saw their child aged 25. Their response was 'college, then a profession or business' with no idea how to implement this vision. Teachers were also asked their views. They saw some kids at 25 being in prison or drug dealing.

Detailed research was then undertaken with 336 parents of children aged 8–9. The long-term goal of 95% was a college degree for their kids, with 68% envisaging graduate or professional training. But only 40% knew how to help their children realize this.

The vision adopted by ERT four years later was 'Kids College Bound'. This was turned into action by:

- Commitment to success for *all* children.

- Strengths of each child appraised at informal work session with child, parents and teachers, and action strategies agreed.

- Workshops for parents, and 'College Bound' Fair.

THE SOURCE

17 Interview with Joel Allison, President and CEO, Baylor Health Care System.

CHART
6.12 View of the future – Baylor Health Care System, Dallas

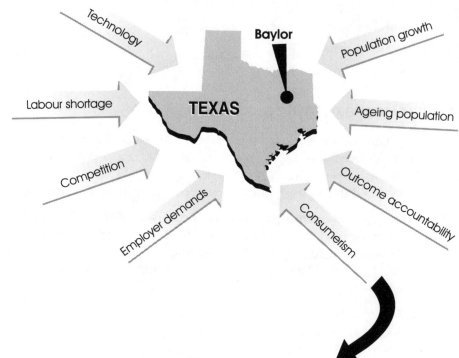

CHART
6.13 Consumer concerns

- Consumers want **more control** of their health care

- Consumers want to **trust** their health care providers, but their confidence in health care has declined

- Consumers express concerns about **convenience** and **wait times**

- Consumers want **more information** that is simple and easy-to-understand

- Consumers want to be able to **access** their physicians – to use the physician they want in a timely, convenient manner

● Parents and teachers lead the vision, in association with San Francisco University.

Will this vision succeed? The natural college percentage for this type of school is 15%. There are good initial signs, but it's very early days.[18]

Estée Lauder[19]   This example demonstrates how to relate a new vision to the original aspirations of the founder:

Leonard Lauder became CEO of Estée Lauder in 1958, and is still Chairman, aged 67. At the beginning, he personally wrote the monthly salary cheques, and his mother, Mrs Estée Lauder, visited every cosmetics store stocking the brand. Estée Lauder is now a world leader in cosmetics with brands like Estée Lauder, Aramis and Clinique.

In 1995, the company went public. The senior management team met to start answering the four key questions. Who are we? What's important to us? What makes us successful? Where do we want to go in future? Task Forces were appointed, and for one and a half years they talked to people throughout the organization, tested thoughts and words, and tried to summarize beliefs and aspirations.

The vision decided upon was 'Bringing the best to everyone we touch'. This harked back to co-founder, Mrs Estée Lauder, who insisted on best quality, and loved touching customers. 'Touch' in the new vision connotes the expression of warmth towards and genuine interest in customers. The vision is backed by nine commitments or values, such as:

● Provide customers with innovative cosmetic products of the highest quality.

● Deliver outstanding service by treating each individual as we ourselves would like to be treated.

● Pursue profit – but never at the expense of quality, service or reputation.

There is also a set of principles, which turn values into practices.

Vision, values and practices are well integrated, although there are too many. Fewer would be more memorable.

Baylor Health Care System, Dallas[20]   The purpose of this example is to illustrate best practice in confronting the future. Baylor has been used earlier in this chapter to demonstrate how to turn vision into objectives and strategies (pages 114–116).

Baylor was founded in 1903 by Dr Truett, a Baptist minister, with this ringing statement: 'Is it not now time to begin to build a great humanitarian hospital, one to which men of all creeds and those of none, may come with equal confidence?'

THE SOURCE

18 Interview with Gini Dold, BASRC Reform Co-ordinator, ER Taylor Elementary School, San Francisco.
19 Interview with Leonard Lauder, Chairman, Estée Lauder.
20 Interview with Joel Allison, CEO, Baylor Health Care System, Dallas, plus Baylor's 'Environmental Assessment', 28 January 2000, and its Strategy/Action Plan.

CHART
6.14 Statement of Purpose – HM Inspectorate of Prisons

STATEMENT OF PURPOSE

To provide independent scrutiny of the conditions for and treatment of prisoners, promoting the concept of 'healthy prisons' in which staff work effectively to support prisoners and to reduce re-offending.

Chart 6.12 summarizes Baylor's view of the future. Each of these eight future issues is reviewed in detail. For instance, advancing technology is studied under four headings – drug therapies, equipment, Internet and genomics. Population growth by county area is estimated, as well as its ethnic composition. Baylor estimates that by 2030, the percentage of Hispanics in Texas will be 46%, and whites will decline from 55% to 37%. A real effort is made to understand changes in consumer needs, as **Chart 6.13** shows.

HM Inspectorate of Prisons UK[21] This example illustrates how vision can be used to expand an organization's impact in a very political environment.

The UK Inspectorate of Prisons is the only independent inspectorate of the treatment of and conditions for prisoners in the world (with the recent exception of Western Australia). The purpose of the Inspectorate is entirely in line with the aim of the criminal justice system, namely to protect the public and prevent re-offending. It does this by monitoring and influencing the treatment of prisoners.

When the new Chief Inspector (CI) arrived in 1997, the Inspectorate was already moving towards a vision of 'healthy' prisons, where its role would not only be to monitor, but also to stimulate improvement. The second half of the statement of purpose in **Chart 6.14** is effectively the Inspectorate's new vision. The CI expands on this vision of 'healthy prisons' as follows:

"In such prisons, the weakest prisoners feel safe, all prisoners are treated with respect as individuals, all are busily occupied and given the opportunity to improve themselves, and all are enabled to strengthen links with their families as part of their preparation for release, with the aim of avoiding re-offending in the future."[22]

The Inspectorate is implementing this by making inspections more effective, and by specifying the quality standards it expects to find.

Prisons now have to develop 9-, 15- and 24-month action plans following each inspection, and performance is checked on follow-ups. The style of inspections has also been changed. It goes beyond monitoring, to help prisons improve operational efficiency and involves experts in education, health, social skills and substance abuse. Twenty-nine 'Expectations' or quality standards have been established, linked to the healthy prison concept.

Building vision involves effort, pain and excitement. If you think an effective vision can be developed at a weekend seminar for senior managers, plus lots of presentations, torrents of brochures, badges and plastic cards, here's some simple advice. Save your time and money. Soldier on without a vision. It is better to be honest and have no vision at all, than go through wasteful motions to create an illusory one.

THE SOURCE

21 Interview with General Sir David Ramsbotham, Chief Inspector of Prisons, UK.
22 HM Inspectorate of Prisons Strategic Plan, 1999–2002.

Chapter

Best Practice ③

Creating hard values for sustainable advantage

Overview

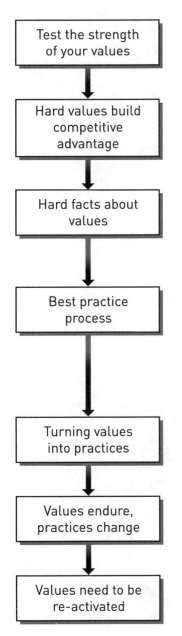

Test the strength of your values	• Are they hard or soft? • Do they withstand pressure? • Are they enduring?
Hard values build competitive advantage	• Define KSF in your category • Select values linked to them • Convert values into practices
Hard facts about values	• 47% moral values, e.g. affecting treatment of people, ethics • 53% performance values, e.g. customer focus, quality, innovation
Best practice process	1. Establish real values 2. Decide future KSF 3. Relate values to KSF and vision 4. Develop draft values 5. Discuss widely, revise 6. Develop practices
Turning values into practices	• Practices describe values in action • They are measurable • Translate them into personal performance targets
Values endure, practices change	• Values can endure for centuries • Practices constantly update the application of values
Values need to be re-activated	• They should guide every action, everyday • They will become passive unless constantly re-activated

CHART
7.1 **Are your values hard or soft?**

- **How do they withstand everyday pressures?**

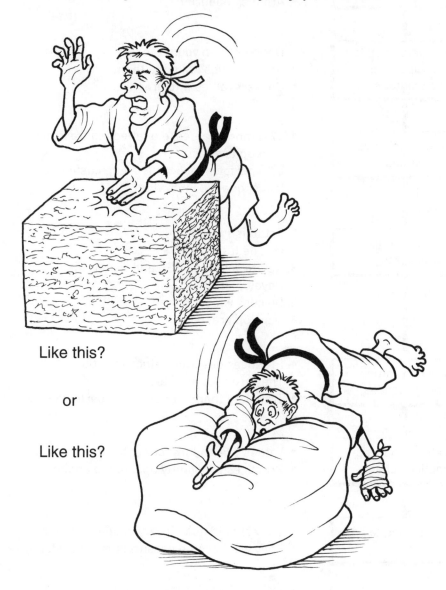

Like this?

or

Like this?

THE SOURCE

1 *FedEx Manager's Guide – Management Leadership Principles and Practices*, September 1998.
2 Lisa Endlich, *Goldman Sachs – the Culture of Success* (Little Brown & Co., 1999).
3 Author's interview.

Are values soft or hard?

Many organizations believe values are 'a good thing'. They see them helping recruitment, and providing useful fodder for the Annual Report – but otherwise remote from the real world, the bottom line.

Do they say, "You're behind on your value targets this year", or, "Breaching values is a sacking offence?" No – but fall behind on your performance targets and you can expect trouble. Organizations like this don't manage values. They play with them. And in regarding values as soft and optional, they usually make three big mistakes:

- They assume that values are generic, and unrelated to the vision.
- They do not link values to key success factors, and gain little impact on performance.
- They do not translate values into practices, so they are not lived or measured.

Contrast this with the best managers of values:

"Federal Express, from its inception, has put its people first, both because it is right to do so, and because it is good business as well. Our corporate philosophy is succinctly stated: People–Service–Profit."

FREDERICK SMITH, FOUNDER CHAIRMAN AND CEO[1]

"Our firm's culture is the most sustainable advantage we have."

BILL BUCKLEY, MANAGING DIRECTOR, GOLDMAN SACHS[2]

"Ethos (or values) provides the context within which you move from A to B. It's the most important aspect of the armed forces, and absorbed into the bloodstream through training. This ethos is timeless and almost unchanged since Wellington's time 200 years ago."

GENERAL SIR MICHAEL JACKSON, COMMANDER-IN-CHIEF, LAND FORCES, UK[3]

Organizations like these not only achieve results, but do so in the right way. People within them won't get promoted unless they live the values, and, yes, they may get fired for serious breaches. Values and performance are mutual partners, not opposed alternatives.

Once values are converted into measurable practices, and personal objectives, they become *hard*, because they strongly influence performance appraisal, rewards, promotion and dismissal. Ethics in particular becomes a hard value, as John Pepper, Chairman of Procter & Gamble observes:

"While ethics may seem like a soft concept – it is in fact a very hard concept. It is tangible. It is crucial . . . values have a tremendous impact on who is attracted to your company and who will stay with it . . . strong corporate values greatly simplify decision-making. It is important to know the things you won't even think about doing – diluting a product, taking a bribe, not being fair to a customer or employee.

CHART 7.2 Hard values build competitive advantage

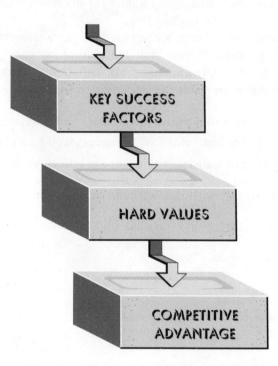

Once or twice a year we may have a problem on ethics. It shows up quickly because the organization knows it's wrong. How you react to these problems tells you things about the organization, and you need to take effective action quickly. If you tolerate one bribe, you're dead. Management needs to give high priority to ethics, to create a climate where they are supported, and people will talk openly. You need to be confident you can go to bed every night knowing that your people are trying to do the right thing."[4]

How hard values build competitive advantage

Organizations that take values seriously are not soft. On the contrary, they are likely to be highly competitive:

"There is a need in business to have strong values, like treating customers and people with respect and care, yet to be voraciously competitive, with a winning outlook."[5]

Competitive advantage is increasingly difficult to sustain because others are quick to copy your products or services. Values provide advantage through people and attitudes – extremely tough to catch up with. They do so by attracting the right kind of people, enabling delegation and focusing on the key factors for success (see **Chart 7.2**).

"It is not difficult to achieve quick success, but this is often followed by problems. Gaining *sustainable* success is difficult, and embedding vision and values are critical to this."[6]

Quick results can often be obtained through short-term expedients, which damage long-term prospects. Hard values ensure that results are got in the right way, so that the future franchise is strengthened. Values also facilitate speed of decision-making, since they enable senior management to delegate with more confidence, while also giving local management a clear picture of how they are expected to approach decisions.

"Today there is greater complexity globally, more need for speed, people on the front line are better trained – and fortunately vision and values provide a framework for much greater autonomy."[7]

SmithKline Beecham (now Glaxo SmithKline) provides a good example of how values can be built in order to achieve competitive advantage:

SmithKline Beckman, a US company, and Beecham Group, UK-based, were merged in 1988. They had different skills and values. Rather than attempt to combine the best of both, the SmithKline Beecham (SB) Management Committee decided to develop a new set of values. It looked ahead to

 THE SOURCE

   4 John E. Pepper, Chairman, Procter & Gamble, 'The BOA Principle – Operating Ethically in Today's Business Environment': address to Florida A&M University, 30 January 1997, plus author's interview.
   5 Interview with Kenny Hirschhorn, Executive VP of Strategy, Imagineering and Futurology, Orange plc.
   6 Interview with Robert Bauman, former Chairman, British Aerospace, first CEO of SmithKline Beecham.
   7 Interview with Terry Leahy, CEO, Tesco plc.

CHART
7.3 Hard values converted into strategies

SmithKline Beecham – hard values converted into strategies	
Values	**Strategies**
Performance	Most efficient producers
Innovation	Leader in new product discovery and development
Customer focus	Most effective marketers
People Integrity	Best managed company

select those values that would make a real difference to SB's performance and competitive position if practised by every employee. Five areas were identified:

- **Performance**. To meet shareholders' expectations, SB had to grow sales and drive down costs. Its productivity per employee was poorer than competitors.

- **Innovation.** This was a critical success factor in pharmaceuticals, SB's main category, and the flow of successful new drugs would have to be accelerated.

- **Customer focus**. The new company needed to become more customer-orientated. Customers were seen as both co-workers internally, and physicians externally. Everyone in the organization had customers.

- **People.** To be successful, SB had to recruit and retain excellent people.

- **Integrity.** The trust of physicians, pharmacists, regulators and consumers was essential for success.

The five chosen values were built around these five factors for success and translated into nine measurable leadership practices. They were also turned into strategies (see **Chart 7.3**).

The values were not distinctive, but the way in which they were executed through strategy and practices was.[8]

In our research, about 60% of organizations linked their values, at least informally, to key factors for future success, and there was no difference between companies and non-profits. However, the general quality of the linkage was not strong.

Hard facts about values

There is little available research analysing the number and type of values organizations have. Based on our survey of 125 organizations, certain conclusions can be drawn:

1 **Only 44% of organizations had written values**. Values always exist whether written or not. If they are not written, there may be confusion over what they are meant to be. Some might argue that everyone knows what the values are, so what's the point of writing them down? However, if it is decided to codify them, people are often shocked to find wide differences of opinion. It is difficult to translate values into everyday behaviour even when they are stated with crystal clarity. Fifty-six per cent of companies had written values, only 29% of non-profits.

2 **The average organization had five values.** This looks about right. Values should be memorable, and more than five becomes a test of memory. One company had 14 values. Having reached unlucky 13, it added another, 'Have Fun'. There was no difference in number of values between companies and non-profits.

THE SOURCE

8 Robert Bauman, Peter Jackson and Joanne Lawrence, *From Promise to Performance* (HBS Press, 1997), an excellent book, plus interview with Robert Bauman.

CHART
7.4 **Hard facts about values**

Breakdown of values by type[9]	
Type	% of total values listed
Treatment of people	15
Ethics/integrity	12
Customer focus	10
Interaction with people	11
Operational excellence	8
Superior quality/service	7
Innovation	7
Social and community	5
Other	25
TOTAL	100

DM
MERLIN
JOBY
DAVE *5
RASO

TC EMP.
NC.
ASSN.
DILOT.
AME.

THE SOURCE

9 This analysis was based on 103 organizations in the research sample for which values could be clearly identified.

3 **Eight types of value accounted for 75% of the total.** Values from all organizations interviewed were listed and broken down by type. Eight predominated, with treatment of people, ethics, customer focus and teamwork the leading types, as **Chart 7.4** shows. There were differences between companies and non-profits. The latter predictably gave more emphasis to treatment of people, less to innovation and customer focus, and had a wider range of values outside the top eight types, as Table 7.1 shows:

Table 7.1

Breakdown of value types		
Type	**% of total values listed**	
	Company	**Non-profits**
Treatment of people	12	(20)
Ethics/integrity	12	12
Customer focus	(13)	6
Interaction with people	10	11
Operational excellence	9	5
Superior quality/service	7	7
Innovation	(10)	4
Social and community	7	3
Other	20	(32)
Total	100%	100%

4 **Moral values accounted for almost half the total, and predominated in non-profits** (see **Chart 7.5**). The difference is important because breaches of moral values tend to be taken most seriously, and can be very damaging to the organization brand. People are more likely to be fired for mistreating people or being dishonest than for falling short on innovation.

Examples of hard values in action

Loblaw is the dominant grocery retailer in Canada and has averaged 27% share price growth annually over the past 24 years. Richard Currie, its former CEO, did the job for 28 years, and observed:

"Loblaw focuses on two main values – competence and honesty. We want both from our people. Many geniuses are dishonest and many honest people aren't smart. Some people are politicians and talk upwards better than downwards. Others are trusted by their people but don't present well to senior management. We have to sort all this out because we only promote people who are both smart and honest.

I've got a veto on hiring, firing, or promoting everyone, to two levels below.

CHART
7.5
7.5 Morality and performance

Breakdown into moral and performance values (%)			
Type	Company	Non-profit	Total
Moral	41	55	47
Performance	59	45	53
All values	100	100	100

> In this school, you fail if you don't care, but caring is not enough. We need caring doers.
>
> **Carole Evans, CBE**
> **Head Teacher, Priory School, Slough, England**

One of the biggest signs of values is whether politicians or demanding hard workers get promoted. People lower down know and can tell whether management is in touch, and applying its stated values."[10]

DuPont is another company with clear values, and its Chairman CEO commented:

"Three of our main values – safety, ethics and respect for people – have been in place since the company was started 198 years ago by the family. The fourth value – environmental stewardship – was adopted a decade ago.

DuPont started life as an explosives company. At that time, all new experiments would be led by a family member, to demonstrate safety in action, and to share the risk. That culture has persisted to this day. We set the highest possible safety standards, above government targets, and are the benchmark used by companies in many industries."[11]

Here are two examples of how quality and teamwork are executed at Johnson & Johnson, provided by a former Group Chairman of Ethicon, who earlier in his career had been a country manager:

Quality: "Highest product quality is one of J&J's most important values. Ethicon manufactures over 600 million needles every year, and its needles and threads are used in over 7 out of every 10 surgical operations conducted in the world, often in life-threatening situations where product quality must be paramount. Every year Ethicon may receive 10–15 product complaints which are taken very seriously.

Some years ago, shortly after I was appointed President of Ethicon USA, we introduced a new quality initiative designed to reinforce our commitment to the highest standards. We were about to introduce a new line of instruments for endoscopic or keyhole surgery, and these were to be launched at a major surgical convention. However, timing was tight and the first batches of the new product only arrived a week before the launch. We had set a standard of 98.4% as a basis for batch acceptance, but the Quality department advised that only 98.2% had passed the test. I was urged to pass the batch, as it was 'nearly' there.

To the horror of the Sales and Marketing people, I told them to reject the batch, and if necessary delay the launch. We had communicated our new quality initiative so broadly within the company I felt it was vitally important we should not be seen to compromise at the first hurdle. Within 30 minutes, the news flashed around the company, and I received calls from all levels even down to individuals on the packing line, congratulating me on my stand, and pledging their personal commitment. 'Now we believe the company is committed to quality, and you have our full support' was a common theme."

Teamwork: "I'd just joined J&J as Managing Director of a small company with 200 employees in Columbia. The good news was high market shares in most of our product segments.

THE SOURCE

10 Interview with Richard Currie, President George Weston Ltd, former President Loblaw Companies Ltd.
11 Interview with Charles Holliday Jr, Chairman and CEO, DuPont.

CHART
7.6 Example of stated values versus real ones

Stated values	Real values
Highest quality	Average quality
Innovation	Limit investment
Teamwork	Blame others
Low cost operation	Seek short-cuts

The bad news – we had virtually no raw materials and were unlikely to receive any for some months. So I called up my new boss in New Brunswick. He said, 'You sort it out. We're a decentralized organization, and this is what we pay you for.' He then hung up, after welcoming me to the corporation.

A bit stunned, but seeing the point, I called in my senior managers for some advice. There were suggestions for using a different raw material which would have reduced quality and other ideas I didn't like. Then someone said 'Every J&J company in Latin America is short of this product, but why don't you call the other Managing Directors to see if they can help.'

So I called up Brazil, Venezuela, and a few others. The response was the same from all countries: 'We're pretty short of supply, too, Philip, but of course we'll help you out, and by the way, you must come and visit us, because we'd really like to meet you.' And they did help me out – a new employee they'd never even met."[12]

An organization with hard values can withstand external scrutiny. Emerson Electric's values are strongly held (though not written down) and include cost reduction through technology, and growth. One day they were unexpectedly tested:

"A reporter from Business Week was doing a feature on Emerson, and asked to speak to five blue-collar employees. In a state of alarm the PR department called the Chairman/CEO. He said, 'It's OK. We should be able to handle this kind of scrutiny. Give him a list and let him choose.'

It was OK. The first interviewee, a plant operative, was asked, 'Why do you work here when you could get $3 an hour more from General Electric, down the road, for similar work?' The reply? 'You're out of touch. GE has had lay-offs over the years, we're beating their butt off in this category, and I like it here.' The next interviewee understood the need for cost reduction. He was redesigning a tool which sold in millions, aiming to save 3 cents per unit. The values stood up to testing."[13]

While organizations have many values, one or two often predominate, as at Loblaws, DuPont, and Johnson & Johnson. Goldman Sachs' two core values are 'clients first' and 'teamwork'. At Home Depot 'entrepreneurial spirit' is the primary value although there are six others. For many schools, 'the children come first' is the most important value.

Identifying what current values really are

The gap between stated values and actual behaviour in organizations is often wide.

This company, with which the author is familiar, constantly underperformed its potential. The gap between stated values and the real ones was wide (see **Chart 7.6**), but never directly addressed. Members of senior management almost relished their widely different views about future destination, and there was no consistency on: 'This is the way we do things around here.'

┌─ THE SOURCE ───
12 Interview with Philip Carne, former Group Chairman of Ethicon, part of Johnson & Johnson, now non-executive director of a number of companies.
13 Interview with Charles Knight, Chairman, Emerson Electric.

CHART
7.7 Best practice process for developing
values

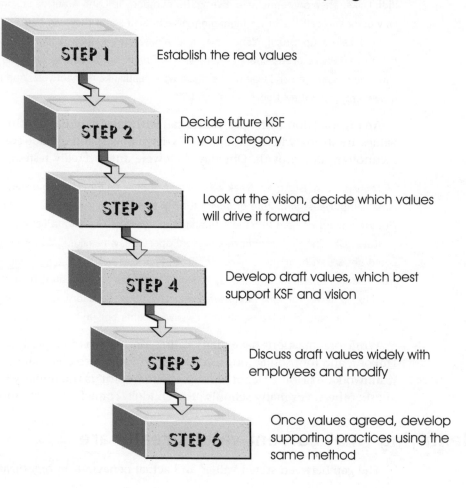

Best practice process for developing values

STEP 1 — Establish the real values

STEP 2 — Decide future KSF in your category

STEP 3 — Look at the vision, decide which values will drive it forward

STEP 4 — Develop draft values, which best support KSF and vision

STEP 5 — Discuss draft values widely with employees and modify

STEP 6 — Once values agreed, develop supporting practices using the same method

Influenced by this, the company marketed average products at premium prices, made poor use of some good people, and allowed them to compete with each other rather than with outside competitors.

So how do you see behind the glossy value statements to the reality? As a new leader, you can set up a confidential employee survey, asking employees what they think values really are, and what they should be. You can check out the same questions with customers. This is especially useful in business-to-business where the whole organization interacts with customers.

Real insights can also be gained from the new art of customer empathy research, where skilled interviewers phone in posing as customers and ask a range of questions that reveal knowledge levels, attitudes and commitment of front-line people. From this, you can tell how the customer is likely to feel about the organization, and how employees *actually* feel.

You can build understanding informally by observing signals from the organization, such as sales literature, websites, buildings and offices, the way people interact, their appearance and dress. Communication through signals is covered in Chapter 8 (pages 159–162).

The task of spotting real values has lately been eased by the publication of heavily researched and unauthorized company biographies, often involving many candid interviews inside and out. They are much more useful than cleverly massaged official histories.

Above all, real values can be seen in the activities and behaviour of people in the company. If the two are not aligned, stated values will be discredited. So when you talk to a CEO who says his most important value is 'respect for people', then discover that he has cleaned out two complete senior management teams since 1990, you can see the gap.[14]

How to develop tomorrow's values

Since strong values endure for decades, even centuries, it should not be necessary to change them. However, in reality many organizations need a new set of values, either because they've never been codified before, or because they are not relevant. The process summarized in **Chart 7.7** is a synthesis of the best approaches observed in the 125 organizations researched. No single one followed this exact process.

Step 5 is frequently overlooked. This example from Tesco, one of the world's leading grocery retailers, demonstrates how to use it:

"Values must be framed in everyday language, so that people can link them to daily work. The draft words for Tesco's values were initially written by senior managers who were graduates. Group discussions with store staff brought about changes. One initial value was 'To have fun'

THE SOURCE

14 Conversation with Chairman/CEO, identity withheld.

CHART
7.8
Turning values into practices

Simply better–SmithKline Beecham's Nine Leadership Practices[15]

1. Find opportunities for constantly challenging and improving personal performance

2. Work with people individually and as a team to determine new targets, and to develop programmes to achieve these higher standards of performance

3. Identify and continuously implement improved ways to anticipate, serve and satisfy internal and external customer needs

4. Stress the importance of developing and implementing more effective and efficient ways to improve SB procedures, products, and services through quality analysis

5. Initiate and display a willingness to change in order to obtain and to sustain a competitive advantage

6. Reward and celebrate significant and creative achievements

7. Develop and appoint high-performing and high potential people to key positions

8. Help all employees to achieve their full potential by matching their talents with the jobs to be done and through quality performance feedback and coaching

9. Communicate with all constituents openly, honestly, interactively and on a timely basis

THE SOURCE

15 Bauman et al., *From Promise to Performance*.
16 Interview with Terry Leahy, CEO, Tesco.
17 Bauman et al., *From Promise to Performance*.
18 Interview with Peter Jensen, former President WSO, SmithKline Beecham.
19 Bauman et al., *From Promise to Performance*.

and operating staff said, 'No, you don't have fun at work. You want it to be enjoyable and fulfilling.' Staff didn't like 'Take Risks' as a value and this was also changed.''[16]

Turning values into measurable practices

Let's take up the SmithKline Beecham (SB) example again, because it is a success story and well documented. Five values, based on key success factors (KSF), have been agreed by senior management: performance, innovation, customer focus, people and integrity (see Chart 7.3 above). Each one has also been described in two or three sentences. For instance, the 'people' descriptor is:

SB employees are all partners, working together in the pursuit of the SB mission and strategy. We strongly value teamwork and we want every employee to be motivated to succeed.[17]

This is useful, but if the process stops at this point, words are unlikely to be turned into action. To ensure they really happen, values need to be turned into measurable practices. SB did this, using the 'Simply Better' way as the internal brand for embedding values. **Chart 7.8** covers the Nine Leadership Practices designed to translate the five values into action. Read them twice and you will see that every word counts, especially Practice Three.

''Values are the way we live, and practices are the way we work.''[18]

These Nine Practices could be improved. They could, for example, cover attitude to risk within innovation, and link the practices more closely with each of the values. However, they are well done, can be translated into personal performance targets, and measured. SB is very good at establishing action processes and measuring them.

Detailed guidelines were developed for the new appraisal system and examples were given of what a practice would look like in action. For instance one question under Practice Three was, ''When did you last sit down with a customer to find out what his/her needs were?'' [See Chart 7.8.]

360° feedback (managers are evaluated by their boss, peers, and subordinates) was also introduced, in line with Practice Nine. This is how the CEO learned that he scored poorly on Practice Six – 'reward and celebrate achievement'. He would say ''Thank you'' and ''Well done'', usually followed by a ''but''. In promising to change his behaviour, he agreed to hand over $10 every time anyone caught him saying ''but''.[19]

SB had hardwired areas usually regarded as soft. If it had merely told people to behave Simply Better without showing them how, little would have been achieved.

In the non-profit sector, Save the Children (UK) followed a similar approach, and the new value of 'child focused' adopted in the mid 1990s, has greatly influenced action.

CHART
7.9 # Communicating what values mean in practice – Save the Children (UK)

Value	Practice
Child focused	• We try to view the world through children's eyes
Independent	• We never compromise our integrity • We are prepared to be radical and outspoken
Accountable	• Responsible to children, families, communities, supporters • Professionally and financially sound, scrupulous, efficient and effective

Note: Extracted from Save the Children's values

There are four others: Ambitious but practical, Open, Collaborative, and a Team

This value means, 'We try to view the world through children's eyes', and 'We put the reality of children's lives at the heart of everything we do'. Here are two examples of how this value has been turned into action:

"First it's enabled Save the Children (UK) to re-focus its activities. In the 1970s, it accepted, like many other children's charities, the logic that helping the community equals helping the child. This led to projects like community health and water. Applying the new value, developed in the 1990s, it became clear that such benefits were too indirect. A new strategy, focusing on six areas of direct benefit to children, was developed.

Second, the 'child-focused' value simplifies decision-making, typified by SC's involvement in difficult issues of child labour. For the 1994 World Cup footballs were hand-stitched, and children were heavily involved, mainly from the Sialkot area of Pakistan. When this was revealed it resulted in bad publicity for manufacturers like Nike, Adidas and others. They asked SC to co-ordinate a project to phase out child labour. SC worked in partnership with UNICEF, local authorities, the chamber of commerce, and global brands.

SC applied one of the practices supporting its 'child-focused' value, which was 'Talk to them and check what they think'. It found that the children couldn't understand why they should stop working. They needed to work, because their mothers and sisters couldn't (religious constraints prevented women working alongside men). The only other work in town was at a surgical instrument factory where there were many injuries. The children viewed stitching work as hard, but safe, while appreciating that they were missing out on education.

SC and its partners wanted to remove the cause of the problem. The key was to phase out child labour rather than bringing it to an abrupt end, to develop a satisfactory education system, and to protect household income. A two-point program was implemented:

- Manufacturers set up all-women stitching plants, with crèches, on-site canteens and bussing in from villages. A bonus was that women could stitch 30% faster than children.

- Funding for children's education was established."[20,21]

Chart 7.9 illustrates practices supporting three of Save the Children's values. If you're still not convinced of the need to translate values into measurable practices, here's one more example.

"One of General Mills' values is high quality products and services. The related practice is: 'We will provide competitively superior products and services to our customers and consumers. This superiority will be measured by rigorous, comparative testing, versus the best competitive offerings, and by growth in market shares.' For the past 10 years, General Mills has set the tough target of winning blind product tests among consumers by a 60:40 margin.

THE SOURCE

20 Interview with Barry Clarke, OBE, Chairman, Save the Children Fund (UK).

21 The International Labor Organization also played an important role in this programme.

CHART
7.10 New York Police Department – what the value of 'professionalism' means[22]

- Acknowledging the rights and dignity of those we come in contact with

- Acknowledging the diversity, traditions and cultures of others

- Being cognisant of the manner in which we speak to others

- Being knowledgeable of our responsibilities and the extent of our authority

- Being adept in defusing volatile situations

- Recognizing the impact that traumatic events can have on the people we come in contact with

- Extending respect to our colleagues, regardless of rank or position

THE SOURCE

22 NYPD – CPR booklet.
23 Interview with Stephen Demeritt, Vice Chairman, General Mills.
24 Interview with Douglas Sweeney, VP Strategy, IBM.
25 Interview with Paul Walsh, CEO, Diageo.

Anyone who has worked in consumer goods will know just how hard that is to sustain. 50% of General Mills' sales revenue now meets this criterion, and the company has recently become No. 1 in USA breakfast cereals, overtaking Kellogg's."[23]

Adjusting values to different cultures

The consensus among global organizations interviewed was that values should be applied consistently across every country and every business, as this comment demonstrates:

"IBM values are global. Many of our customers are also global and share similar values to our own. Our key values and metrics to measure them are mandatory. However, our countries are run by nationals, so they understand local cultures, and issues like working hours and dress code are local decisions."[24]

Global values which may run counter to local cultures include integrity (vs corruption), diversity (vs discrimination), equal opportunity (vs untouchables, promotion by seniority, exclusion of women), and academic independence (vs political influence).

While the best global organizations retain their core values everywhere, they may communicate them differently by country or vary the supporting practices:

"At Diageo, there are no exceptions anywhere to our four values, but we may stress or de-emphasize specific aspects by region or country."[25]

Of course, different cultures *within* countries are also important in applying values. This applies to the New York Police Department (NYPD):

"New York City has 7.5 million people from 178 countries. NYPD's vision is to reduce crime and to do it in a way the community feels happy with.

The key factors for success in police work are simple – cut crime while maintaining public support (for information and co-operation) and political support (for funding). The two key measures are results and complaint levels, and these are closely monitored, using the COMPSTAT system.

Performance (crime reduction) has always been a strong value. Serious crime in New York is down by 60% (versus a national drop of around 25%) since 1993, and civilian complaints have declined by 43% since 1996. Three values were introduced in 1996 – courtesy, professionalism and respect (CPR). [See **Chart 7.10** for what 'professionalism' means.]

CPR was developed with NYPD by people from different cultural backgrounds, including local community groups, advocacy people, police critics and religious groups. They comprise a CPR Board, monitoring results and providing feedback. Each of the city's 76 precincts has developed a demographic profile, and there are 7 videos on ethnic mores, demonstrating, for instance, that it's quite normal for Chinese Americans to indulge in sword practice.

CHART
7.11 Values need to be constantly re-activated

Values will become passive unless re-activated

Reactivate by:

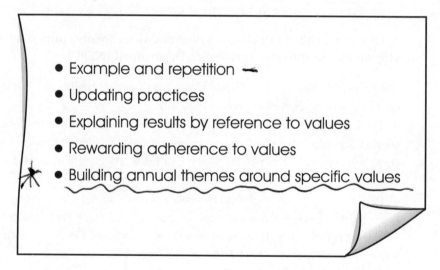

- Example and repetition
- Updating practices
- Explaining results by reference to values
- Rewarding adherence to values
- Building annual themes around specific values

CPR is therefore tailored to the specific culture of each precinct, though its essential core is applied throughout New York."[26]

If you think it's easy to adjust values to different cultures, consider this story, about a Western global company, as described by its CEO:[27]

"You need to allow for different cultures. Some are more driven than others, and the balance between home and office life varies. In Japan, our country manager felt some of the executives were working themselves to death, and he decided to forbid weekend working. He got everyone together one Friday afternoon, explained his thoughts, and said he was locking the office for the weekend. Driving by the office on Saturday morning, he was confronted by the sight of a ladder resting against a second floor window and employees within, working as hard as ever."

Hard values drive change

It is easy to allow values to become passive, and part of the background. Even companies with long established values, and supporting practices, find it hard to bring them alive on an everyday basis. Procter & Gamble uses values and practices to address things it wants to change:

"Values of ownership, integrity and high calibre people have been in place at P&G for almost 100 years, but only recently codified. Many of the codified practices (called 'principles') are designed to create real change. For instance:

- 'We are honest with people about their performance.' In the past, people were not sufficiently candid in personal appraisals. This is unfair to those assessed and impedes development.

- 'We learn from both our successes and our failures.' Failures used to be glossed over and we didn't learn from them. Now we insist on being candid.

- 'We take pride in results from reapplying others' ideas.' P&G had a big 'not invented here' syndrome. We want to change that."[28]

THE SOURCE

26 Interview with Howard Safir, former Commissioner, NYPD. Also CPR booklet, and article on former Commissioner Bill Bratton, 'Lessons from the man who tamed New York', *Daily Telegraph*, 21 July 2000.
27 Name and company withheld.
28 Interview with Durk Jager, former CEO, Procter & Gamble.

Chapter

Best Practice 4

Emotional activism – communicating by action, signals and words

Overview

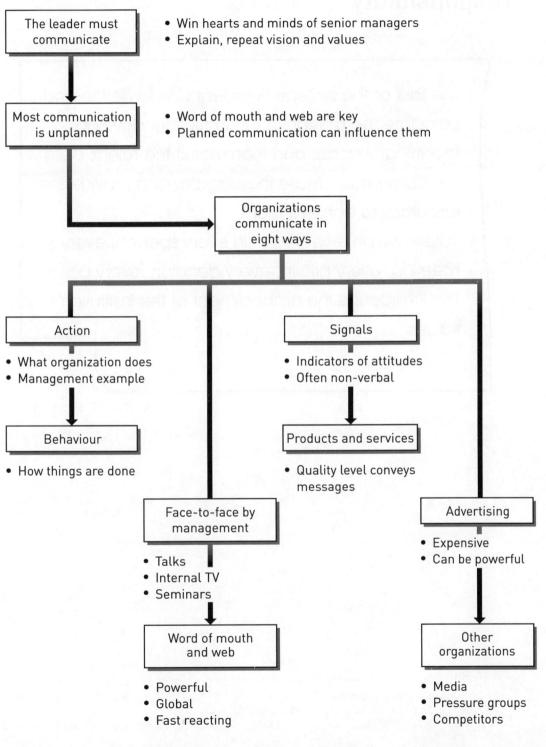

The leader must communicate
- Win hearts and minds of senior managers
- Explain, repeat vision and values

Most communication is unplanned
- Word of mouth and web are key
- Planned communication can influence them

Organizations communicate in eight ways

Action
- What organization does
- Management example

Signals
- Indicators of attitudes
- Often non-verbal

Behaviour
- How things are done

Products and services
- Quality level conveys messages

Face-to-face by management
- Talks
- Internal TV
- Seminars

Advertising
- Expensive
- Can be powerful

Word of mouth and web
- Powerful
- Global
- Fast reacting

Other organizations
- Media
- Pressure groups
- Competitors

8.1 Communication is the leader's personal responsibility

The task of the college President ... is to define and articulate the mission of the institution; develop meaningful goals; and then recruit the talent, build the consensus, create the climate, and provide the resources to achieve them.

Values will be reflected ... in every speech, every meeting, every priority, every decision, every policy. The President is the embodiment of the institution's values.[1]

THE SOURCE

1 Dr Frank H.T. Rhodes, President, Cornell University, 1977–94, 'The Art of the Presidency', in *The President*, American Council of Education, Spring 1998.

Communication is the leader's personal responsibility

Chart 8.1 relates to universities, but describes the task of every organization leader. Dr Rhodes elaborates on how to do this:

"By building on the traditions of the institution, harnessing its strength, recognizing emerging needs, seizing new opportunities, developing new niches, and building new constituencies, the vision and mission gradually take shape, to be tested, refined and sharpened in active debate with all the stakeholders, both on and off the campus."[2]

A key role of organization leaders is communication. They communicate all the time by what they say, do and don't do. Nothing has the same authority as the Chairman/ CEO, Hospital President, or Head Teacher talking to you personally. Communication of vision and values may be cascaded below CEOs, but it can't be delegated by them.

Leaders must either win the hearts and minds of senior managers or replace them. Those who ultimately can't agree with the vision and values, after extended discussion, should be given the opportunity to leave, as in this example:

"When I became CEO, there were 65 senior managers. The biggest group was articulate profes-sional types, who were bright but risk-averse, and poor implementers. Some had to go. A smaller group (mostly ex-sales people) was low on intelligence, high on risk-taking. They were dangerous and all had to go. I brought in 15 intelligent risk-taking implementers from outside and combined them with the core of the original team. They soon earned most of the leadership positions.

Once the vision and values were agreed, I said to the senior managers: 'If any of you is unhappy about our future direction, come and tell me privately, and we'll be generous and helpful in moving you on.' Three left. We just didn't have the time to carry senior people who weren't convinced."[3]

Effective leaders operate by example, and communicate frequently through action and words, like this chairman:

"The message from the top has to be consistent and constantly repeated until you're thoroughly bored with it. This is when the message starts to penetrate, because you have to tell people seven times before they hear for the first time.

Layers of management can be a problem. There are always patches of shadow below managers who are ineffective communicators, areas where the vision and values don't penetrate. That's why I encourage all of my management team to attend meetings two levels down."[4]

THE SOURCE

2 Interview with Dr Frank Rhodes, President Emeritus of Cornell University and Director of GE; article on 'The Art of the Presidency', in *The President*, American Council of Education, Spring 1998.
3 Chairman/CEO, identity withheld.

CHART
8.2
Cascading the vision and values message will fail if there's not a critical mass of support at the top

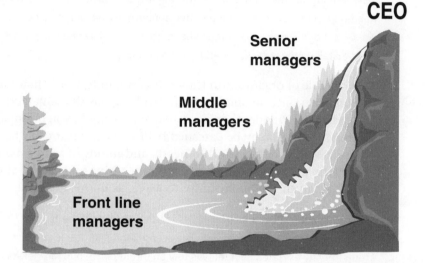

CEO

Senior
managers

Middle
managers

Front line
managers

CHART
8.3
Actions communicate more powerfully than words

"One of my long-standing beliefs is commitment to low cost.
In many organizations it's hard to stop people becoming extravagant.
I emphazise that all costs of running a business have to come from the customer – there's no other source.
So if the company wants to spend £X, you ask, 'Would the customer think that was value for money?' Our pay and conditions are not excessive and we don't own private planes.
Senior Management must lead by example.
You can't have unnecessary spending in a world of intense competition."

**Sir Brian Pitman
former Chairman, Lloyds TSB**

William Stavropoulos, Chairman of Dow Chemical, repeatedly demonstrates the connection between vision and values, growth and the bottom line; and the idea of consequences – for living and not living the vision and values.[5]

In smaller organizations like schools, communication will be mainly face-to-face by the Head. In global companies, with perhaps 300 000 people worldwide, leaders remain personally responsible for communication, but have to operate through others. A key issue is how many people you require, inside the circle of wagons, before feeling confident enough to cascade the message through others:

"You need a critical mass of senior managers who are believers before you start cascading. Otherwise the message will dilute or reverse as it goes down the line [see **Chart 8.2**] and the readiness of senior managers to sell the message erodes if they see decisions or behaviour which conflict with it."[6]

Percy Barnevik, Chairman of ABB, talked to 5000 employees and 100 major customers each year when he was CEO, and had 10 people directly reporting to him who did the same.[7] Capitalization of the company increased dramatically during his years as CEO.

Actions by managers are more important than words

This obvious fact is frequently ignored. Managers' actions may be out of line with the words of the vision and values because they are not committed. Or perhaps they are true believers yet fail to understand how others will interpret their actions (see **Chart 8.3**).

You can avoid the problem by explaining how decisions fit the vision and values. The content and tone of the communication should vary between qualified professionals and blue-collar workers, customers and environmentalists, security analysts and government officials. The overall message must be consistent and true. You can't say opposing things to the different stakeholders any more.

Some of the best statements about words and action were written in the sixteenth century – the twenty-first century has some catching up to do:

Suit the action to the word, the word to the action.[8]

All words and no performance.[9]

Deeds, not words, shall speak me.[10]

THE SOURCE

4 Interview with Sir Alan Rudge, CBE, FRS, Chairman, W.S. Atkins.
5 Interview with Bill Stavropoulos, Chairman, Dow Chemical.
6 Interview with Sam Younger, Director General, British Red Cross.
7 Interview with Percy Barnevik, Chairman, Asea Brown Boveri (ABB).
8 William Shakespeare (1564–1616), *Hamlet*, Act III.
9 Philip Massinger (1583–1640), *The Parliament of Love*, Act I.
10 John Fletcher (1579–1625), *The Lovers Progress*, Act I.

CHART
8.4

"Communication always occurs but often it's not deliberate"

Planned communication

- Vision, value statements
- Face to face by management
- Advertising

- Web sites, e-mail
- Actions and behaviour
- Products, services
- Performance
- Signals

| Some control |

Unplanned communication

Word of web

Word of mouth

Editorial comment

Behaviour

Unexpected events

e-mail

Actions

| Little control |

CHART
8.5

Organizations communicate in eight ways

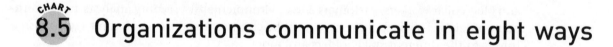

1. Actions
2. Behaviour
3. Face-to-face by management
4. Signals
5. Products and services
6. Advertising
7. Word of mouth and word of web (including e-mail)
8. Comments by other organizations

"Communication always occurs, but often it's not deliberate"[11]

Chart 8.4 breaks down communication into planned and unplanned. There is always overlap between the two. Senior management would like every employee to reflect the organization's vision and values all the time, and to be innovative as well. This never happens because people are individuals. Planning can only reach so far, and the unpredictable is always lurking ahead.

Well-planned and honest communication will influence unplanned communication. An exciting vision creates word of mouth of its own accord. Bold actions to uphold values become legends. Meticulously planned new products communicate concern for quality and innovation.

In reality, only a small proportion of an organization's communication can be planned, and even less can be controlled.

Organizations communicate in eight ways

Communication by organizations works in eight main ways, as summarized in **Chart 8.5**. This section takes a brief look at each way. Later ones examine all eight in more depth.

- **Action.** This what the organization does. There are hundreds or thousands of actions each day.
- **Behaviour** describes *how* things are done, how people treat others, especially colleagues and customers.
- **Face-to-face communication by management** covers talks, meetings, debate, one-to-one conversations and questions asked. Questions by managers communicate what they think is important. If superior quality is a key value, but the CEO only asks people about costs, quality will soon be replaced by cost as the priority.

This head teacher communicated through questions:

"For us, the most important thing is a happy environment, and academic achievement by children who do lots of things. Happiness is an intangible value and hard to evaluate. So at the end of conversations or interviews with parents, I always ask: "Is he/she happy?"[12]

- **Signals** are actions or objects which convey information about an organization. For instance, in schools, signals include the way children look, behave, play and dress. An experienced Head could get a good feel for the values of a new school just by walking around and observing signals for a couple of hours.

THE SOURCE

11 Interview with Vice-Dean Eitan Zemel, Stern Business School, NYU.
12 Interview with Claire Oulton, then Head Teacher at St Catherine's School, Bramley, now Head of Benenden School.

8.6 Communication through action

Action of *Titanic* orchestra in continuing to play signalled its commitment to values of entertaining and relaxing passengers

THE SOURCE

13 Interview with CEO of leading company, identity withheld.

14 Activism: the use of vigorous campaigning (*The New Oxford Dictionary of English*, Clarendon Press, 1998).

15 Interview with Head Teacher, name withheld.

Here is an original CEO approach to signals:

"I used to run a farm. Early every morning I'd look at the animals' noses, eyes, coats. I do the same here. First thing, I walk around the offices and talk to people, look at their eyes, the way they move, or sit, listen to their tone of voice. Running a farm and a company have a lot in common."[13]

- **Products and services.** Their quality and style embody the organization's vision and values. Poor quality or service says people don't care.
- **Advertising** covers the whole gamut of paid-for communication. While advertising output is planned and controlled, reaction to it isn't.
- **Word of mouth and web.** Next to action and behaviour, this is the most important way organizations communicate. It's heavily influenced by the other seven ways.
- **Comments by other organizations** such as the media, pressure groups, governments.

We'll look at each of the eight ways in which organizations communicate. Managing and influencing them requires emotional activism – the use of vigorous campaigning.[14]

Communication through action

This has already been covered indirectly, and **Chart 8.6** provides a famous example of how action communicates values. Those musicians were heroes. Like innovation, action comes in two forms – the daily drip feed, and the big hits.

The first matters most. The momentum of daily actions only moves values minutely, but over time, inches become miles. The big hits will gain you a mile in a moment. Big hits occur when values collide with events. The organization's response to these moments of truth will heavily enhance or erode values. Everyone is watching the leader. Will the values stand up or fall apart when really tested?

This school had a policy of expelling pupils who took drugs. The son of the Chairman of the Board of Governors (also a major donor) was discovered with drugs. The Head Teacher had to decide what to do. He consulted senior colleagues, and expelled the pupil. The Head said to me, "It was the right thing to do, and I thought I might get fired myself." He wasn't, and the Chairman, who didn't oppose the decision, resigned.[15]

Big hits have a disproportionate impact, and may remain on the word of mouth network for years, like Procter & Gamble's decision to shut down its Pampers plant in Nigeria rather than pay a bribe to a customs inspector; and Merck's decision in 1987 to donate supplies of Mectizan, a drug preventing river blindness, to equatorial countries, since the governments had neither the funds nor the delivery systems to treat those affected.

CHART 8.7 Communication through behaviour

Values	Behaviour	Communication
Treat everyone with respect	Tolerate bullying	
Unimpeachable integrity	Allow bribery	*Management doesn't care about values*
Superior service	Accept mediocre customer service levels	

Such moments of truth are usually created by unforeseen events, and the way they are resolved becomes folklore... one way or the other.

Communication through behaviour

Behaviour is one of the most important communicators of values, especially those affecting people, quality and integrity. News about behaviour makes good conversation, and spreads fast by word of mouth or e-mail. Mismatches between values and behaviour (as in **Chart 8.7**) are soon picked up.

What conclusions do you draw from this story, told by the Chief Executive of Eurostar, the rail service connecting Britain to Europe beneath the Channel?[16]

There are different internal cultures at Eurostar, reflecting the three countries involved, UK, France and Belgium. Shared values are a strong belief in the Eurostar product and a determination to be at the leading edge.

In the early days, differences emerged in attitudes to customers that had to be, where possible, ironed out. The UK side saw the physical product as the base, people as the differentiator. It viewed people as intrinsic to the product and a level of flexibility was therefore accepted in delivering service to customers. In general, the French and Belgians were more inclined to view efficiency as paramount and to enforce rules rigidly.

Three overseas passengers from London to Paris were convinced that they had booked and paid for first-class tickets, yet were given economy ones. They complained to the English Purser. She decided to adopt the flexible approach. She said she believed them but they still only held economy tickets. However, as an exception, and because there was plenty of room in first class, she would allow them to upgrade. At this point the French Train Manager was passing and intervened.

He took the 'efficiency' approach and, after a brief discussion, told the passengers that if they didn't leave first class at once they would be removed. Neither staff member was 'wrong' in their stance and the 'rules' had been correctly observed. However, their different approach to the same situation produced a poor customer experience.

Building on this experience and others, Eurostar dramatically increased investment in customer service in all countries, recognizing the need for a single culture to which everyone was committed, and substantial progress has been made.

Eurostar is not an exception. In most organizations, vision and values tend to be applied differently between countries, locations and even departments. For instance those dealing directly with customers, like sales or service people, are usually more enthusiastic about vision and values than staff insulated from the market place, like R&D workers or actuaries.

THE SOURCE

16 Interview with Hamish Taylor, then Chief Executive, Eurostar.

CHART
8.8

Face-to-face communication by management

- Talks
- Visits
- Seminars
- Internal TV
- E-mail
- Meetings
- Questions
- Debate

THE SOURCE

17 Interview with Frederick Smith, Founder Chairman and CEO, FedEx Corporation.
18 Interview with John Neill, CBE, Founder CEO, Unipart Group of Companies (UGC).
19 Interview with Joe Weller, CEO, Nestlé, USA.
20 Interview with Dr Michael Karpf, President, UCLA Medical Center.
21 Interview with Ani Magill, Head Teacher, St John the Baptist School, Woking, UK.

Face-to-face communication by management... and especially the leader

Some organizations do this in a comprehensive and sophisticated way, and **Chart 8.8** gives some examples. FedEx Corporation owns and operates a major satellite-based TV network, and broadcasts daily via TV screens or computer monitors. It covers service levels achieved, problem areas like weather, training, and transmits messages from the Chairman/CEO. There is lots of targeted and interactive communication.[17]

Unipart is an international service organization, and has the vision of 'Building the World's Best Lean Enterprise'. It launched Unipart University in 1993, and every employee attends for at least 10 days per year. The CEO conducts a 3-hour course on Unipart's mission, vision and values twice a week. He felt he had to do this, to justify asking his Directors to do the same. Every Unipart employee has attended the CEO's course.[18]

As the expectation of openness grows, leaders increasingly participate in 'no holds barred' Q&A sessions, either in person or on closed circuit TV. The CEO of Nestlé USA has 'Town Hall' meetings with employees at plants or head office every 30 days. These give him the opportunity to explain and illustrate the vision and values: "It can be uncomfortable, but it's worth it."[19] At UCLA Medical Center, the President[20] does 'Town Hall' Q&A meetings quarterly in every building, has 'Breakfasts with the Boss' for mixed groups of 10–15 people and a Q&A session for his top 100 managers every few weeks. Terry Leahy, the CEO of international grocery retailer Tesco, conducts 'Town Hall' meetings with customers:

"I usually do two Road Shows a year, meeting consumers in groups of 150 in Town Halls. Reactions differ by meeting and by country. I was recently in Hungary, where reactions were very positive, and in Korea, where customers were tougher, more questioning and even hostile."

Consistency and sincerity is more important than sophistication. An inspired talk by a Head Teacher on her philosophy of education, with no visual aids, may be much more effective than a global Q&A session on closed circuit TV, by a CEO. Here is an example of imaginative communication by a leader:

"When I became Head, I decided to do one of the most unpopular jobs in the school – supervising the lunch queue. It involves getting 600 kids fed in 50 minutes, and is a way to see them all personally every day. One of our values is 'positive approach'. We have a 4:1 policy... for every negative comment there must be four positive ones. The lunch duty gives me a chance to demonstrate this.

I'd only intended to do this for my first year, but I'm still at it 5 years later, because surveys of the children showed they liked my visibility."[21]

CHART 8.9

Communication through signals

- Executive salaries and bonuses
- Executive offices and cars
- Dress, uniform
- Advertising and brochures
- How people talk to each other
- How people treat customers
- Internal layout
- Style of reception area and welcome

Communication through signals

Chart 8.9 gives examples of signals. Some are intended, others not. They provide a quick impression of an organization. When studied in detail by an expert eye, signals reveal a great deal.

Let's visit a company CEO and observe signals en route:

- Is the building old or modern? Is it located in an expansive green park with fountains and sculptures (bad news – out of touch), or a busy suburban area surrounded by ordinary customers?

- Are there car parking spaces for customers and suppliers? How plush are senior executives' cars and do they have reserved parking spaces? (bad news). Are there uniformed drivers hanging around? (bad news). If you arrive by local taxi, ask the cab driver what he thinks of the company. He's probably driven lots of its executives and customers.

- What's the feel and atmosphere of the reception area? Pretentious, friendly or impersonal? Is the receptionist welcoming, helpful and efficient? Are there any employee Newsletters? What's their style and tone? One of the worst reception areas was at BBC Worldwide – it used to be sub-contracted to a security organization and you had to queue up to receive surly service, signalling arrogance, lack of care. Fortunately, it's now vastly improved.

- Talk to the receptionist and security guard. How long have they been here? How do they like it? Mention the CEO, and listen for any reaction.

- Ask if you can have a cup of coffee in the canteen, and observe how people behave. Are they animated in groups or sitting alone? Watch how people interact when walking through the lobby. Are they friendly and relaxed or tense? How do they dress?

- Are you kept waiting, and if so, does anyone keep you informed?

- Talk to the secretary on the way up in the lift, and ask a few simple questions, like, 'How many people work here?', 'Do people stay long?' and 'How long have you worked for the boss?'

- What's the CEO's office like? Massive with acres of space and full of valuable art (bad news) or small and practical?

You will already have visited the company's website and read its Annual Report. By looking at and listening to signals, you can build up a picture before meeting the CEO.

A similar exercise can be done more easily in a school or hospital, because you see the customers (children, patients) as well as employees. A tour of a school, including classroom visits, and fifteen minutes in the staff room during the coffee break, will produce hundreds of signals.

By sitting in the lobby of a hospital observing staff and patients, walking round the shops and down passages, visiting the canteen and the toilets, reading the staff newsletter, you will rapidly form an impression of the organization.

8.10 Andy Grove's signal at Intel on punctuality

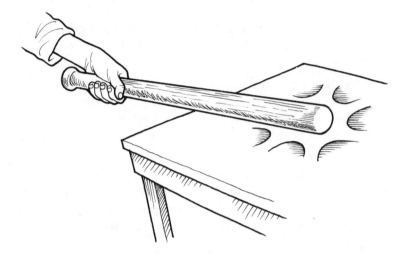

"Five minutes after the hour, when the last participant arrived (at the meeting) there was a deafening crash.

Andy Grove, CEO of Intel, was sitting there, holding a stave of wood the size of a baseball bat... he had just slammed the wood onto the surface of the meeting room table – and was now shouting at the top of his lungs:

'I don't EVER want to be in a meeting with this group that doesn't start and end when it's scheduled!'"[22]

THE SOURCE

22 Tim Jackson, *Inside Intel – How Andy Grove Built the World's Most Successful Chip Company* (HarperCollins, 1997).

Signals are powerful communicators of vision and values in practice. **Chart 8.10** illustrates a signal on the importance of punctuality at Intel. Here are two other examples. First a family company:

Mars is owned equally by the three grandchildren of the founder – Forrest Jr, John and Jackie. The company is No. 1 in world confectionery, and first or second in petfoods, where it dominates the European market. Sales are around $20 billion.

Mars has five values – quality, freedom, mutuality, responsibility and efficiency. While they sound like platitudes, they are vigorously practised (although 'freedom' is perhaps misleading, because the family can be autocratic). Equality is also an important value, though not one of the five official ones.

Signals about quality include:

● Millions of products are rejected daily for minute defects, like not printing the letter 'M' right in the centre of M&Ms.

● Any employee is authorized to stop the production line for quality reasons.

● The Mars family and executives regularly taste petfood to check quality.

And here are some signals about equality:

● No private offices, personal secretaries, executive washrooms, or reserved parking spaces.

● Everyone, including the family, clocks in daily and everyone earns the same % bonus (variable) each month.[23]

Secondly, signals at a school:

"When I arrived as Head, I found a school with good atmosphere, mediocre results and no ambition to change. I told the staff there was no room for just another average school, pointed out that other private girls' schools had gone bust recently, and said that we had to get more pupils. We had lots of staff meetings and there were quite a few dissenters at first.

Visible changes had to be made quickly. We removed all the old school photos along the corridors, replacing them with pupils' artwork. This was well received by staff and pupils, but not by the Old Girls' Association.

During the rest of the first term, we revamped the senior girls' centre inexpensively with rugs, posters and new chair covers, and developed a new school prospectus."[24]

┌─ **THE SOURCE** ───

23 Joel Glenn Brenner, *The Chocolate Wars* (HarperCollins Business, 1999), plus interviews with current and ex Mars executives.

24 Interview with Claire Oulton, Head Teacher, St Catherine's School, Bramley.

8.11 Communication through products and services

American customer satisfaction is declining, complaints have doubled:[25]

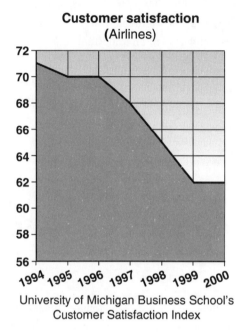

Customer satisfaction
(Airlines)

University of Michigan Business School's
Customer Satisfaction Index

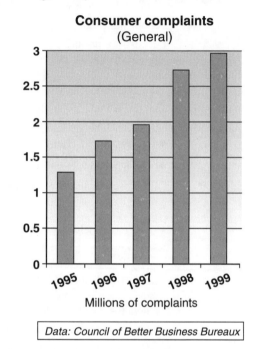

Consumer complaints
(General)

Millions of complaints

Data: Council of Better Business Bureaux

8.12 Communication through advertising

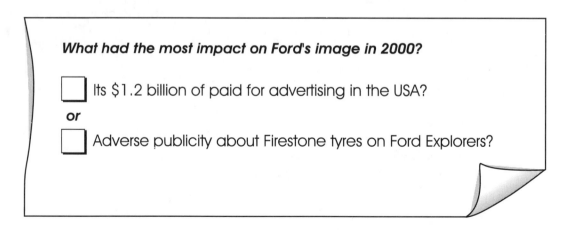

What had the most impact on Ford's image in 2000?

☐ Its $1.2 billion of paid for advertising in the USA?

or

☐ Adverse publicity about Firestone tyres on Ford Explorers?

Communication through products and services

People make products and provide services. These represent the output of organizations, and communicate their values. Products which are shoddy, unsafe, poor value for money or just mediocre, convey a message, to both customers and employees.

Picture a tele-sales operator for a Housing Loan Company. She has received first-rate training, and had it drummed into her that excellent customer service is the primary value. After two weeks work at the understaffed tele-sales centre, she knows this value is a lie. Customers are kept waiting for an average of three minutes, and then offered a truly uncompetitive loan rate. The message to staff and customers is clear – this company doesn't care about customer service or value. How long before our enthusiastic and well-trained tele-sales operator quits?

Communication through products and services criss-crosses all shareholders. Customers have direct experience and feed it back to employees. Employees, frustrated by their company's lack of customer commitment, let their standards of service slip. At the weekend, they'll meet customers socially, and get more playback. Finance providers may also be customers, and the smart ones will want to see numbers on customer satisfaction.

Unfortunately, this is declining, as **Chart 8.11** shows, leading to lots of unplanned adverse communication. The irony is that technology and understanding of customer relationship management (CRM) has dramatically improved in recent years, yet service has worsened. That's because CRM has been used to cut cost rather than help customers.

Communication through advertising

Advertising is important, but it's only one method of communication. Skilfully used, by organization brands like Intel and American Express, or product brands like Budweiser or Marlboro', it can have great impact.

Advertising also influences communication through products and services, by altering perceptions, and it stimulates word of both mouth and web. Advertising can change employees' views of themselves and their organization. This affects their actions and their behaviour. Much advertising for service organizations like airlines or retailers is directed at employees as well as customers. If you work for Nike, or The Gap, how can you fail to be influenced by their advertising?

Communication through advertising, however, can't be viewed in isolation as **Chart 8.12** shows. It's part of a complex web, linked to the seven other ways to communicate. Advertising for the organization brand must reflect and be consistent with vision and values. Chapter 10, Branding the Committed Enterprise, covers this.

THE SOURCE

25 'Why Customer Service Stinks', *Business Week*, 23 October 2000.

8.13 Communication through word of mouth and web

- Consumers filter out most adverts, but listen to friends and colleagues
- There are more than 1000 Ford Mustang-related websites
- The Internet connects word of web globally – very fast
- Bad news is spread between two and six times more widely than good[26]

8.14 Communication about you by other organizations

TYPE OF COMMUNICATION	→	EXAMPLE
Media news and editorial comment	→	Monsanto and GM foods
Consumer and environmental groups	→	Greenpeace and Exxon
Stock market and debt analysis	→	Moody's Credit Ratings
Suppliers	→	Firestone and Ford
Competitors talk	→	Sun, Oracle and Microsoft
League tables for schools, hospitals	→	US News and Reports
Government, regulators, law courts	→	Microsoft legal case

Communication through word of mouth and web

Word of mouth is exchanged with people you know, face-to-face or by phone. Participants are friends, relatives and colleagues. Word of web is much wider, global rather than local, and involving networks of people.

What is the implication of this for leaders communicating vision and values? Do people spend lots of time discussing vision and values statements? Of course not – two-thirds of conversations revolve around social issues: "Who's doing what with whom... who is in, who is out, and why."[27] Action and behaviour by leaders and managers will be observed, dissected and discussed more widely than ever, not only by employees but also by customers. Unforeseen events that collide with values to expose moments of truth will happen ever faster; and stories good and bad will spread like wildfire.

Note from **Chart 8.13** that bad news spreads two to six times more widely than good, and emotional involvement is a good predictor of how many people will be told about an experience.[28] Word of web and word of mouth are like a gigantic global police force, monitoring how well organizations live up to their stated vision and values. They heighten the rewards for communicating by action and behaviour, and multiply the penalties for not doing so.

The web is always hungry for ammunition, so organizations need to keep pumping their own good (and true) stories into this vast network:

The Jeep Jamboree spawns stories. It's an off-road weekend trip designed for Jeep owners only. They may take the Rubicon Trail, from Georgetown, California to Lake Tahoe – nine miles of rough country that takes nine hours to complete. A Jamboree makes a good cocktail talk.[29]

Communication about you by other organizations

Other organizations are monitoring yours, and most carry the authority of apparent objectivity. **Chart 8.14** lists some. Monsanto, over 100 years old, with strong values, was virtually destroyed in 2 years by adverse editorial comment about genetically modified food. A non-competing CEO observed: "They worked for years to come up with a break-through discovery – weed resistant seed – and were treated by the media as if they'd murdered their mother-in-law."[30]

Analysts, suppliers, competitors, governments, regulators and law courts, are constantly communicating with others about *your* organization, and quick to criticize any deviation from promises, especially those associated with vision, values or performance.

THE SOURCE

26 Emanuel Rosen, *The Anatomy of Buzz* (HarperCollins Business, 2000).
27 Ibid.
28 Ibid.
29 Ibid.
30 Interview with Chairman/CEO, identity withheld.

Chapter

9

Best Practice (5)

Creating systems to embed vision and values

Overview

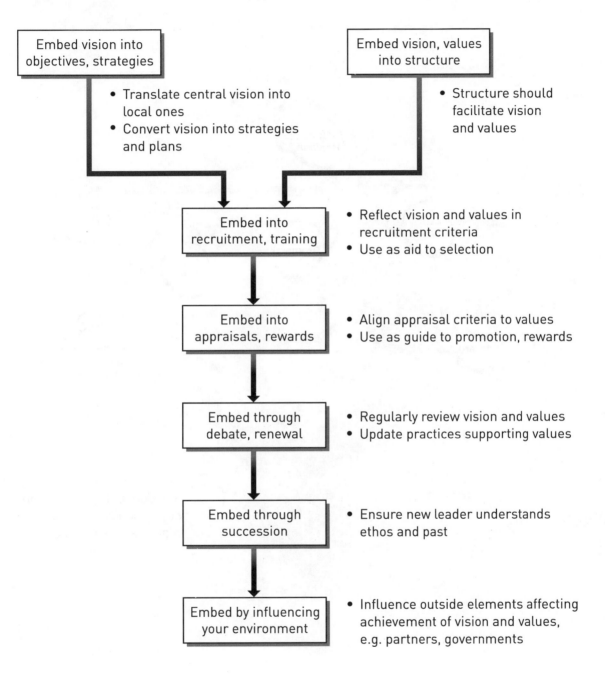

Embed vision into objectives, strategies
- Translate central vision into local ones
- Convert vision into strategies and plans

Embed vision, values into structure
- Structure should facilitate vision and values

Embed into recruitment, training
- Reflect vision and values in recruitment criteria
- Use as aid to selection

Embed into appraisals, rewards
- Align appraisal criteria to values
- Use as guide to promotion, rewards

Embed through debate, renewal
- Regularly review vision and values
- Update practices supporting values

Embed through succession
- Ensure new leader understands ethos and past

Embed by influencing your environment
- Influence outside elements affecting achievement of vision and values, e.g. partners, governments

CHART
9.1   The influence of founders

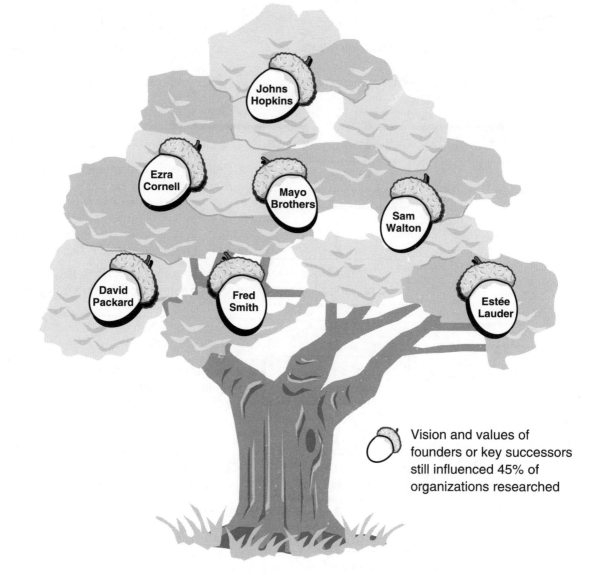

Vision and values of founders or key successors still influenced 45% of organizations researched

THE SOURCE

1 Interview with Robert Bauman, founding CEO of SmithKline Beecham, former Chairman, British Aerospace.

Sustaining vision and values

Too many vision and values programmes glide over the surface, produce a few ripples and drift away, forgotten. They have no anchor at a deep level.

In our research, American companies strongly outperformed other groups on systems to embed vision and values, an area of weak delivery by non-profits (Figure 9.1).

Figure 9.1 Percentage of organizations achieving best practice on systems to embed

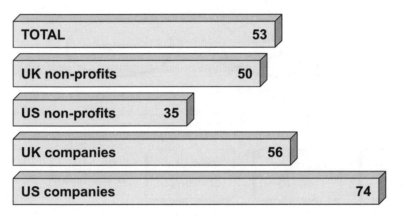

TOTAL	53
UK non-profits	50
US non-profits	35
UK companies	56
US companies	74

The primary reason for American companies' superior performance was quality of systems to translate vision and values into strategies and practices; and success in linking these to individuals, through personal objectives, appraisal and reward.

Most organizations performed poorly on training to make vision and values work, and fewer than 20% used annual themes to promote them:

"It's not enough to gain acceptance to vision and values. It's essential to train people in how to implement them in practice and this includes training in process management... Organizations are always ready to stabilize, rest on their oars, take a breather – you need to keep moving things forward."[1]

Among the few organizations to run effective vision and values promotions or themes were BP, PepsiCo, General Mills, Unipart, FedEx and Centrica.

The influence of founders

Founders or their notable successors often achieve legendary status in organizations. Their vision and values are frequently distinctive and deeply felt. This combination of personal reputation and resonating vision is a powerful embedder. In our research, founders or key past leaders still influenced vision and values in 45% of organizations, and 17% were still active. **Chart 9.1** gives examples of influential founders.

CHART
9.2 Systems to embed vision and values

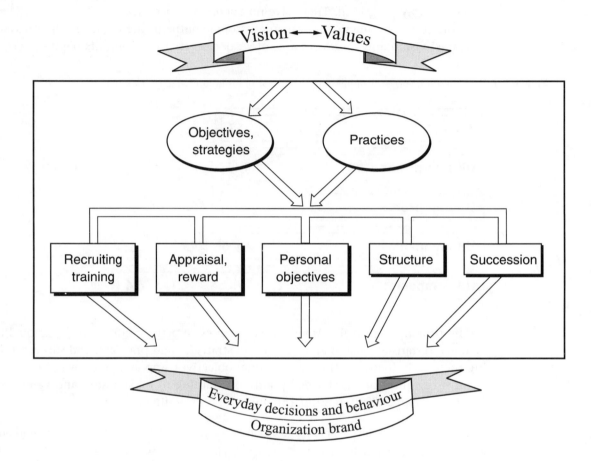

- Systems for translating vision and values into everyday behaviour are shown inside the box above

Notable successors include Robert Woodruff (Coca Cola), Jack Welch (GE), Jim Burke (Johnson & Johnson), Sidney Weinberg (Goldman Sachs) and Lou Gerstner (IBM). Outstanding people in non-profits are equally well remembered in their organizations.

As major new companies spring up, and mergers create new organizations, so the importance of founders is increasing. But there's a danger with new companies that large egos inflated by media attention will create 'Me' values and erode teamwork.

Will the visions created by individuals like Larry Ellison (Oracle) outlast them? Will they become deeply embedded in the heartbeat of their organizations? The answer depends partly on the quality of vision and values, partly on the people and systems to embed them.

Systems embed vision and values

'Embedding' is fixing firmly and deeply, or ingraining. While anchoring future direction, embedding may also stimulate change.

"Embedding is critical to sustainable success, which moves beyond a response to crises."[2]

Embedding systems are illustrated by the box in **Chart 9.2**. They start with vision and values at the top, and end with everyday decisions and behaviour that determine the quality of the organization brand. In between are the working systems that transform vision and values from top-level intentions into everyday activity.

Here's a brief summary of embedding systems:

- **Objectives and strategies.** Visions will float above the action unless they are translated into hard-edged targets and plans. These need to be developed right through the organization, from global to local, from departments to individuals. Personal objectives establish responsibility, provide a sense of direction, and guide behaviour, for everyone.

- **Practices** do the same for values as objectives and strategies do for vision. They convert aspirational words into behaviours that enable people to judge themselves and others, and were covered in Chapter 7.

- **Structure.** How people are organized affects their ability to apply vision and values. It's difficult to practise teamwork if you're trapped in a silo.

- **Recruitment and training.** Those entering the organization should be attracted to its vision and values, and trained in how to apply them. Recruitment criteria will screen out people who don't fit the values.

- **Appraisal and rewards.** Best practice appraisal will evaluate results, and *how* they are achieved, versus personal objectives. Development, recognition and rewards will follow.

THE SOURCE

2 Interview with Robert Bauman, founding CEO of SmithKline Beecham, former Chairman, British Aerospace.

CHART
9.3 Embedding values into plans at BP

Sequence for decision-making

1. How safe?
2. Environmental impact?
3. Effect on people?
4. Financial effect?

- **Constructive debate** keeps vision and values fresh. Annual themes, built around one or more values, helps to embed them.

- **Succession.** Well-planned succession provides continuity in vision and values.

- **Influencing the organization's total environment.** By spreading your values to those outside, like suppliers or partners, you can reinforce them. For example, Mayo Clinic educates and trains 20 000 physicians a year on subsidised courses.[3] McKinsey keeps on good terms with ex-employees, who are usually still committed to its values and standards, and many become clients. The Dragon School (Oxford) runs courses for staff in other schools, in pursuit of its vision to 'set an example of teaching skills, pastoral care, and breadth of program'.[4] Other examples are given later in this chapter.

The systems boxed in Chart 9.2 will be covered individually in the remainder of this chapter.

Embedding vision into objectives and strategies

Chart 9.3 shows how BP's vision and values are translated into everyday decision-making. Not harming people or the environment are crucial elements in its vision; 'to play a leading role in meeting needs for safe energy... without damaging the environment'.[5]

The vision of Nestlé USA is 'to be the very best food company in the USA'. It was agreed in 1998, a modification of its 30-year-old advertising campaign: 'Nestlé makes the very best'. On its own, the vision sounds bland. Nestlé USA gave it teeth by converting it into four strategies and 13 key initiatives.[6] The strategies, which use too many long words, were, in order of priority:

- **Renovation/innovation.** Continuously revitalize our brands and products, and, through portfolio management, prioritize and launch successful new products that drive consumer needs.

- **Product availability.** Whenever, Wherever, However. Invest to ensure that our brands and products are in the widest distribution possible.

- **Consumer communications.** Increase communications spending and effectiveness (especially advertising), communications integration and co-marketing activities to drive demand and strengthen our brand loyalty.

- **Low cost – highly efficient operations.** Follow a disciplined continuous improvement process that optimizes our ability to fuel our growth initiatives, by improving our delivered product costs and reducing overhead costs.

THE SOURCE

3 Interview with Dr Hugh Smith, President, Mayo Clinic.
4 Interview with Roger Trafford, Headmaster, Dragon School, Oxford.
5 Interview with Lord Browne, CEO, BP.
6 Interview with Joe Weller, CEO, Nestlé, USA.

CHART
9.4 Localizing visions

"When I ask people where DuPont will be in ten years' time, they usually talk about their plant, unit, or country, not the total company ... it's important to think locally, resource globally."

Chad Holliday
Chairman and CEO, DuPont

THE SOURCE

7 Interview with Sir Alan Rudge, FRS, Chairman, W.S. Atkins.

8 John Katzenback, *Real Change Leaders* (Nicholas Brealey, 1997); see ch. 2 which covers working visions very well.

9 Interview with John Neill, CEO, Unipart Group of Companies.

10 Interview with Ronald Peterson, President, Johns Hopkins Health System.

11 Interview with Merrill Vargo, Director, BASRC.

Key initiatives go into more detail on each strategy. Drilling down below the renovation/innovation strategy, for instance, are these initiatives:

Prioritize and accelerate new product development to ensure that our resources are spent against our greatest opportunities.

Profitably renovate our key base businesses, investing in our No. 1 and No. 2 brands and in our strategic niche businesses, striving for 60/40 consumer preference.

Implement e-business opportunities that achieve efficiencies, drive sales growth and build relationships with our consumers, customers and suppliers.

Build a core competency in branded active ingredients and nutrients so that they are integrated into our product lines, resulting in enhancing the health and well-being of our consumers.

They spell out simple guidelines for all employees, and say:

- We're going to be selective in our new product development. (No messing around on small opportunities or minor brands.)
- We will focus on our leading brands and develop superior products.
- e-Business is a high priority for everyone.
- We're going to develop distinctive ingredients for our brands, and build health and nutrition into them.

Using these objectives, strategies and priorities as a guide, each Nestlé Division and Department will then develop action plans. And the key question senior managers will ask when they see these are, "How do these plans advance our vision and reflect our values?"[7]

Vision and values also need to be translated into working versions,[8] consistent with the central one, and with real meaning for people at a local or department level, as **Chart 9.4** implies. The final step is to convert all these elements into personal objectives for which each individual is responsible, as the basis for appraisal. What you want to hear is this: "Everyone has a personal development plan."[9]

The need to ensure that strategies and plans implement the vision is common to all organizations, for example:

- **Hospitals:** "All strategies and plans must be relevant to and support the vision and values." *Johns Hopkins Medicine.*[10]
- **Schools:** The key questions always are, "Have you moved closer to the vision? Will this strategy or that action move you closer?" *Bay Area School Reform Collaborative (BASRC), San Francisco.*[11]

9.5 Embedding value of customer focus at Nordstrom[12,13]

Customers

Sales and support people

Department Managers

Store Managers, Buyers, Merchandise Managers, Regional Managers, General Managers

Board of Directors

- Sales people at Nordstrom are the heroes

- They get paid mainly by commission, but turnover of people is low for the industry

- Sales people can accept returns, reduce prices, sell across every department

- They are encouraged to build long-term customer relationships by personal contact, phone, e-mail or direct mail[14]

Interview with John D Whitacre, former Chairman and CEO, Nordstrom.
Robert Spector and Patrick McCarthy, *The Nordstrom Way* (Wiley, 1995).
Interview with John D Whitacre, former Chairman and CEO, Nordstrom.

- **Charities:** Save the Children (UK) is very decentralized, with Programme Directors responsible for their own countries. But each one has to show how his/her plans are aligned to the central vision and values.[15]

Embedding vision and values into structure

Best practice structure facilitates the application of vision and values. If an organization's key value is customer focus, a structure based on products or factories will undermine it. A senior executive who joined a leading retailer highlights this:

"When I got involved, in the late 1990s, the structure consisted of many product groups. Signs on office doors said, 'Director of Men's Suits', 'Director of Ladies Knitwear'. These people were very expert in design, material and production of their specialized products, but rarely talked to each other, and didn't see the consumer as a total person. It was like a factory landscape of many chimneys.

We were selling products to people who visited our stores, rather than consumer benefits to individuals."

If teamwork is a key value, a silo structure, built around inflexible departments, will frustrate teamwork across functions. One of the Mayo Clinic's core values is 'Work Atmosphere'. This means collaboration across disciplines, and elimination of barriers between them. The distinctive structure, summarized in Chapter 1 (p. 12), facilitates teamwork. Space is a barrier at the Mayo, because there are 23 000 employees in 16 buildings in Rochester, Minnesota, plus new locations at Scotsdale (Arizona) and Jacksonville (Florida). So all buildings are tele-linked, with many hours of teleconferencing daily.

The Mayo recently opened an integrated transplant centre, where experts in liver, pancreas, heart, kidney and bone marrow transplants work in adjoining offices, to capitalize on cross-learning between disciplines. Its brand logo of three shields overlapping, with no words, symbolizes collaboration.

Chart 9.5 illustrates how the structure at Nordstrom embeds the value of 'customer focus', with its inverted pyramid.

"The idea is for us to adapt to the customer not the other way round."[16]

Nordstrom encourages an entrepreneurial approach and has few rules, as demonstrated by its 'employee handbook' (**Chart 9.6**).

THE SOURCE

15 Interview with Barry Clarke, OBE, Chairman, Save the Children, UK.
16 Ann D McLaughlin, Director of Nordstrom, quoted in Spector and McCarthy, *The Nordstrom Way*. Nordstrom demonstrates that strong vision and values do not guarantee results. Financial performance at Nordstrom has been weak in recent years, influenced by problems of inventory management, IT issues and too great a decentralization of buying.

CHART
9.6
Freedom to act: Nordstrom's one rule

Our only rule:

USE GOOD JUDGEMENT IN ALL SITUATIONS

Please feel free to ask your department manager, store manager or personnel manager any question at any time

NORDSTROM

CHART
9.7
Embedding values into recruitment at New York Central Park

Key values	Key recruitment criteria
Preservation Improvement	Desire to learn about horticulture
Customer contact	Skills with people
Love for Central Park	Love for Central Park

Embedding into recruitment and training

People entering an organization should be checked both for competency and alignment with the vision and values. If this is done successfully, you'll be keen to keep them and they'll want to stay. At Central Park in New York, criteria for recruitment reflect its values (see **Chart 9.7**). The Chief Operating Officer observed:

"The main things we look for in people are love for Central Park, good attitudes, people skills, and acceptance of training. Horticultural skills are not critical initially and can be taught. Some very good horticulturists may not be very sociable and dislike the non-horticultural aspects of cleaning garbage, and contact with park users. Each person is responsible for his/her Zone – its condition, development and customer contact. Many users walk through specific Zones regularly, and we expect Zone Managers to build social contact."[17]

In the 1970s, New York Central Park was desolate and crime-ridden. In the 1990s it moved closer to the vision of its founder, F.L. Olmsted, "A haven of repose, relaxation and recreation for the masses of ordinary people".

Central Park's recruitment criteria emphasize attitudes above formal skills, and this approach is spreading. It's in tune with the concept of Emotional Intelligence,[18] an important building block for Committed Enterprises. Emotional Intelligence consists of attitudes and character. Things like the ability to motivate yourself, to empathize with others, to put aside self-centred focus and really listen. "At best, IQ contributes about 20 percent to the factors that determine life success, which leaves 80 percent to other forces."[19] Emotional intelligence is a lot easier to change than IQ.

It's stimulated by vision and values, and actively drives them. That's why best practice recruitment criteria feature a combination of skills, attitudes and character, linked to values.

Try this test. Get an outsider to read your recruitment criteria, and, based on these, write down what he/she thinks your organization's values are. If they can't do this reasonably accurately, the criteria are wrong.

ASDA, a UK grocery retailer owned by Wal-Mart, focuses strongly on personality in hiring people. It asks recruits to operate on the floor for half an hour, and gives preference to those who talk to customers and colleagues, and smile.[20] At Home Depot, the new hiring system was led by the Senior Vice President for Values and achieved a better match between people selected and values like excellent customer service, entrepreneurial spirit.[21]

Here's another example:

THE SOURCE

17 Douglas Blonsky, Central Park Conservancy (CPC).
18 Daniel Goleman, *Emotional Intelligence* (Bloomsbury Publishing, 1996).
19 Ibid.
20 Interview with Allan Leighton, former CEO, Wal-Mart Europe.
21 Interview with Faye Wilson, Senior VP Values, and Director, Home Depot.

CHART 9.8 Embedding values into appraisal at UC, Berkeley

Key values	Key appraisal criteria
• Excellence • Forefront of technology	Academic excellence is No.1, teaching next
• Collaboration • Ethical and civic responsibilities	Being collegiate, mentoring, intellectual exchange across faculties

Egon Zehnder is the leading executive search firm in Europe and has a global presence. Its values, structure and style differ widely from competitors like Korn Ferry, and it has traditionally never hired from competition. Like Mayo and Goldman Sachs, it stresses the value of teamwork, and shuns the cult of individual 'stars'. The firm's structure and recruitment criteria support this value.

The firm is non-hierarchical. Everyone is called a consultant, and there are no titles on business cards. There is only one profit centre – worldwide – and this encourages teamwork across countries... important, because many searches are multi-national. Remuneration is based on the firm's results, not on revenue generated or handled by individuals.

Each successful recruit is interviewed by 20–25 people. This extended process attracts individuals with the necessary skills and values. Egon Zehnder is open about its values, structure and remuneration system, which are highly attractive to some, less so to others.[22]

Embedding into appraisals and rewards

Criteria for appraisals will be linked to those used in recruitment. When you hire people, you buy potential. When you appraise them, you evaluate how far this potential is being realized. New York Central Park appraises potential customer service skills when it recruits people, and it's logical to include this in on-going personal evaluation. The same applies to Egon Zehnder and teamwork.

Within organizations, detailed appraisal criteria may differ by type and level of job. For example, scientific skills are more important for an R&D worker than for an office cleaner. However, a common thread in any Committed Enterprise is appraisal both of what's been done (vision and performance), *and* how it's been done (values). The 'what' will vary by job type, while the 'how' will apply to everyone. Personal objectives, aligned to vision and values, provide the framework for appraisals.

In our research, few organizations fully reflected their values in appraisal systems, and there were many mismatches and inconsistencies. University of California, Berkeley, was an example of good practice[23] (see **Chart 9.8**).

Appraisal is taken very seriously. There is a very strong Academic Personnel Committee, consisting of the very best Faculty members who serve for 2 years, with a full time Chairman. The committee covers 1000 cases per year. Criteria are linked to values. Academic excellence is the key ingredient, teaching next. There is a strong reward for being collegiate, and a focus on intellectual exchange and vitality. That's why there are more cross-discipline projects at UC Berkeley than at other leading universities.

For organizations stressing openness and transparency, the 360° appraisal, where people are assessed by bosses, peers and subordinates, is best suited. A highly effective Head Teacher practised an original version of this for her own 360° appraisal:

THE SOURCE

22 Interview with David Kidd, Partner, Egon Zehnder.
23 Interview with Robert Berdahl, Chancellor, University of California, Berkeley.

CHART
9.9 Embedding through debate and renewal

- Everyone promoted to the Board of any of the 190 Johnson & Johnson companies attends a 2-day 'Credo Challenge' at head office

- These occur twice a year for 35–50 people

- Chairman or Executive Vice President discusses the Credo, opens and closes the meeting

- Group reviews the famous Credo (see page 184), considers any conflicts with current behaviour, and agrees how to change

"All the names of the governing body, teachers and other staff – over 100 people – are put into a hat and four are picked out to appraise me. Last year they were a cleaner, a teacher, a parent and a governor."[24]

Appraisal is also the basis for recognition, rewards and promotion or dismissal. It's sometimes viewed by non-profits as a satanic art, but, well used, it's a positive tool for self-improvement and self-development.

Companies like Lufthansa[25] and Cisco Systems[26] link bonus levels to customer satisfaction levels as well as financial results. Few organizations are more thorough in policing their values than the FBI:

"Honesty is a key value. Every FBI employee has a full internal investigation every 5 years. Checks are made with neighbours, credit agencies, banks and on visible spending (e.g. cars, houses) related to what's likely to be affordable on salary. Word gets around about this... I've been with the FBI for 32 years now, and have never been offered illicit drugs."[27]

Goldman Sachs says, "Talk alone doesn't work for values. You need a system which embeds them", and uses appraisal, promotion and rewards to embed the core values of 'client first' and 'teamwork':

"The 360° appraisal is a cornerstone of our culture and no one is exempt. It's a way of reinforcing values. People can be exceptionally talented in mergers and acquisitions, but if they're not team players, they won't progress. Compensation is heavily influenced by how clients rate you and your 360° review."[28]

Embedding through debate and renewal

Chart 9.9 demonstrates embedding through debate and renewal at Johnson & Johnson (J&J). Its 'Credo', a combination of constituent priorities, values and practices, is justly famous, but lengthy, so only the first six lines are quoted below:

We believe that our first responsibility is to the doctors, nurses, hospitals, mothers, and all others who use our products.
Our products must always be of the highest quality.
We must constantly strive to reduce the cost of these products.
Our orders must be promptly and accurately filled.
Our dealers must make a fair profit.[29]

THE SOURCE

24 Interview with Ani Magill, St John the Baptist School, Woking.
25 Interview with Dr Holger Hätty, Senior VP, Lufthansa.
26 David Bunnell, *Making the Cisco Connection* (Wiley, 2000).
27 Interview with Rex Tomb, and Philip Edney, FBI.
28 Interview with John Powers, Managing Director, Goldman Sachs.
29 Interviews with Robert Darretta, Chief Financial Officer, Johnson & Johnson; and Philip Carne, formerly Group Chairman of Ethicon at J&J.

CHART
9.10 Embedding through succession

- Planned succession helps sustain vision and values

- Jack Welsh, Chairman/CEO of GE, spent many years selecting his successor, from a corps of internal candidates

- Average state school head has no role in choosing a successor, and so vision and values are often lost

The other four constituents – workers, managers, communities and stockholders – have their own paragraphs. Notably stockholders are mentioned last, although J&J share performance has been stellar, and sales have grown by over 10% per year since 1887.

The Credo was written down by General Robert Wood Johnson in 1943. It has only been changed slightly since.

Soon after the Tylenol crisis in the mid 1980s (see p. 312), it was decided to introduce two initiatives to embed the Credo into daily practice at J&J – the Credo Challenge and the Credo Survey. J&J is very decentralized, with 93 000 people working in 190 different companies. Each has 10 or so Directors, and all attend a Credo Challenge when promoted. The Credo Survey is covered in the next chapter on measurement.

Many organization leaders stressed the importance of real debate about vision and values to embed them, even though this slowed things down. Here is an example:

"We spent 9 months reviewing the vision and values throughout the company, and fought over every word. To make them work you need to have genuine debate, test the elements, and ensure that people believe the results. This applies particularly to senior managers, because they have to present and lead the process, handle any objections."[30]

Embedding through succession

For organizations doing well, succession will be planned ahead, and the baton passed on to a new leader, to refresh the vision and renew the values. He/she may well update the vision, and sharpen practices, but the original values will likely remain.

This is the probable scenario at GE, where Jack Welch has just retired after 20 years as CEO (see **Chart 9.10**).

Many organizations are not doing well, and change CEOs often. "Two-thirds of all major companies world-wide replaced their CEO at least once in 1995–2000."[31] The average CEO tenure in the top 200 US companies is now 4–5 years. This volatility may cause companies to look more closely at their future vision . . . if they ever find time to do so. It also produces pressure to change for change's sake. Vision and values may not be the cause of the problems, but they are often changed anyway.

Longer-tenured CEOs and well planned succession provide more fertile ground for embedding vision and values.

Schools appear to be particularly weak in planning succession. Responsibility for succession rarely belongs to the existing leader – a total contrast to companies – and the successor is not often homegrown.

┌─ THE SOURCE ───

30 Interview with Sir Anthony Cleaver, Chairman, AEA Technology.
31 Anthony Bianco and Louis Lavelle, 'The CEO Trap', *Business Week*, 11 December 2000. Research figures from Drake Beam Morin Inc.

CHART
9.11 Using vision and values to influence the total environment

- Association for a Better New York (ABNY) was set up by Lewis Rudin, a major property developer, in the early 1970s, when the city was in crisis

- He knew you can't be a successful developer if a city is failing ... and you can't move your buildings

- ABNY worked with the mayor, police, business, labour, sport and the community, and acted as a catalyst

- It mixed lobbying, networking, publicity and philanthropy.

- Following the tragic events of 11 September 2001, ABNY has helped to lead the fight-back to business and cultural revival in New York.

THE SOURCE

32 Interview with Lewis Rudin, Chairman, ABNY, and Co-Chairman Rudin Management.

33 The importance of the FBI's international role was highlighted by the tragic events on 11 September 2001.

Embedding by influencing your environment

Organizations survive by influencing and benefiting those outside, especially customers. Vision and values are constructed on this assumption. The challenge for leaders is to focus on those outside elements that enhance the vision and values, and to neutralize those undermining them.

We will explore four examples of embedding vision and values by influencing the external environment (Table 9.1):

Table 9.1

Organization:	Influence on:
ABNY	Success of New York
FBI	Police forces outside USA
US and UK Army	Societal attitudes
Global companies	Employees overseas

Association for a Better New York (ABNY)[32]

Chart 9.11 summarizes what ABNY is and has done. It was started up in 1971 by Lewis Rudin, a leading property developer, whose family company owns 40 major buildings. The motive appeared to be a mix of philanthropy and good commercial sense. In the early 1970s New York was in decline and so were its properties.

ABNY has a full time staff of only five, and 300 contributing organizations, but it's very influential. Its results have been achieved through a mixture of lobbying, networking, linking, publicity and provision of finance. Among initiatives to which it has contributed are:

- Concorde landing at Kennedy Airport in 1976, when the Mayor was prepared to cede it to Boston or Washington owing to noise.
- Help with crime prevention programmes, clean-up campaigns, educational improvements, public transport lobbying; supported sport and culture.
- Lobbied for Gun Control Legislation, helped supply police with bullet-proof vests, created NYC Police Foundation, Operation Bright Lights, Dial a Teacher.

ABNY focused on things it was practical to change – e.g. clean sidewalks, two-way radios for office security staff, statues on streets – and not interest rates or national policy.

Federal Bureau of Investigation (FBI)

The FBI is an American organization, but its mission includes 'providing leadership to international agencies, and investigating violations of criminal law'.[33]

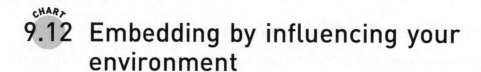

9.12 Embedding by influencing your environment

Federal Bureau of Investigation

- To fulfil its vision in the USA and spread its values, the FBI educates other police forces globally, because major crime is now international

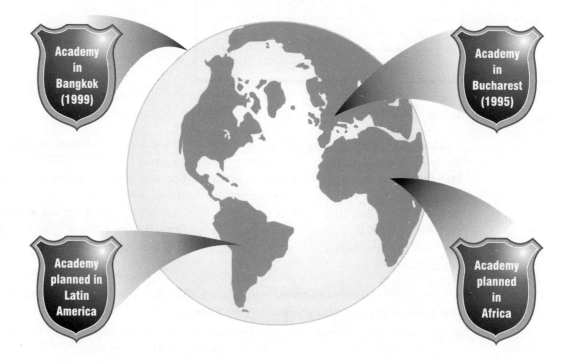

THE SOURCE

34 Interview with Dr Gerald Lynch, President, John Jay College of Criminal Justice, New York.

35 Interview with General Sir Michael Jackson, Commander in Chief, Land Forces, UK.

It has therefore developed a worldwide vision, to educate and influence other police forces, since financial fraud, drugs and criminal cartels are global. Unless policing is strong in developing countries, the FBI will be outflanked in the USA, and unable to fulfil its mission.[34]

Following this through, Police Academies have been set up in Budapest (covering East Europe), Bangkok (covering China, Laos, Philippines and Cambodia). Academies are planned for Africa and Latin America (**Chart 9.12**). These Academies help the FBI to educate, embed its vision and values more widely, and build local relationships.

US and UK armed forces

Key values are teamwork, self-sacrifice, and discipline ('discipline is the best antidote to fear'). These values run counter to modern social trends, which focus on individuals and rights. "Society may change, but the reality of the battlefield does not. Our ethos needs to be acceptable to society, but there is pressure for us to reflect it. If we do this, we may become unable to defend society."[35]

To counter the pressure of society's values on its own, the armed forces have to communicate their role in sustaining democracy, and why their values differ from those of civilian society. This is sometimes done badly. A recent TV ad campaign for the US Army actively erodes the teamwork value with its slogan "I am an Army of one" and dramatic footage of a lone soldier running through the desert. The comments of great commanders like Patton, Julius Caesar or Grant would be unprintable.

Global companies

There is sometimes a clash between the values of Western companies and the societies in which they operate. Here are some examples:

- Giving and taking bribes. This is common in some countries, and often viewed as a normal cost of doing business. It runs counter to Western values of integrity and ethics.

- Openness and transparency. There is growing pressure for this in the West, especially the USA and Northern Europe. Efforts to cover up uncomfortable facts now usually end in tears. However, this is alien to many countries, especially those where public opinion is stifled. A leading US company had difficulty in communicating its value of 'intellectual integrity' to its Chinese executives.

- Equal opportunity. In some countries, discrimination against women or minorities is standard. For example, Western pharmaceutical companies in Japan have some excellent female medical representatives, but some doctors won't see them, on principle. Promotion by seniority not merit, caste and tribal systems, are also counter to equality of opportunity.

What do global companies do to uphold their values in this context? Here are two typical responses, one from Dow and the other from Gillette:

^{CHART}
9.13 **Embedding vision and values**

"At Dow Chemical, we respect the local customs, but have the same values globally. If discrimination is common in a particular country, we will still apply our own non-discriminating values. Dow people are proud of this."[36]

"Fairness and civility to employees are two of our most important values." (Gillette is also committed to personal growth based on merit.) "Societal values in some of the countries we operate in are opposed to our own (e.g. tribalism, untouchables), but we apply our values globally."[37]

In summary, creating systems to embed vision and values requires imagination and persistence, as well as sound process. There are many different ways to embed, and best practice companies use them all.

THE SOURCE

36 Interview with William Stavropoulos, Chairman, Dow Chemical.
37 Interview with Michael Hawley, former Chairman and CEO, Gillette.

Chapter

Best Practice 6

Branding the Committed Enterprise

Overview

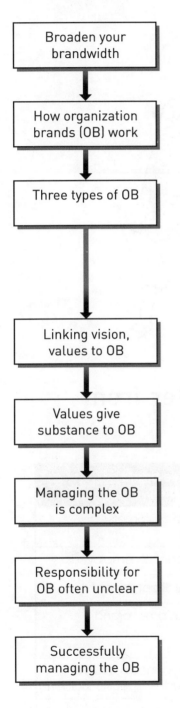

Broaden your brandwidth

- How organization brands (e.g. Diageo) differ from product/service brands (e.g. Smirnoff)

How organization brands (OB) work

- Every organization also a brand
- Target all stakeholders, not just customers
- Mechanism a continuous process

Three types of OB

- Type 1: Single name across all stakeholders (e.g. Goldman Sachs, Princeton University)
- Type 2: As for Type 1, plus additional brand name for customer (e.g. Sony Playstation 2)
- Type 3: Single name across all stakeholders except consumers (e.g. Procter & Gamble)

Linking vision, values to OB

- Vision, values and branding should be closely aligned, across all stakeholders

Values give substance to OB

- Best to build vision, values first, then brand them to outside world

Managing the OB is complex

- Different stakeholder managed by different internal departments
- Hard to achieve consistency of message

Responsibility for OB often unclear

- Normally spread across many functions
- Result is ineffective micro-management

Successfully managing the OB

- Allocate responsibility to one senior person
- Establish OB Board
- Agree OB proposition and strategies
- Coordinate, and measure results

CHART 10.1 Broaden your brandwidth

CHART 10.2 How organization brands differ from product/service brands

Organization brand (e.g. Procter & Gamble)	Product/service brand (e.g. Tide or Ariel)
• Impacts all stakeholders	• Marketed to customers/consumers
• Flag for all employees	• Limited impact on employees
• Brand for Wall Street	• Limited Wall Street impact
• May or may not be customer brand (IBM is, Procter & Gamble is not)	• Always a customer brand
• Brand for media, NGOs, regulators	• Low interest to media, NGOs, regulators, unless specific incident
• May not be advertised at all (e.g. Procter & Gamble)	• Likely to be heavily advertised

Broaden your brandwidth

Everyone would agree that Tide or Ariel is a brand. What about its owner, Procter & Gamble? Is it a brand? You have to search hard to find Procter & Gamble in small print on the back of the package. And if you ask for the "Procter & Gamble detergent please" in a store, you will get a bemused response, as illustrated in **Chart 10.1**. Yet to Wall Street, company employees, suppliers and distributors, Procter & Gamble is an important 'organization brand'.

Chart 10.2 shows how organization brands differ from product/service brands. An **organization** brand is what stakeholders transact with. A product/service brand is what a **customer** buys.

This chapter will concentrate on the 'organization brand' and branding the Committed Enterprise.

Bill Gates, Chairman of Microsoft, is reputed to evaluate people on their intellectual 'bandwidth'.[1] They may fail the test by thinking too narrowly. His test can also be applied to branding, hence 'brandwidth'. Many view branding superficially as a communications device, or narrowly, as applying only to customers. Chart 10.2 demonstrates how wide-ranging the organization brand is. It influences every aspect of an organization's activity. And the opinion of all stakeholders, not just customers, is what matters.

A 'brand' summarizes people's perception of products, services and organizations. Brands started as a way of differentiating products, and then extended into services like insurance, banking and leisure. A later development was the 'corporate brand'. In theory, this represented the company to the world at large. In practice it has been an excuse for self-indulgent corporate advertising of doubtful effectiveness.

A recent and more useful concept is 'the organization brand'.[2] This represents the impression people in and outside the organization have of it. Every company is a brand in this sense. Every college, school and hospital is too.

Brand image will differ between stakeholders. For example, Wall Street and customers may be great admirers of a company, while employees and suppliers are not. Staff may think the school is wonderful – the children may hate it.

THE SOURCE

1 'Bandwidth' is 'the transmission capacity of a computer network', *The New Oxford Dictionary of English* (Oxford University Press, 1998).
2 Simon Knox and Stan Maklan, *Competing on Value* (F.T. Pitman Publishing, 1998). This is the landmark work on the organization brand and introduces the concept of the UOVP – the Unique Organization Value Proposition.™

10.3 Organization brands have many stakeholders

Organization brands

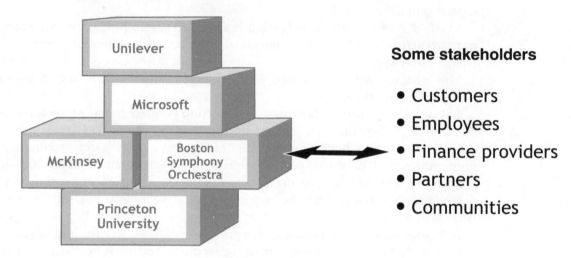

Some stakeholders

- Customers
- Employees
- Finance providers
- Partners
- Communities

THE SOURCE

3 Interview with Mark Volpe, President, Boston Symphony Orchestra.

Brand image can change as sharply as the wind, especially if the organization is involved in a highly publicized event like discrimination, environmental scandals, product glitches or child abuse.

'Brandwidth' summarizes the scope of the organization brand. It involves leveraging *all* the organization's assets, skills, and values through its brand, and targeting *all* stakeholders, as Figure 10.1 demonstrates.

Figure 10.1 The organization brand

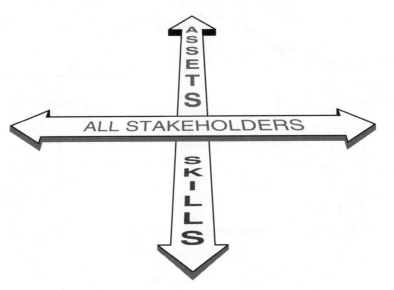

How the organization brand works

Organization brands vary in complexity, and have many possible stakeholders. **Chart 10.3** shows this through five organization brands. They all differ.

- **Unilever** is targeted at all stakeholders except consumers, to whom the organization brand is hardly visible. Like Procter & Gamble, it markets to consumers through hundreds of individual brands, like Magnum or Calvin Klein.

- **Microsoft** targets all stakeholders. It also uses individual customer brands like Windows and Office, branded together with Microsoft.

- **Princeton University** and **McKinsey**, the management consulting firm, target all stakeholders and have no sub brands.

- **Boston Symphony Orchestra** is a non-profit organization brand, targeting all stakeholders. It also uses individual customer brands like Boston Pops (lighter orchestral music) and Tanglewood (summer festival in Berkshire),[3] targeted at particular groups.

CHART
10.4 The mechanism of the organization brand

Stakeholder reaction to brand

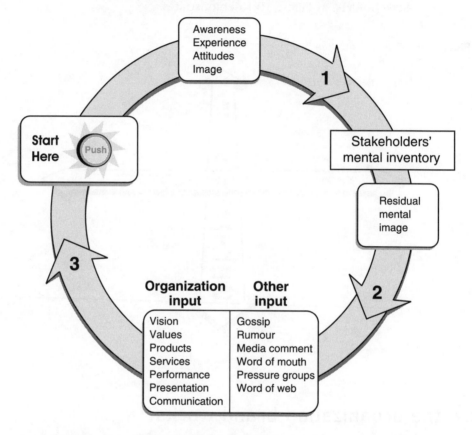

Awareness
Experience
Attitudes
Image

1

Start Here Push

Stakeholders' mental inventory

2

Residual mental image

3

Organization input	Other input
Vision	Gossip
Values	Rumour
Products	Media comment
Services	Word of mouth
Performance	Pressure groups
Presentation	Word of web
Communication	

- Stakeholder reaction to the organization brand changes daily

- The mechanism for this is a continuous process

While organization brands have many stakeholders, their needs vary widely, as do their views of the organization. Oakland Arts School demonstrates this:

This innovative school integrates art into all subjects, and achieves above average SAT[4] scores. The vision is that students should regard themselves as creative people, whatever they do. Many take non-arts jobs like business. Students are 20% Caucasian, 30% Afro-American, and 40% multi-racial. There are 200–300 applicants for 25 places annually. Selection is by lottery, adjusted to reflect Oakland's ethnic breakdown.

The school (or organization brand) is highly regarded by parents and students. However, others view it as maverick, and eccentric. The District School Board finds it difficult to categorise.[5]

So how does the organization brand work? **Chart 10.4** demonstrates its mechanism. There are three stages in this continuous process. First, stakeholders react to information or experience of the organization brand. This may consist of advertising, media comment, word of mouth; or direct experience of people, products, or services.

These are translated into attitudes, which take us to stage two – the residual mental image. Think of it as a mental filing cabinet of brands. Some brand 'folders' will only have a label, with nothing inside. Others will be bulging with information: experiences, attitudes and image, good and bad.

In the third stage stakeholders absorb further data about the brand (see Chart 10.4). This comes both from the organization, and outside it: word of mouth with fellow employees, friends and relatives, e-mail and word of web. The process is like a non-stop production line.[6] Raw materials are fed in from inside and outside the organization. The stakeholder processes these into attitudes and images, and files them in the mental inventory. The process never ends. Word of web in particular can be disconcertingly far reaching:

A junior employee of a top international legal firm received a hot e-mail from his girlfriend full of graphic sexual detail. He proudly e-mailed it to five colleagues, who, suitably impressed, passed it on. Within days, the e-mail circled the globe, and was read by millions. The media added fuel to the fire by naming the legal firm employing this young man. Awareness of this firm's brand by the general public had therefore multiplied one-hundredfold – though not in a context it would have chosen.

The Internet and word of web is rapidly reducing the level of control organizations have over their brands, and increasing the importance of 'other input' in Chart 10.4.

THE SOURCE

4 SAT, Scholastic Aptitude Test, used for admission to American colleges.
5 Interview with Mary Hurley, Teacher Leader, Oakland Arts School, Oakland, California.
6 Adapted from *Even More Offensive Marketing* (J. Hugh Davidson, Penguin, 1997).

CHART
10.5 Three main types of organization brand

Three main types of organization brand		
Types of brand	**Organization brand**	**Individual brands**
Type 1: Single name across all stakeholders	IBM Mayo Clinic Harvard University Greenpeace Goldman Sachs	None
Type 2: Single name across all stakeholders, plus individual brand for customers	Microsoft Sony McDonalds	Windows PlayStation 2 Big Mac
Type 3: Single name across all stakeholders, different brand names for consumers or customers	Procter & Gamble Pfizer Woodruff Arts Center	Pampers Viagra Atlanta Symphony Orchestra

The three main types of organization brand

Chart 10.5 gives examples of the three types. The USA's Top 100 Advertisers split evenly between them in 1999,[7] but most non-profit organizations are Type 1.

Type 1: Single organization brand name across all stakeholders IBM is one example – it's the brand employees, customers, shareholders and every other kind of stakeholder look to. Brand attributes are reliability, trust, quality and, perhaps, innovation. These are true of IBM's people, products and services. The brand proposition, 'e-business advantage', applies to all.

Type 1 branding is increasing in importance. Most new companies use it – Cisco Systems, Amazon, Yahoo, Sun Microsystems, Dell, Oracle, Nokia, Intel and Starbucks for example. Its appeal is simplicity and concentration of resources on a single brand. No one could afford to build a portfolio of strong individual brands from scratch, like Philip Morris and PepsiCo have done over the past few decades.

It is no coincidence that new companies are service rather than product marketers. The single organization brand name is suited to this. It works well for service categories like airlines, retailing, energy, financial services and telecom.

Most non-profit organizations use Type 1 branding since they offer services like education, policing or health care. **Chart 10.5** gives some examples – Mayo Clinic, Harvard University and Greenpeace.

Type 1 brands have a dual role. They are organization brands, targeted at all stakeholders, and also customer brands, marketing products and services. The two roles need to be understood and managed separately, since they can be easily confused.

Type 2: Single name across all stakeholders, plus individual brand for customers Sony is a familiar organization brand to all stakeholders, and sometimes adds individual consumer brands like Walkman or PlayStation 2 to the Sony brand. It operates in many categories and individual branding is a useful way to differentiate distinctive products. Like Microsoft, it's a Type 2 brand.

Few non-profit organization brands are Type 2.

Type 3: Single name across all stakeholders except consumers Many famous product marketers, like General Motors, Procter & Gamble, Diageo and Pfizer, are Type 3. The organization brand covers all stakeholders except consumers, who are targeted via individual brands. These give little or no prominence to the organization brand.

Very few non-profit organizations are Type 3 brands. An exception is the Woodruff Arts Center in Atlanta,[8] one of the USA's few integrated performing arts centres. Woodruff Arts Center is the organization brand, and there are four individual consumer brands – the Atlanta Symphony Orchestra, Alliance Theatre Company, High Museum of Art, and Atlanta College of Art – all on the same greenfield site.

THE SOURCE

7 USA Top 100 Advertisers, 1999, *Advertising Age*, 17 July 2000.
8 Interview with Shelton Stanfill, President and CEO, Woodruff Arts Center, Atlanta.

10.6 Three different views of the same person

Triple Portrait of Charles 1
(1635) Van Dyke

- The organization brand is like this painting
- Different stakeholders view it from different angles

10.7 Three different views of the same brand – its value lies inside the stakeholder's mind

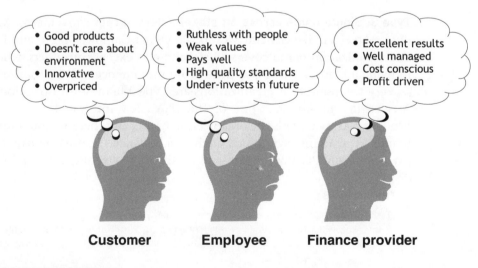

- Good products
- Doesn't care about environment
- Innovative
- Overpriced

- Ruthless with people
- Weak values
- Pays well
- High quality standards
- Under-invests in future

- Excellent results
- Well managed
- Cost conscious
- Profit driven

Customer   **Employee**   **Finance provider**

Different stakeholders view the brand from different angles

Everyone associated with an organization brand will have a different view of it, as we saw with Oakland Arts School (p. 200). That's because they approach it with different needs, have different experiences, and may interpret identical information in different ways.

Different needs among stakeholders   Shareholders are uncomplicated people – they simply want superior returns on their investment. They have little interest in how companies treat employees (unless so scandalous as to affect the share price) and may support ruthless downsizing with meagre redundancy payments. Employees, by contrast, expect to be well treated and rewarded, and demand job satisfaction too. Customers insist on superior value from goods and services.

Table 10.1 summarizes the different needs of stakeholders.

Table 10.1

Different needs of organization brand stakeholders	
Stakeholder type	**Likely needs**
Customers	Superior value
Resource providers	Superior return
Employees	Superior satisfaction
Suppliers	Fairness
Outsiders	Responsible behaviour

Different experiences   Stakeholders see organizations from a variety of angles – inside, or outside; upwards or downwards; close up or far away. Employees experience the brand from the inside. Their experiences are numerous because of daily involvement. Business-to-business customers may also have frequent contact with the organization brand, both the inside and outside (e.g. Compaq purchasing Pentium chips from Intel).

Different responses to the same experiences   Witnesses often give very different accounts of car accidents, because each sees the incident from a different perspective. The same applies to stakeholders. A price increase may be good news for shareholders, bad news for customers. An environmental report may interest NGOs greatly yet bore shareholders to death.

Chart 10.6 visualizes this. Van Dyke's famous triple portrait of King Charles I shows three different faces, each portraying a different side of the king's character. People see the same person in different ways. **Chart 10.7** shows the mental inventory of three stakeholders, influenced by varying needs, experiences and interpretation of events.

CHART
10.8 The organization brand visibly expresses vision and values for all stakeholders

The organization brand		
Vision	**Values**	**Organization brand proposition**
Lufthansa: To become a leading aviation services group, with the airline as the core	• Safety • Reliability • Teamwork • Efficiency	• Safe • Reliable/punctual • No gimmicks • Efficient
Johns Hopkins Medicine: To be the world's pre-eminent healthcare institution	• First rate patient care • First in discoveries • Teach next generation	• First rate patient care • First in discoveries

Note: The values of Johns Hopkins Medicine (which includes America's No. 1 rated hospital) are more complex than the above chart would suggest.

Linking vision and values to the organization brand

Committed Enterprises have a seamless link between vision, values and branding. The brand is the external expression of internal values, for all stakeholders. This is much more difficult to achieve than it sounds, and **Chart 10.8** illustrates how two organizations have done so.

Lufthansa's brand proposition echoes its Germanic internal values of safety, reliability, teamwork and efficiency. The airline's aim is to achieve the best safety and punctuality record in the industry, at the lowest cost, and the brand proposition is delivered by all staff in a straightforward way. It's also consistent with the new businesses specified in Lufthansa's vision. All of these are aviation-related services where operational efficiency is critical (e.g. pilot training, transport consultancy and engine testing).[9]

Johns Hopkins Medicine's brand proposition is closely aligned to its vision and values – all three emphasize excellence in patient care and discovery.[10]

As Chapter 8 shows, the organization communicates in a variety of ways – planned and unplanned – mainly through the behaviour and decisions of its employees.

"The FedEx brand closely reflects our values. FedEx couriers and customer service agents deliver the promise of our brand to the market place, through their day-to-day performance."[11] In service companies like FedEx, the values of the people determine the properties of the brand. A single incident, seen as out of character with accepted values, can erode the impact of a $200m consumer ad campaign.

Linking vision, values and branding is hardest for Type 3 organization brands (see page 202). Much of the difficulty is self-created. These organizations are often led by sophisticated marketers, and focus on heavily advertised individual brands. Many of their senior managers barely acknowledge the existence of an organization brand, since, in their minds, brands are synonymous with consumers and heavy marketing support. Consequently, Type 3 organization brands are often neglected, and weakly linked to vision and values. This is a paradox because Type 3 CEOs often have exceptional knowledge of branding techniques.

A typical interview with a Type 3 CEO will go like this:

Q How is your organization brand managed? Perhaps you call it the corporate brand?

A All our marketing is done through individual brands, with strong consumer franchises. And we don't believe in advertising the corporate brand. It's a waste of money.

Q But surely your corporate brand is important to employees, and Wall Street?

⌐ THE SOURCE ⌐

9 Interview with Dr Holger Hätty, Senior VP, Lufthansa.
10 Interview with Ronald Peterson, President, Johns Hopkins Health System.
11 Interview with Frederick Smith, Chairman and CEO, FedEx Corporation.

10.9 The organization brand iceberg

Appearance — Brand name, Advertising, Products, Promises, People

Substance — Customer focus, Integrity, High quality, Skills and values, People development, Cost consciousness, Treatment of people, Measurement, Innovation, Teamwork

- The appearance above the waterline should reflect the substance (below it)

- Mismatch between appearance and brand substance are potentially lethal

A Not really. We are judged by how well our individual brands do. If they flourish, so does the organization.

You can see the questioner's frustration. CEOs of this type can't mentally widen their brandwidth beyond consumers and heavy advertising.

Values give substance to the organization brand

"What you see is what you get" is a good motto for an organization brand, and **Chart 10.9** illustrates this. Promises must be kept and expectations met. No organization brand can tolerate gaps between promise and performance. If an organization has values of integrity and care for people, these will be implicit in its brand. Failure to live up to them will be noticed, first by employees, and then by customers. Chart 10.9 also illustrates that appearance should be based on substance.

Above the waterline of the brand iceberg are promises, symbols and experiences. These are created by products and people, words and pictures. Below the waterline, the skills and values of the organization provide substance for the appearance above. If these are weak, or inconsistent with the appearance, the iceberg will melt from the bottom up, and eventually capsize.

That's why it's wise to build vision and values internally first, and tell the world about them later. Once they are solidly embedded within the organization, the brand will have the substance to withstand the pressures of outside examination. Save the Children understood this well:

Save the Children (SC) is a Type 1 organization brand with a compelling heritage. It was founded in 1919, by Eglantyne Jebb, for children in Austria, and soon became international.

By the early 1990s, SC management recognized its brand had been neglected, since individual countries were taking different approaches, yet using the same brand name. With global sponsors and almost instant communication, a mis-step in Nigeria could negatively impact the brand in USA or vice versa. The media wouldn't know or care that they were different organizations.

Before sorting out the brand, common vision, values and structures had to be agreed internationally, in order to provide substance and protection. How could you write a sensible branding brief if you didn't have clearly applied vision and values?

The International Save the Children Alliance, which already existed, was strengthened, and now consists of 30 countries, including the largest ones. Its vision and values, previously informal, were codified. Most of the individual SC members now have their own purpose, vision and values, which are broadly similar to those of the Alliance. When this groundwork was completed, it was feasible for the Alliance and SC member countries to develop a more differentiated organization brand proposition, with real substance.[12]

THE SOURCE

12 Interviews with Barry Clarke, OBE, Chairman, Save the Children UK, and Dr Charles MacCormack, President, Save the Children USA.

10.10 The complexity of managing an organization brand across stakeholders

Stakeholder targets	Stakeholder needs	Organization contact point
Shareholders	• Security • Performance	• Finance Department • Board
Distributors	• Meets specification • Margin • Superior value	• Sales Department
Consumers	• Superior value • Good service	• Marketing Department • Distributors
Employees	• Security • Motivation • Reward	• Every manager • Human Resources Department
Suppliers	• Fair dealing • Confidence	• All Departments, especially Operations

Some organizations have taken the reverse approach, and this seems wrong. They reason that they are customer-driven, and should therefore start in the market place. "Yes," they say, "there is a time-lag between making the brand claims and being sure of delivering them in practice, but you must take a long-term view."

This is rather like trying to fly a balloon over a rifle range. It is possible, and has been done, but it's not advisable.

Managing the organization brand is complex

Managing an individual consumer brand like Budweiser is challenging, yet straightforward. The brand's targets are clear – consumers and distributors. There is a sales, spending and profit budget. And there will certainly be objectives, strategies and plans, rigorously measured.

The organization brand has little in common with this picture of clarity and good order. It will have many stakeholders, and they are unlikely to be well defined, prioritized, or linked. Responsibility for managing it will be widely spread across many internal departments (as **Chart 10.10** indicates). There is unlikely to be much co-ordination among these micro-managers, many of whom know little about the techniques of brand management. If there is a budget, it will be dispersed across many departments, and not viewed as a totality. No one will have any idea of its size or how it's broken down by stakeholders.

Finding clear objectives, strategies and plans for the organization brand, covering all stakeholders, is a challenge rarely handled with complete success.

Table 10.2 contrasts the management of the typical consumer brand (effective), and the organization brand (ineffective).

Table 10.2

How consumer and organization brands are managed		
Factor	Consumer brand	Organization brand
Stakeholders	Consumers Distributors	Very wide range
Targeting	Clear	Fuzzy
Management responsibility	Brand manager	Widely spread, uncoordinated
Location of budget	Marketing department	No specific budget
Clear objectives/strategies	Yes	No
Performance closely measured	Yes	No

Type 1 and 2 organization brands also double as consumer brands, and the consumer role is usually much better managed than that of stakeholders.

10.11 Who's responsible for managing the organization brand?

10.12 Where responsibility for managing the organization brand usually lies

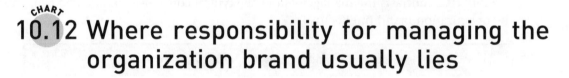

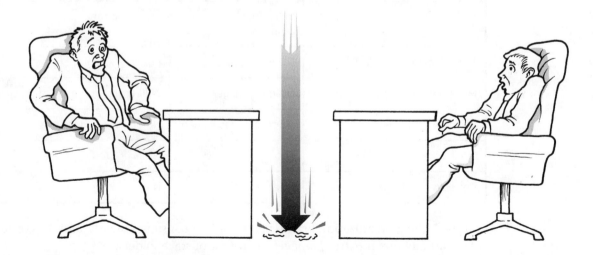

Table 10.3 provides a simpler model to demonstrate why management of the organization brand is diffused and confused – a striking example of unaligned micro-management.

Table 10.3

Responsibility for managing the organization brand	
Stakeholder	**Responsibility for organization brand**
Consumers ←	Marketing Department
Distributors/retailers ←	Sales Department
Employees ←	Human Resources Department
Shareholders ←	Finance Department
Opinion-formers ←	External Affairs Department
Suppliers ←	Procurement Department

So who's responsible for managing the organization brand?

Many organization brands are either not managed at all, or managed badly. Often they are a highly valuable asset, accounting for the majority of a company's capitalization. For non-profits, their value is inestimable, since they guard (or undermine) reputation. They should be macro- not micro-managed.

Figure 10.2 Macro-manage the organization brand

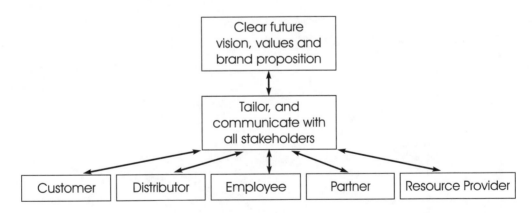

Two questions can strike terror among senior executives, especially for Type 3 brands. "Who is responsible for managing the organization brand?" And, "Who is responsible for setting objectives and measuring the performance of the organization brand?" Answer: the CEO.

10.13 Successfully managing the organization brand

1. Allocate responsibility and authority to one Director

2. Establish organization brand 'Board'

3. Agree Brand proposition and strategies

4. Implement consistently

5. Measure results rigorously, and improve

Successfully managing the organization brand

Chart 10.13 lists the keys to success, and here's a close-up on three of them.

Allocate responsibility and authority to one Director The Chairman/CEO, Head Teacher or President, is the best candidate, since he or she has cross-departmental authority, is responsible for the success of the organization brand, and personally answerable for any problems. The buck stops here.

When Johnson and Johnson learned of customers being poisoned by deliberate in-store tampering with Tylenol packs, the then Chairman/CEO, Jim Burke, immediately took charge, and appeared on network TV within hours of the discovery. When Coca Cola faced a range of problems in Europe, on product quality and relations with the EU, the then Chairman/CEO was slow to react, and subsequently resigned.

The main role of the Chairman/CEO, Head Teacher or President is to manage the next two steps.

Establish an organization brand 'Board' This would consist of those responsible for managing the brand with each constituent. The group would likely include the VPs of Marketing (consumers or customers), Sales (distribution channels), Operations (suppliers), Human Resources (employees), External Relations (media, communities) and the Chief Financial Officer (Wall Street, shareholders, regulators). The Head of Investor Relations might also be involved. Each member would be responsible for contributing to the overall proposition for the organization brand, and tailoring this to stakeholders. Each would be expected to understand their stakeholders' needs deeply, and to satisfy them with the overall brand proposition.

The Mayo Clinic has a Brand Management Committee to protect brand quality. There is no advertising, but lots of word of mouth. Staff are not allowed to operate in 'grey' areas. Quality must go in before the brand name goes on.

The Mayo trains and educates 20 000 physicians per year. These courses are subsidised and therefore a form of advertising.

Agree organization brand proposition and strategies Like any consumer brand, the organization brand deserves a one-page Brand Positioning Statement (BPS). Unless the overall proposition is crystal clear, the organization brand will be managed in darkness. Here is a format that works:

CHART
10.14 **How to manage the organization brand: Brand Positioning Statement (BPS) for United Parcel Service**

Elements	Issues (max. 50 words)
1. Brand name	UPS
2. Key stakeholders	Customers, employees, shareholders, communities
3. Brand proposition	The enabler of global commerce
4. Linkage to vision and values	Vision same as brand proposition, values provide substance
5. Brand differentiation	Ownership (80% of shares owned by present or former employees) Attitudes, technology, speed
6. Brand personality	Caring, urgent, innovative, trusted, reliable
7. Measurement	Customer and employee satisfaction Sales, profits, share price

(See link to Table 10.4 opposite)

THE SOURCE

13 Interview with Claire Oulton, then Head Teacher, St Catherine's School, Bramley, now Head of Benenden School.
14 Derived from interview with Jack Duffy, Senior VP Strategy, United Parcel Service, and material related to UPS vision and values.

Table 10.4

Organization brand: Brand Positioning Statement (BPS)	
Elements	**Issues**
Brand name	What name do stakeholders use?
Key stakeholders	List stakeholders and link
Brand proposition	e.g. "A happy school for bright girls"[13]
Linkage to vision and values	Demonstrate linkage
Brand differentiation	How is the brand different?
Brand personality	Image and associations
Measurement	What measures and by whom?

Chart 10.14 provides a completed example for United Parcel Service (UPS).[14]

When the overall BPS has been agreed, a BPS should be developed for each stakeholder. The leader is responsible for ensuring consistency of proposition across all stakeholders. A budget and programme for the organization brand, broken down by stakeholder, can then be agreed.

Tailoring the organization brand to different stakeholders

The theory of managing the organization brand is straightforward. The practice is much more difficult. As Chapter 1 (pages 5 and 8) shows, all those stakeholders want different things, and they're liable to pick a fight with each other. One American CEO said, "Conflicts between stakeholders here are like a religious war." Many different inside people are communicating with just one of the warring sects.

The process of converting these differing needs into a holistic response is like completing a badly designed jigsaw puzzle. The pieces don't exactly fit and they are distributed among up to a dozen people (your organization brand 'Board'). To make the thing work at all, you need to have a clear picture on the jigsaw box (the organization brand proposition), to know who has which pieces, and to get them to build the jigsaw. The best you can expect to come up with is a slightly jumbled picture, where some pieces overlap a bit, but approximate to the picture on the box.

Chart 10.15 demonstrates how to tailor the Orange organization brand to its different stakeholders.

10.15 Orange brand alignment among different stakeholders[15]

Orange brand values	Translation to stakeholders:		
	Shareholders	**Consumers**	**Employees**
Honest	Keeps promises	Open and fair	Open and fair
Straightforward	Simple and clear	Simple and clear	Speed and results
Friendly	Confident and trusted	Trusted partner	Respect for people
Dynamic	Innovative and energetic	Innovative	Innovative and exciting
Refreshing	Bright and customer focused	Delights customers	Delights customers

THE SOURCE

15 Derived from interview with Kenny Hirschhorn, Executive VP Strategy, Imagineering and Futurology, Orange plc.

Orange was launched in 1994 and now operates in 20 countries. It is the international mobile arm of French Telecom, which paid $37bn for Orange in 2000.

As Chart 10.15 shows, Orange has five brand values. These are tailored to the needs of stakeholders in slightly different ways, but consistent with the overall brand proposition. For instance, 'Straightforward' means easily understood and consistent information to shareholders; simple propositions and clear communication to consumers; and focus on clear structure, speed and results to employees.

Orange's consumer brand claim is 'The future's bright – the future's Orange'. The company aims to align its external values towards consumers with the internal values practiced by employees, so that outside and inside values are closely aligned.[15]

A measure of Orange's success is the highest customer loyalty and revenue per customer in the industry. Will its vision and values be maintained under its new owner, France Telecom? I hope so, but doubt it.

Best Practice 7

The hard-edged organization – measurement

Overview

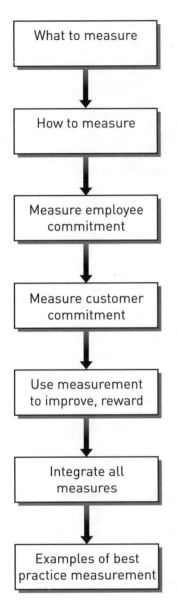

What to measure
- Customer commitment
- Employee motivation
- Satisfaction of resource providers

How to measure
- Description of what will be measured
- Selection of measurement type
- Commitment by those responsible
- Measurement and action to improve

Measure employee commitment
- Quality of recruitment
- Retention levels
- Employee attitude surveys
- Performance appraisal

Measure customer commitment
- Market share
- Share of all customer purchases in your category
- Customer loyalty
- Customer attitude surveys

Use measurement to improve, reward
- Take action on all survey feedback
- Communicate action taken to employees
- Link bonuses to customer and employee satisfaction

Integrate all measures
- Plan integrated measurements of all stakeholders
- Ensure common timing
- Review results before start of annual planning process
- Action to improve in new plans

Examples of best practice measurement
- PepsiCo
- New York Police Department

11.1 What you're measuring

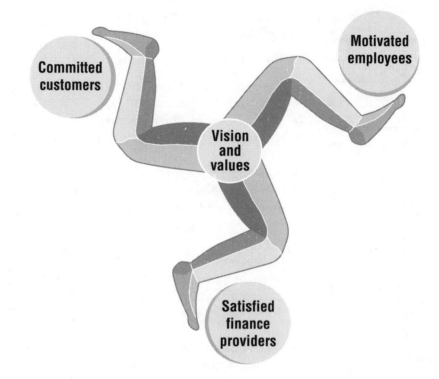

Why measure?

In our research, companies scored much better on best practice measures than non-profits (see Figure 11.1).

Figure 11.1 Percentage achieving best practice on measurement of vision and values

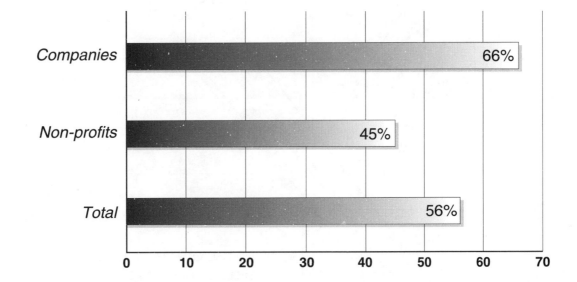

Many organizations performed unevenly, with, for instance, good measures for customer commitment, weak ones for employee motivation, and vice versa. Non-profits had less rigorous processes for measuring people, activities and results.

Why bother to measure vision and values? Because measures create consequences for good or poor performance, and provide a basis for improvement. They send out an important message to everyone: management is serious about making vision and values work. People will do what you measure. If you can't measure it, you can't manage it.[1]

Those who openly commit to measures for success at the outset of a programme are more likely to succeed, because they know their performance will be evaluated.

Who and what to measure

You are measuring whether you have succeeded in creating a Committed Enterprise. That means committed customers, motivated employees and satisfied resource providers, as **Chart 11.1** reminds you. Of course there are other constituents, such as suppliers, partners and the general public, to be considered as well. But if you're on song with the main ones, the others will usually be satisfied.

THE SOURCE

1 Interview with Sir Anthony Cleaver, Chairman, AEA Technology.

11.2 Sequence for measurement

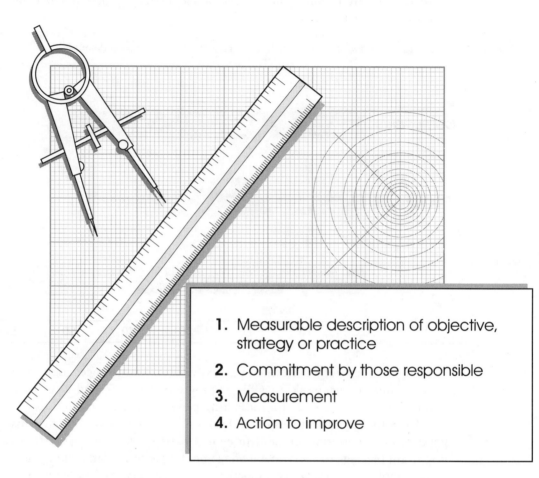

1. **Measurable description of objective, strategy or practice**

2. **Commitment by those responsible**

3. **Measurement**

4. **Action to improve**

THE SOURCE

2 Interview with Percy Barnevik, Chairman, Asea Brown Boveri.
3 Interview with Sir Anthony Cleaver, Chairman, AEA Technology.
4 Derived from conversation with Managing Partner of leading international legal firm.

How to measure

Measurement has a logical sequence, summarized in **Chart 11.2.**

Measurable description   Vision and values are unlikely to be strong unless translated into measurable strategies and practices. If the action or behaviour expected of people is not clear, it will not be measurable, however sophisticated the tools used. That is why bland or contradictory vision and values never work.

Commitment to action   People need to understand what's expected of them, and how they will be measured. Otherwise they will respond, "Nothing to do with me, Boss", "That's the first I've heard of it" or "That's not fair".

At ABB, Percy Barnevik would typically give each of his senior managers up to ten bonus-related personal objectives. These would relate to vision, values and performance and were simply spelt out:

- Hire three senior Asians (in a Western country)
- Take over two plants in Russia, transfer technology and build them to ABB quality standards by the end of the year.[2]

To be actionable, measures need to be simple. If they are complex, they will not be remembered or understood.

"It's easy to be put off by superior intellectual attitudes, especially in high technology businesses, and objections like 'What we do is so complex it's hard to measure'. Crude measures usually take you down the right track. You may well put in some wrong measures at first, but that doesn't matter as long as the trend is improving and you're learning what the right measures are."[3]

Measurement   If the method of measurement has been pre-agreed, there will be less room for argument about the results.

Here is a reconstructed[4] conversation on measurement between the new managing partner of a legal firm and her senior tax partner. It's based on fact:

Lucinda: I know you weren't happy at the last partners meeting when it was agreed that all partners would be appraised.

John: It's a ridiculous idea. I've been with this firm for 30 years, and we've done fine without appraisals. Anyway, I'm one of the top five tax people in the country. Who could possibly appraise me?

Lucinda: Your clients.

John: Just HOW do you propose doing that?

Lucinda: We'll do interviews with them.

John: You mean to say some outsider is going to talk to MY clients?

Lucinda: OUR clients... yes, that's right. I'll send you a copy of the interviews, because I'd appreciate your comments. But you need to understand, John, that we're going ahead with this, and there'll be no exceptions.

11.3 St Bartholomew's Church, Park Avenue, New York[5]

Using quantitative and informal measures:

Values	Measures	
Growth	Membership and attendance	Quantitative
Giving	Revenue	
Excellence	Quality of activities	Informal
Salvation Compassion	Spiritual growth	

THE SOURCE

5 Interview with Rev. William Tully, Rector, St Bartholomew's Church, Park Avenue, New York.

Action to improve   The purpose of measurement is to decide what has been accomplished versus expectation, to harness recognition and reward, and to stimulate improvement for the individual and the organization. Without subsequent action, measurement is pointless.

Quantitative versus informal measurement of organizations

Some leaders use a run of quantitative measures. Others prefer to walk, listen and talk. The two styles are not opposed, and the ideal is to mix them. Personal observation adds perspective to the numbers.

The larger and more complex an organization, the greater the need for quantitative measures. As leader of a global company with hundreds of thousands of people in scores of countries, you are unlikely to meet more than a few thousand each year. However, schools are more like family businesses. A head teacher often sees all the staff and pupils daily in morning assembly, and can walk around all the locations (classrooms) in an hour, like this one at Fessenden School in Boston:

"I take the temperature all the time. Do the children look you in the eye? How do they interact with each other and the staff? Are they lively and happy? Are they polite and considerate? My wife also gives me feedback. We do research among leavers, and talk to those who return."[6]

Looking at internal e-mail is a useful method of informal measurement. People at EDS use many quantitative measures, but also 'walk and talk' electronically:

"We have open e-mail among all employees. You can get a feel for tone, issues, and the morale of the place by looking at them. Our Chairman/CEO also visits numerous places each week – customers or EDC units – and writes about them in his bi-weekly letter to all 127 000 employees. He gets thousands of e-mail responses and replies to many personally. Some are passed on to his 125 senior managers, but he always gets a copy of their replies, sometimes commenting further."[7]

Some values are very difficult to measure, such as 'innovation'. 'Spiritual growth' is also tough to assess, as **Chart 11.3** indicates:

Bill Tully became Rector at St Bartholomew's Church in 1994, and since then attendance has increased by a factor of 4 to 5, donations by much more. Sunday morning congregation is 600–700, and it has changed from mainly white middle class to a more diverse mix. The Rector says 'spiritual growth' is very hard to measure. "I rely mainly on anecdotal feedback. People now talk about the quality of welcome at St Bart's. And when a person comes here to worship for the first time, I want the response to be 'Wow!' not 'That was nice'."[8]

THE SOURCE

6 Interview with Frank Perrine, Head Teacher, Fessenden School, Boston, a private school for boys aged 5–14. It is heavily over-subscribed.

7 Interview with Troy Todd, Executive VP, Leadership & Change Management, EDS.

8 Interview with Rev. William Tully, Rector of St Bartholomew's Church, Park Avenue, New York.

11.4 How quantitative measures differ between companies and schools

Companies	Schools
Sales	Growth in numbers
Profits	Exam results, SAT scores
Share price	Applications per place
Objective rankings (e.g. Fortune's Most Admired)	Objective rankings (inspections, league tables)
Employee turnover	Employee turnover
Customer satisfaction	Pupil and parent satisfaction

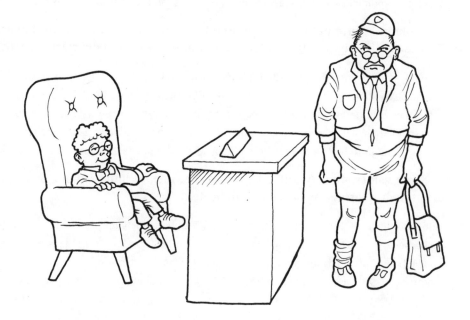

THE SOURCE

9 Interview with Lord Browne, CEO, BP.

10 Interview with Dr Tom Everhart, President Emeritus, California Institute of Technology.

Measuring quantitative results

Quantitative results are important to all stakeholders, especially resource providers. Whether they are shareholders, private donors, or governments, they want to know what's being achieved with their resource. Employees and customers also like to be associated with successful organizations.

Each organization selects a set of measures that fit its own situation. Companies have different requirements from schools, as **Chart 11.4** shows. And a consumer products company has a different list from a mining company. The main requirement is to highlight whether key objectives and priorities are being met. This is how BP measures its quantitative results:

The sequence is Purpose [i.e. vision], Values, Strategies and Targets. We use underlying targets. These are unaffected by the changing oil price, which people can do little to influence. Underlying targets get across, when a cold wind blows, that we can do better, and when a warm wind blows, avoids a feeling of complacency. They remain firm, irrespective of external circumstances.

The core theme at BP is performance. All aspects, including safety, health, environment, customers, employees, as well as sales, profits and costs, are measured monthly by operating companies and presented to me quarterly.[9]

The measures used by Caltech, a university, are different from BP's, but also enable it to check whether its vision is progressing, and its values practised:

Caltech employs a range of quantitative measures such as:

● SAT scores for entry students. Caltech is often No. 1 in maths and science.

● Assessment by American Association of Universities.

● Percentage of PhDs to total students.

● Student appraisals of classroom teachers after most courses. These are fed back to staff faculty but not published.[10]

You must measure what's important, not what's easily measured. Some things can only be assessed by listening and observation.

Measuring employee commitment

Employee and customer commitment (see below) are so important in building vision and values that they have separate sections.

Measures of employee commitment include quality of recruitment, retention rates, attitude surveys and performance appraisals.

● **Quality of recruitment.** This is a useful measure in its own right, and an indirect reflection of employee commitment. A Committed Enterprise will attract first class talent. Quality of recruitment can be assessed by number of applications for each position, calibre of candidates and acceptance rate.

CHART
11.5 Baylor Medical Center – employee attitude survey[11]

Structure	Confidential self-completion questionnaire
Frequency	Annual
Comparisons	Previous years and other health care organizations
Communication	Summary sent to all employees, results for individual units reviewed with their people
Action	Initiatives to improve personal development plans, training and to reduce employee turnover

THE SOURCE

11 Interview with Joel Allison, President and CEO, Baylor Medical Center.
12 Interview with Charles Knight, Chairman, Emerson Electric.
13 Interview with Roger Trafford, Headmaster, Dragon School, Oxford.
14 Interview with Robert Youngjohns, VP, Sun Microsystems.
15 Interview with Douglas Sweeney, VP Strategy, IBM.

Trend of scores on internal intelligence or attitude tests are worth tracking. A Committed Enterprise will evaluate recruits through a combination of skills and attitudes.

- **Retention levels. Chart 2.9** (see page 33) gives examples of annual executive turnover at four companies. Some turnover is healthy and promotes change, but a high level indicates employee dissatisfaction. The raw numbers only tell part of the story. Are you losing stars or average performers? Are people moving to bigger jobs? What is the attitude of leavers to the organization? Here are two examples of looking behind the numbers. First, a company:

Emerson Electric employs 117 000 people, and has had 42 successive years of profit growth – unmatched among major US companies. Here are the Chairman's views on turnover: "Among our top 800 people, we have 3–5% annual turnover. Most get recruited out to bigger jobs. If someone is not performing to our standards, we'll try to find them another job, or help them look outside. We're tough but fair. 'Tough' means being demanding, not cruel. We wouldn't put anyone out on the street."[12]

Second, a school:

"We've got 82 teachers, with an average age of 36. Some department heads are only 30. We aim to produce one head teacher for another school every year. There is movement three ways – up and out, internal promotion or move on. If people don't fit here, we persuade them to move on and help them do so."[13]

- **Employee attitude surveys.** These are widely used by companies, less so by non-profits. **Chart 11.5** summarizes the Baylor Medical Center's approach. Here are the key tests of a survey that Baylor passes.

  Confidentiality – this is essential, otherwise few people will complete the question-naire, and responses may be less than frank. *Frequency* should be at least annual to enable comparisons of trends. *Benchmarking* should be conducted against comparable organizations – in Baylor's case a dozen or so recent surveys in other healthcare centres, conducted by Avator International. *Communication* – everyone benefits by seeing the report for the total organization and for their own unit. And, finally, *Action* to be taken as a result of the survey.

  One thing missing in the Baylor survey is measurement of all five of its values. Servanthood, quality and stewardship are well covered, but the other two values – integrity and innovation are not.

  Employee surveys are increasingly conducted on-line. Sun Microsystems[14] uses an Employee Quality Index (EQI). This consists of an anonymous web-based questionnaire on attitudes and satisfaction with the company and its managers. IBM[15] also does on-line surveys, with 140 questions applied over an 18-month cycle to 165 countries.

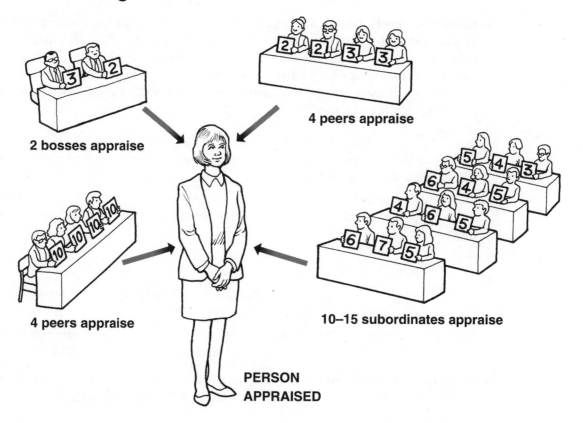

CHART 11.6 General Mills 360° appraisal of senior managers[16]

2 bosses appraise

4 peers appraise

4 peers appraise

10–15 subordinates appraise

PERSON APPRAISED

- Individual appraisals confidential

- Results analysed externally, ratings versus other senior executives on each criterion

- Suggestions for improvement and development given

- Appraisal given by one or more bosses, often including CEO

THE SOURCE

16 Interview with Stephen Demeritt, Vice Chairman, General Mills.

17 *Federal Express Managers' Guide*, *1998*, and *SFA Guide*, plus input from William J Cahill, VP Personnel, FedEx Corporation.

Topics covered include IBM as a place to work, job content, responsibility, ability to make a full contribution, view of manager and opinion of rewards. These are then translated into a Morale Index, broken down by area.

Federal Express has surveyed its employees annually since 1979. Here is the crux of its Survey–Feedback–Action (SFA) programme:

There are 123 000 employees in 66 countries who complete the survey annually. It's viewed as a way to get improvements for customers and in the workplace. The approximately 30 questions are grouped into six topics – direct boss, corporate leadership, attitude to organization, rewards, co-operation and job conditions.

Results are broken down by work group, and employees work with their managers to find solutions to problems identified. An action plan is then developed and implemented.[17]

- **Performance appraisal**. In our research, companies had much better systems for appraising people than non-profits. Some used the old 'This is what the boss thinks of you' approach; most got people to appraise themselves and used the subsequent discussion for self improvement; and an increasing number used 360° appraisals at least for senior management – see the example from General Mills in **Chart 11.6**.

Appraisals, when done well, reveal *what* a person has achieved and how. The 'how' tells you whether they are living the values. Equally, people who get good results the right way tend to be more emotionally committed, and their performance is more sustainable. It is worthwhile tracking appraisal trends, and feasible to do so, because most organizations have a ranking system, placing everyone in one of four or five boxes. To make this meaningful, you have to ensure that appraisals are conducted objectively, to an unchanging standard.

Measuring customer commitment

This can be assessed by checking both what customers *do* about your organization, and how they *feel* about it.

What customers do   Perfect commitment is where a customer uses all your products and services exclusively, for ever. So, if you marketed two vehicle ranges, one a luxury car, the other an off-road vehicle, all your customers would buy both, and remain loyal to future models. This of course never happens. But what's the best way to measure how close you are to the impossible ideal?

There are three main measures of commitment by doing – share of market, share of all customers' purchases in your category and customer loyalty. The last two overlap.

- **Market share** is a rough guide. In highly competitive markets, it's a good indicator of customer confidence, since every purchase made is a vote in your favour. In other sectors, where there's limited choice, or where it's inconvenient or expensive to switch, high market share has less meaning. Your school, gas station or discount warehouse may be the only one in a rural area.

CHART

11.7 Measuring customer commitment

Organization	Method
Oakland Arts School[18]	• Two attitude surveys per year • Younger children give oral tape, older ones complete questionnaire
SBC Communications[19]	• Speed of answering, service, repair • Customer attitude studies – courtesy, knowledge, speed • Complaint line analysis

THE SOURCE

18 Interview with Mary Hurley, Teacher Leader, Oakland Arts School, Oakland.
19 Interview with Edward Whitacre Jr, Chairman and CEO, SBC Communications.
20 Tim Ambler, *Marketing and the Bottom Line* (FT/Prentice Hall, 2000), pp. 65–8.
21 Interview with Dr Gerald Lynch, President of John Jay College of Criminal Justice (part of City University of New York).

- **Share of all customer purchases in your category** is a better measure of commitment. A credit card company may feel a customer spending $10 000 a year was committed, but if it discovered he was spending $30 000 a year on other cards, this opinion would be revised, since share of his purchases is only 25%.

- **Customer loyalty** is useful, but can be deceptive. People may be loyal out of habit, even though they feel lukewarm about your offer, and when something better turns up, they will leave in droves.

Each organization will use the most relevant measures of commitment. For instance, some schools use number of applications per place as one indication of parent attitudes, and level of attendance by pupils as another.

What customers feel   **Chart 11.7** shows two ways to monitor this. Oakland Arts School conducts two attitude studies every year. SBC Communications uses attitude studies, complaints analyses and factual checks on speed and service.

Other organizations also favour the mystery shopper technique, where a researcher poses as a customer, and visits locations, calls by phone, or writes. Over time, they track quality of customer care.

The most important areas to check are relative customer commitment and relative quality.[20] Relative means 'in comparison with similar or competing organizations'. Are you seen as better, worse or similar? Would customers recommend you to a friend? And what's the trend?

The majority of companies operate in business-to-business markets, where they market to other organizations, not individual consumers. For the minority who are consumer marketers, like Nestlé or Unilever, finding out what consumers feel about them is more complex, since their consumers do business with many brands, not with the organization. Each major brand needs to be measured individually. This is a big task, because both companies have hundreds of major brands worldwide.

Using measurement to improve and reward

Measurement reveals both good and poor performance, and always identifies opportunities to improve organizations. It must lead to action:

The John Jay College of Criminal Justice is a leading centre for the continuing education of professionals in criminal justice. It was the top ranked US university in its subject in 1999. It places graduates with over 200 organizations, and measures its effectiveness by interviewing their managers about their graduates' performance, especially on writing skills, decision-making, communications and building relationships.

Feedback in 1999 was that writing skills were not good enough. Since this is fundamental to the judicial process, the College increased its focus on improving writing skills across all disciplines, including maths and computers, and ensured that everyone got lots of practice.[21]

11.8 Using measurement to improve and reward[22]

Givers and Receivers

"Great managers develop people and offer them to others in the organization.

Givers create more candidates than they need, and can earn 20%–30% of their bonus by doing this.

Receivers take people from elsewhere or recruit externally – they're a drain on the organization."

Percy Barnevik
Chairman, Asea Brown Boveri

THE SOURCE

22 Interview with Percy Barnevik, Chairman, ABB and Investor, AB.
23 Interview with Allan Leighton, former CEO, Wal-Mart Europe.
24 Robert Kaplan and David Norton, *The Balanced Scorecard* (HBS Press, 1996).
25 Interview with Stephen Demeritt, Vice Chairman, General Mills.
26 Interview with John Powers, Managing Director, Goldman Sachs, New York.
27 Interview with Dr Holger Hätty, Senior VP Strategy, Lufthansa.

If you don't take action as a result of employee surveys, people won't bother to fill in the questionnaire next time round. ASDA, part of Wal-Mart Europe, is very aware of this:

ASDA gives 20% of its 200 000 employees a self-completion questionnaire each month, and the response rate is 95%.

There is a section for optional comments and 30% contribute to this. Half the comments are negative. The CEO reads most of the comments personally.

The response rate is high because:

● People know their comments are read.

● There's often quick follow-up action.

● $16K is allocated annually to each store, for local action, and this often results from questionnaire comments by local store personnel.

In the last six years, the score given by employees on the measure 'enjoyment at work' has increased from around 35% to 89%.[23]

Measurement also provides a basis for recognition and reward, as **Chart 11.8** on Givers and Receivers shows. Many organizations have moved to a 'balanced scorecard',[24] where people are rewarded not just for achieving financial results, but for a wide range of activities. At General Mills, for example, senior executives can earn up to 100% of salary in bonuses, and these are based half on hard measures like sales and profits, half on softer measures.[25]

In Wall Street, the philosophy of 'eat what you kill' – remuneration tied to short-term revenue generation by individuals – is getting stronger, and bonuses can amount to 10 to 30 times salary. Goldman Sachs runs counter to this approach, and remuneration is based on things like how a person is viewed by clients, how good he or she is at building relationships, as well as revenue (see Chapter 9, p. 184). People are categorized into A, B and C rankings. You can earn an 'A' by well-rounded performance in mentoring, people development, recruitment and commercial performance, even though you aren't a top revenue generator.[26]

Some companies link bonuses to performance on employee surveys and customer satisfaction studies:

Lufthansa does employee surveys annually, using self-completion questionnaires. These are sent in confidence to analysts at the University of Mannheim, and broken down by department or area, to a minimum of 10 people. Results are then compared with previous years, and with other companies surveyed by the University. Manager's bonuses are linked to their employees' scores.

Bonuses are also linked to the monthly Customer Service Index, where customer views on Lufthansa's reliability, friendliness, in-flight service etc. are monitored.[27]

CHART
11.9 Integrating measures and constituents

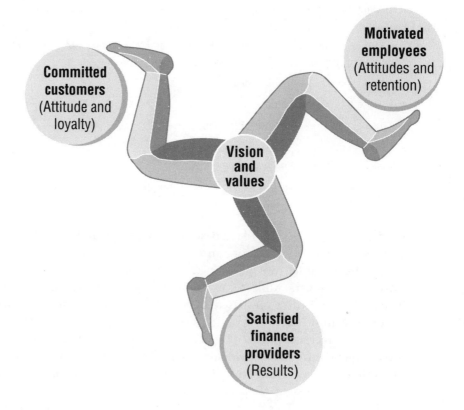

IBM operates to similar principles. Everyone agrees personal objectives, and values are reflected in these, e.g. raise customer satisfaction index by 1 point, employee morale index by 2 points in your business unit.

Integrating all measures to evaluate vision and values performance

This is the one step the vast majority of organizations fail to take. They may have all the information available, on a piecemeal basis, but it's not put together. Therefore nothing happens.

Chart 11.9 gives a simple illustration of the data to be integrated. If it's so simple to do why is it so rarely done well? Because the various tasks are done by different departments, at different times, in an unconnected way. Employee surveys may be co-ordinated by the Human Resource Department in October, customer satisfaction studies done by the Marketing Department in May, and neither integrated with the other. It's the same problem as described in Chapter 10 (p. 210) on Managing the Organization Brand.

The starting point in successful measurement is to make three key decisions:

1 We *will* measure progress on the vision and on each individual value.

2 We *will* do so on a cross-departmental basis every year, at the very beginning of the annual planning process.

3 The Chairman and CEO *will* be responsible for ensuring that this is done, and appropriate action taken.

It makes sense to involve the whole Board in the review, since strong non-executive Directors have breadth of experience and objective judgement. Once the date of this annual review of vision and values has been set, the measurements required, their timing and interaction can be planned.

Differences in employee and customer views on similar issues are illuminating and actionable. That's one of the reasons why some of the questions in the employee and customer surveys need to be considered together.

Here are questions the annual review of vision and values should answer:

- Is our future vision well understood?
- Are people convinced by it?
- Does it need clarifying or changing?
- Are there differences in view among different constituents?
- What awareness is there of our values?
- What is the perception of how they're practised?
- Which values score best or worst?
- What are the views of different constituents by value?
- How can commitment to vision and values be strengthened?

11.10 Best practice example of measurement – PepsiCo[28]

Stakeholder	Measure
Customer commitment	'Market place' P&L, covering: • Quality (product blind test) • Customer attitudes, monthly • Retailer attitudes • Market share
Employee motivation	• Same questionnaire in every country, rolling monthly results • Results and action published in 'Operation Talk back'–see chart 11.11
Resource provider	• Shareholder value (share price and dividend) • Financial P&L

┌─ THE SOURCE ───

28 Interview with Martin Glenn, President, Walkers Snackfoods, UK. (Walkers in UK is equivalent to Frito Lay in USA, and part of PepsiCo.)

- What changes should be made in future strategies or plans?
- What changes should be made in the practices that support values?
- What changes are needed in systems to embed – management of the organization brand or measurement?
- Is any other action required?

Once these questions are answered, action can be included in the 3-Year Plan and next year's budget.

Best practice example of measurement – PepsiCo

PepsiCo was formed in 1965 by the merger of Pepsi-Cola, the No. 2 drinks brand, and Frito Lay, the world's largest snacks brand. At the time the Pepsi-Cola CEO said to his snacks counterpart, "You make them thirsty and I'll give them something to drink", and that was the rationale.[29]

Today Pepsi-Cola soft drinks are significant in the USA, and a few selected international countries, but PepsiCo is powered by Frito Lay, which accounts for almost 50% of the global snacks market and 60% of PepsiCo's profits.

PepsiCo's measurements are hard-edged and very strong. The group's vision is something like 'the world's favourite snack break company'. It's centred on the strategy of building both drinks and snacks, and combining their strength: "The soft drinks bring the customer traffic in, and the snacks give you the margin."[30]

Values include superior product quality, differentiation and excellence in executing. Innovation is not a core value, since PepsiCo is better at adapting and improving (like the Japanese) than at developing radical new ideas. Its measurement system is summarized in **Chart 11.10**.[31] Points to note are:

- There is clear measurement of each of the three major stakeholders.
- Attitudes of retailers as well as consumers are measured under the 'customer' heading.
- Measurements are applied consistently across countries, so that country comparisons can be made.
- A number of separate measurements are combined to produce 'Market Place' Profit and Loss (P&L). This balance sheet consists of volume sales, market share, product quality, brand equity and attitudes of employees, retailers and consumers.
- 'Market Place' and financial P&L must both be met in each country. It is unacceptable to hit profit targets, while missing Market Place P&L targets, because, for instance, employee attitude scores have declined.

THE SOURCE

29 Don Kendall, quoted by Betty Liu, 'Cola Warrior with a new Recipe for Success', *Financial Times*, 23 January 2001.
30 Roger Enrico, Chairman and CEO PepsiCo, quoted in 'Cola Warrior' as above.
31 Interview with Martin Glenn, President, Walkers Snackfoods UK.

11.11 Results and action areas based on employee surveys – PepsiCo

WALKERS ➡ *Operation Talk Back*

➡

	Red	Orange	Green
I am satisfied at Walkers		✓	
I am proud to work at Walkers, and plan to stay here		✓	
I understand what my team and I have to do in our jobs			✓
➡ **I have the tools and support I need to do my job**	✓		
I understand what the Company is doing and how I can have an impact		✓	
I understand how our business operates and who our competitors are			✓
My Manager cares about me, my work and my opinions		✓	
We work well as a team and treat each other with respect			✓
People are committed to doing their jobs well			✓
The Company considers my safety to be important		✓	
➡ **My achievements are recognized and my performance is rewarded**	✓		
➡ **I receive regular coaching, feedback and development**	✓		

Our goal is to score green against all 12 statements – they define what we should expect from the Company we work for

Key:	
Red	= Need to fix
Orange	= Could be better
Green	= Pretty good

THE SOURCE

32 This is a simplified version of NYPD's weekly 'Compstat' reporting system. Results in Table 11.1 are city-wide, but they are also available for each of the 76 precincts.

33 Interview with Howard Safir, New York Police Commissioner 1996–2000.

- Action follows measurement. **Chart 11.11** reproduces a plastic card given to every employee. It demonstrates communication and action stemming from the latest employee survey at Walkers (name used by Frito Lay in the UK). It also shows that strong companies are open and self-critical.

Best practice example of measurement – NYPD

New York Police Department's (NYPD) vision is to continue reducing crime and in a way the community feels happy with, respecting civil rights and not being seen as an occupying army.

NYPD's two major performance measures are therefore crime and complaint levels.

Table 11.1[32]

Reported Crime	Week to Date (5/24/00)			Longer Term % Change		
	2000	1999	% Change	Year to date	2-Year	7-Year
Murder	8	9	−11.1	+8.4	+15.9	−62.8
Rape	52	28	+85.7	+2.7	−18.7	−32.3
Robbery	594	615	−3.4	−8.4	−17.0	−62.6
Fel. Assault	501	510	−1.7	−3.4	−11.8	−37.1
Burglary	726	784	−7.3	−11.3	−25.5	−62.7
Gr. Larceny	949	994	−4.5	−5.4	−9.6	−44.2
G.L.A.	711	767	−7.3	−9.6	−25.7	−69.5
Total	**3541**	**3707**	**−4.4**	**−7.7**	**−18.4**	**−58.4**

Precinct Commanders (PC) are responsible for results and values. Every 5 weeks, each PC meets with the Commissioner and his team, to review results. A 10-foot screen maps all crimes committed in the past 5 weeks, and level/trend is compared with similar precincts. The PC has to analyse, draw conclusions and recommend a 5-week plan, with resource allocation. If, after four to five reviews, there is no positive improvement, personnel are moved. In the past 4 years, 54 PCs have changed, some promoted.

Complaints are also analysed overall, and by type. There are 6 million police contacts with the public every year. The number of complaints is down from 7000 in 1996 to 4000 now. A civilian review board decides which are valid and substantiated. Validated complaints have declined from 400 a year to 250.

"Accountability means consequences following results. You can't shoot blanks. If someone is not getting results, you need to pull the trigger." Anyone subject to over five complaints is automatically called to head office, interviewed by a panel, and a decision made whether to retrain, discipline, or dismiss.[33]

Chapter

Why most vision and values programmes fail

Overview

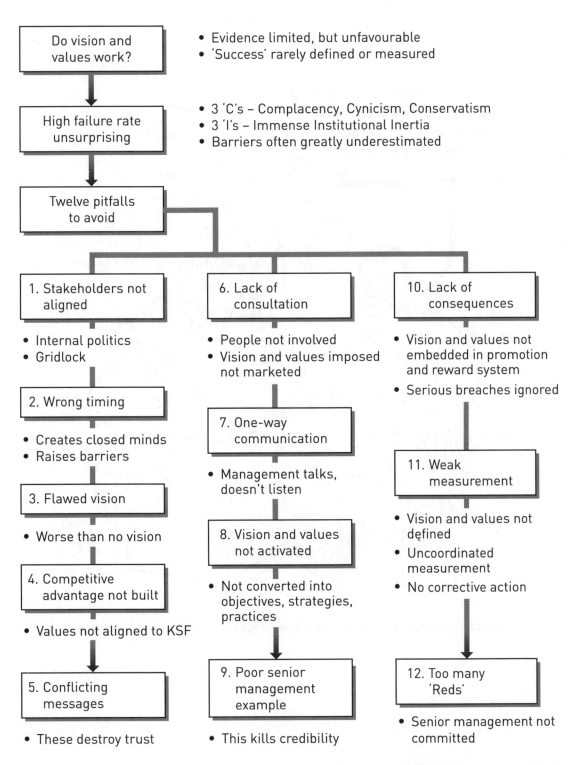

```
Do vision and        • Evidence limited, but unfavourable
values work?         • 'Success' rarely defined or measured


High failure rate    • 3 'C's – Complacency, Cynicism, Conservatism
unsurprising         • 3 'I's – Immense Institutional Inertia
                     • Barriers often greatly underestimated


Twelve pitfalls
to avoid
```

1. Stakeholders not aligned
- Internal politics
- Gridlock

2. Wrong timing
- Creates closed minds
- Raises barriers

3. Flawed vision
- Worse than no vision

4. Competitive advantage not built
- Values not aligned to KSF

5. Conflicting messages
- These destroy trust

6. Lack of consultation
- People not involved
- Vision and values imposed not marketed

7. One-way communication
- Management talks, doesn't listen

8. Vision and values not activated
- Not converted into objectives, strategies, practices

9. Poor senior management example
- This kills credibility

10. Lack of consequences
- Vision and values not embedded in promotion and reward system
- Serious breaches ignored

11. Weak measurement
- Vision and values not defined
- Uncoordinated measurement
- No corrective action

12. Too many 'Reds'
- Senior management not committed

CHART
12.1 Visions frequently attract derision

Source: Adapted from Alec, *The Daily Telegraph*, via Robert Youngjohns

The questionable track record of vision and values

Most organization leaders can quote at least one example of failed vision and values. Front-line people gain vast amusement from platitudes emerging from the corridors of power after months of frenzied effort. They would recognize the cartoon in **Chart 12.1**

What proportion of vision and values programmes succeeds? This is a trick question because in order to answer it, you have to define 'success'. What is it? At best, you'd expect a clearer sense of direction, more motivated employees and more committed customers. At least you'd look for visible change in behaviour and approach to decisions. An acid test would be to visit the organization 3 years later, and check whether you can spot any differences.

Using these rough criteria, let's repeat the question. The honest answer is that no one seems to know. It's not too difficult for outsiders to tell how successful a company's **new product programme** is. And you can gauge the success of **acquisition and merger programmes** by looking at the trend of shareholder value. But the only people who really know whether a **vision and values programme** is working are company insiders, and insiders who talk to the outside world have a vested interest in claiming success.

The limited amount of research around is not encouraging. One source[1] reported that 60% of mission programmes failed to generate the expected benefits. Research[2] among 429 UK companies showed that as few as 39% thought that values 'really do make a difference'. And only 6% of the 125 organizations interviewed for this book attained all seven best practices in vision and values management. There is a steady flow of stories about failed vision and values programmes.

Because they are rarely turned into hard objectives, their effectiveness is difficult to measure. If success is neither defined nor measured, it's unlikely to occur very often. The probability is that most programmes fail. The failure rate is probably higher than for mergers and acquisitions (50% plus),[3] but lower than for new products (80–90%).[4]

Senior management often labours hard to make vision and values work and finds failure puzzling, even humiliating. A good analogy is a children's party where the parents conscientiously blow up balloons, then discover them burst or deflated a few hours later. Figure 12.1 illustrates a typical top-down deflation scenario:

THE SOURCE

1 Geoffrey Nightingale in *101 Great Mission Statements*, compiled by R.V. Foster (Kogan Page, 1995).
2 Quoted in *101 Great Mission Statements*.
3 A number of studies suggest a 50–70% failure rate for acquisitions.
4 New product failure rates:
  • K. Clancy and R. Shulman, *The Marketing Revolution* (Harper Business, 1991). This estimates 75% failure rate for new products.
  • R.G. Cooper and E.J. Kleinschmidt, 'New Product Processes at Leading Industrial Firms', *Industrial Marketing Management*, May 1991. This estimates 80%.
  • Bill Ramsey, consumer products expert, suggests over 90% failure rate.

CHART

12.2 High failure rate is not surprising

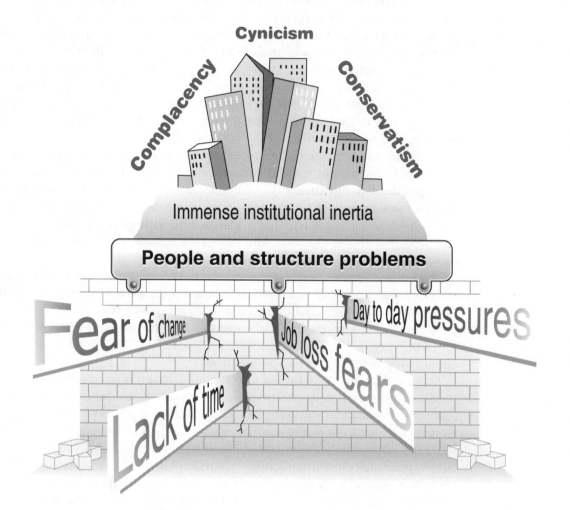

Cynicism

Complacency

Conservatism

Immense institutional inertia

People and structure problems

Fear of change

Day to day pressures

Job loss fears

Lack of time

THE SOURCE

5 Interview with Percy Barnevik, Chairman of ASEA Brown Boveri (ABB) and Investor AB.

Figure 12.1 How vision and values deflate

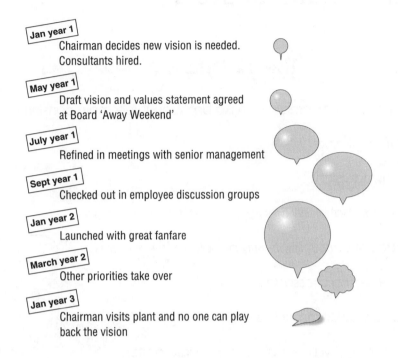

Jan year 1	Chairman decides new vision is needed. Consultants hired.
May year 1	Draft vision and values statement agreed at Board 'Away Weekend'
July year 1	Refined in meetings with senior management
Sept year 1	Checked out in employee discussion groups
Jan year 2	Launched with great fanfare
March year 2	Other priorities take over
Jan year 3	Chairman visits plant and no one can play back the vision

High failure rate is not surprising

Some organization leaders seriously underestimate the size of the barriers to be surmounted in making vision and values work, and creating a Committed Enterprise. They think it's like driving the organization down a gently sloping straight road. In reality it's like storming a heavily fortified walled city, and takes more time and resource than anyone could imagine.

Chart 12.2 summarizes the main barriers mentioned in our research – cynicism, complacency and conservatism (the three 'C's); immense institutional inertia (the 3 'I's), wrong people and structures.

Most of these barriers are general ones, reflecting resistance to change, and inability to allocate sufficient time to it. These are the most difficult to overcome. Specific structural problems like physical plant (e.g. school too small), incompatible IT systems, or internal organization, may slow down change, but can usually be fixed.

To overcome these barriers, vision and values have to fight hard for their share of time when they're being developed. Once they're well established in hearts and minds, they generate their own momentum. The effort needed to surmount barriers is immense. "A degree of obsession, strong enthusiasm, and real desire is needed."[5] And this is harder to achieve in the USA and Western Europe than elsewhere, as this story by Percy Barnevik shows.

CHART
12.3 Twelve pitfalls to avoid

The 12 Pitfalls

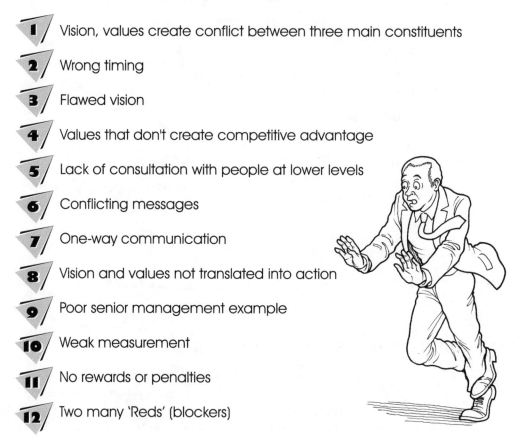

1 / Vision, values create conflict between three main constituents

2 / Wrong timing

3 / Flawed vision

4 / Values that don't create competitive advantage

5 / Lack of consultation with people at lower levels

6 / Conflicting messages

7 / One-way communication

8 / Vision and values not translated into action

9 / Poor senior management example

10 / Weak measurement

11 / No rewards or penalties

12 / Two many 'Reds' (blockers)

┌─ THE SOURCE ───

6 Interview with Percy Barnevik.
7 Interview with Dick Brown, Chairman and CEO of EDS (Electronic Data Systems), and Troy Todd, Executive VP Leadership and Change Management.
8 See Chapter 2, pp. 13–21.

"During a presentation to 400 of ABB's most senior people, I asked everyone to indicate when they'd last read our 20 page vision and values Strategic Guide, by pressing 'Yes' or 'No' electronic buttons which produced percentages on the screen. Most had read the guide in the past few weeks. But 5–10% read it *daily*. They were zealots, converts, who almost knew it by heart, and came from countries with shorter histories in business – Poland, Hungary, Slovakia, Brazil and some Asians. The screen showed that 2% had never read the Guide. I said 'Please stand up' . . . but they didn't!"[6]

Leaders need not only to be very committed to vision and values, but also hard-edged in pursuing them, as this example shows:

EDS was founded 37 years ago by Ross Perot, and is a world leader in information systems with sales of around $20 billion. Dick Brown joined as Chairman and CEO in early 1999, and worked with his senior people to develop new vision and values. Every word was interrogated and debated over.

Six weeks later he led a meeting of the top 125 most senior managers. He asked each one to put his/her name at the top of a piece of blank paper, to write down the new vision from memory, to fold over the page and hand it back to him. Eleven failed to produce even an approximation of the vision. Each was subsequently spoken to individually after the meeting. The word quickly got out that the CEO was serious about the vision.[7]

Twelve pitfalls that cause failure

The twelve pitfalls to avoid are summarized in **Chart 12.3**. A good organization leader, thinking about developing or changing vision and values, might have a session like this with colleagues:

Q   What are the main benefits of successfully changing our vision and values?

A   More committed employees, customers and therefore finance providers.[8]

Q   What are the chances of success?

A   Moderate.

Q   How much will it cost?

A   A lot, and most of it will never appear in any budget, because it consists of a massive diversion of executive time. It's a heavy short-term investment with a medium-term payback.

Chairman: [*summing up*] The benefits look worthwhile, but cost and chance of failure are high. We'd better get this right, because if it doesn't work, penalties in loss of morale, time and resources will be immense. We'll start by looking at what others have done and learning what not to do. Then we'll identify a series of best practices and follow them.

CHART
12.4 Flawed vision

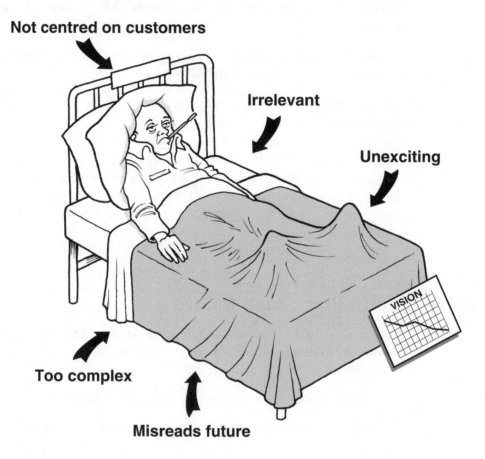

Why some visions never come to life

Not centred on customers

Irrelevant

Unexciting

Too complex

Misreads future

VISION

THE SOURCE

9 CIBA is now part of Novartis.

Action Agreed: Review 125 organizations and enumerate the main pitfalls to avoid.

You have already seen the results of the research. The remainder of this chapter is a reminder of the key points in other chapters. It reinforces the essence of the Seven Best Practices by spelling out the consequences of not following them. Chapters dealing with each pitfall topic are shown in brackets after each heading below.

Pitfall No. 1: Conflict between three main stakeholders (Chapter 1)

Remember the Three Legs of Mann on page 9, representing customers, employees and resource providers? If they are not united behind the vision and values, the three legs will kick each other and keel over. To succeed, vision and values have to meet the needs of all three.

Pitfall No. 2: Wrong timing (Chapter 6)

In some cases, it's essential to introduce new vision and values right away. In others, it's better to wait for a couple of years, and then introduce them gradually.

Let's suppose that you're the new CEO of a global company, and after 3 months have drawn these conclusions:

- This year's profit figures look adequate, but there's trouble ahead next year.
- Of 100 senior executives, 60 look competent, but only 30 of these recognize the need for radical change.
- The company is not strongly committed to its customers.
- Costs are too high and internal morale too low.
- Structure is creating mindless internal competition.
- There is no vision for the future.

New vision and values are clearly needed. Should you introduce them now or wait? In this example, it's better to sort out your senior people, change structure and cut costs first. New vision and values can then be introduced in a positive environment.

At the other extreme of timing, the new Principal of a failing school, threatened by closure, would be wrong to wait. He or she should outline their philosophy to the staff on day 1, discuss things vigorously for the next two weeks, and have the school moving in a new direction by week 3. Otherwise the term will be lost.

Pitfall No. 3: Flawed vision (Chapters 5 and 6)

Well-meaning and intelligent people are quite capable of producing visions that induce narcolepsy. Can you avoid yawning as you read this one?

CIBA[9] – flawed vision: We strive to achieve sustainable growth by balancing our economic, social and environmental responsibilities. Empowered employees and a flexible organization support our commitment to excellence.

If the vision is flawed, it will never come to life, as displayed by **Chart 12.4**.

CHART 12.5 Values that don't create competitive advantage will fail

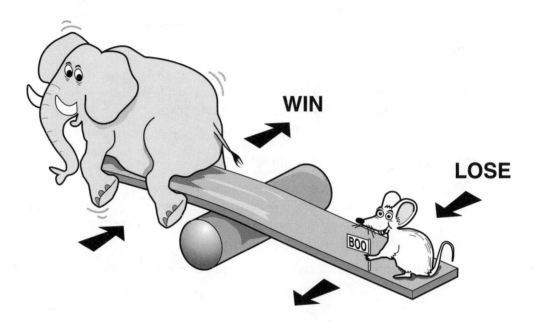

Key factors for success:

- Teamwork
- Risk-taking
- Innovation
- Excellent quality
- Speed

Values (real ones):

- 'Me' culture
- Avoid mistakes
- Results today
- Low cost
- Bureaucratic

Pitfall No. 4: Values that don't create competitive advantage (Chapter 7)

It's easy to compile a list of values that sound nice and everyone agrees with. That's exactly what many organizations do and why so many sets of values are bland. Such exercises are a complete waste of time.

Chart 12.5 illustrates a mismatch between key factors for success and values.

The big tests for values are: 'Do they make a difference to the way people behave?' and 'Do they create competitive advantage?' You pass the tests by analysing the key success factors in your category and by building values that address them. If innovation were a key success factor for your organization, you would adopt it as a value, and translate it into practice.

In our research sample of 125 organizations, key success factors (KSF) were developed and compared with values. In 59% of cases, there was a fair alignment between the two, with UK non-profits and US companies doing best, as in Table 12.1:

Table 12.1

Alignment between KSF and values in research sample[10]			
USA companies	65%	US non-profit	52%
UK companies	54%	UK non-profit	72%
All companies	**59%**	**All non-profit**	**59%**

Few organizations followed a deliberate process of identifying KSF, then building values around them. In most cases, the link between KSF and values was instinctive rather than planned. Among the better performing organizations, level of alignment was reasonable, with some pockets of best practice.

Two types of KSF – low cost operation and executional excellence – were least well reflected in values. Both these KSF are growing in importance, since differentiation as a strategy is becoming harder to sustain, and organizations increasingly rely on low cost, high quality execution. This gap was therefore a serious weakness. In addition, innovation was a KSF for many organizations, but not strongly reflected in values.

Values closely aligned to KSF are more likely to be practised, because people can see their relevance to everyday activity and observe how they contribute to better results.

Pitfall No. 5: Lack of consultation (every chapter)

The day of the autocratic leader is almost over. For vision and values to work well people throughout an organization need to be consulted, and involved. Inspirational leadership is still required, however. Vision starts and finishes at the top.

THE SOURCE

10 Only 107 of the 125 organizations researched were included in this analysis; 18 were excluded because their values were unclear and could not be linked.

12.6 Hypocrisy in action

Hypocrisy in action?

Pitfall No. 6: Conflicting messages (Chapter 8)

A harsher description is 'hypocrisy in action'. Some organizations spend heavily on publicizing new values, but never change inbred practices.

Chart 12.6 provides an example of values and practices in conflict. Such conflicts make failure inevitable, and success will only be achieved if practices are changed.

Pitfall No. 7: One-way communication (Chapter 8)

Senior management's idea of communication is often just to talk. If they are 'out there', talking furiously, leading from the front, they think they are communicating. Not so. The best way to communicate is to listen hard, and to demonstrate understanding by being prepared to change what you do. Here is a true story, slightly disguised to save the CEO's blushes:

Conversation between Enthusiastic CEO and Wise Chairman:[11]

CEO: Anne, I just can't understand it. I've travelled 500 000 miles and given 200 presentations in 90 countries in the past two years on our vision and values. But the results of our latest employee attitude survey have just come out, and they're worse than last year! Can you believe it!

Chairman: Perhaps you should stop talking and start listening, Ed?

[One year later]

CEO: That listening tour idea of yours, Anne – It worked. I asked our people: 'How can we make life easier for our customers?' The new employee survey shows attitudes are up 30%.

Chairman: Listening is much harder than talking – especially at our level.

Pitfall No. 8: Vision and values not turned into action (Chapter 9)

Agreeing a set of vision and values is only a small first step. The challenge and the benefits come from translating them into everyday decision-making and behaviour. Two quotes from interviews with organization leaders illustrate this:

"There is no secret recipe for making vision and values work. It's 95% implementation."[12]

"Progress here is glacial. One hundred years is not a long time. We are a sophisticated workers' control organization. Twenty years ago, change came from the bottom. Now government is pouring a fire hose of control through the top." **University Chancellor**[13]

THE SOURCE

11 Interview with Chairman, identity withheld.
12 Interview with Percy Barnevik.
13 Despite working in a difficult environment, this University Chancellor has achieved outstanding results.

CHART 12.7 Senior business management's values are not widely admired

- 73% of people think senior executives are paid too much

- Only 33% think companies treat employees well

- 65% say companies do a fair to poor job in providing job security

- 74% think companies have too much political influence

Source: Harris poll of 1009 adults, *Business Week*, 11 September 2000

┌─ THE SOURCE ───

14 Ferdinand de Bäker, in *101 Great Mission Statements*, compiled by R.V. Foster (Kogan Page, 1995).

15 Interview with Executive Vice President.

16 The average CEO at 365 of the largest American companies earned $13.1m in 2000. Source: *Business Week*, 16 April 2001.

17 Interview with Terry Leahy, CEO Tesco, an unusually insightful CEO.

18 Interview with Charles Knight, Chairman and CEO, Emerson Electric.

Pitfall No. 9: Poor example by senior management (every chapter)

"The problem with some value statements is that employees read them and then look around. And it is here that... most programmes are being killed... because management's behaviour is constantly benchmarked against its values."[14]

"There are still some people, including our CEO, who can't accept a value as a standard to live by... the most important part of communicating values is behaviour, and that's where our problem lies."[15]

Some senior managers think values are for others and don't apply to them personally. Others are simply out of touch with the ordinary people who are their customers and employees, as **Chart 12.7** illustrates. If you are paid over 300 times the average USA salary,[16] spend most of your time with peer CEOs, security analysts and investment bankers, you're unlikely to share the mindset of ordinary people. Even clear-sighted managers, who genuinely live the values, can still sometimes look like hypocrites:

"You won't always look great when your behaviour is checked against the company values, since you may have to act pragmatically, or in ways not obviously aligned to the values. Common sense and constant explanation are essential."[17]

Lack of example is less of an issue in non-profit organizations.

If senior managers do not strongly believe and act upon the vision and values, they have no chance of succeeding. The old proverb 'practice what you preach' applies. That's why it's important for leaders to ensure all their senior managers are true believers, and instil belief in others by words and example.

"If you compromise with excellence, your whole organization will."[18]

Pitfall No. 10: Lack of consequences (Chapters 9 and 11)

If vision and values aren't embedded in personnel appraisal and reward systems, and an indelible part of any promotion decision, they won't work. Consequences need to be attached to attitudes so that active support for vision and values is rewarded, and serious breaches penalized.

Where smart people with weak values get promoted, a headline signal is transmitted across the organization, saying: "Values are optional around here. They don't really matter as long as you're talented and get good results."

Pitfall No. 11: Weak measurement (Chapter 11)

Vision and values are often neither measurable nor measured. Making measurement feasible is the first step; ensuring that it actually occurs is the second.

CHART
12.8 Too many Reds

Green	Orange	Red

Status	Enthusiasts	Fence-sitters*	Blockers
Your action	Support	Convert to Green	Turn some Pink Move out the rest

*For obvious reasons, in this company, Orange plc, fence-sitters are called 'Whites' rather than the customary 'Oranges'

Pitfall No. 12: Too many Reds (see Chapter 14)

"I divide people into Greens (supporters and drivers of change), Whites (they're ambivalent about change, roll along and eventually follow Greens) and Reds (donkeys, naysayers, doubters). We try to turn the Reds into Pinks, since they can be useful in questioning instinctive or emotional moves by the Greens."[19]

Too many Reds means too many blockers of change. A certain number of vision and values blockers have to be converted, or removed, so that there is a critical mass of support. However, it is also useful to retain a number of Pinks – critics who question the vision and values constructively, and prevent complacency. A small proportion of Reds and Pinks provide useful grit in the oyster, and a challenge to conventional thinking.

Many organization leaders remarked that, in order to make vision and values work in practice, you need 30% of your people to be Greens, including all senior management. They will eventually convert most of the Whites. Many Reds will leave of their own accord, some will be pushed, others will become Pinks. Greens also need to move fast, as this excerpt from the Infantry Manual of General Rommel, an outstanding military leader, shows:

"Never forget that a section can do in the first hour what by nightfall would require a company, the following day a battalion, and, by the end of the week, an Army Corps."[20]

An organization consisting of 100% Greens however, would be unpleasant to work for, and prone to arrogance or complacency.

⌐ THE SOURCE ══

19 Interview with Kenny Hirschhorn, Executive VP Strategy, Futurology and Imagineering, Orange plc.
20 Quoted in *The Tories*, by Alan Clark (Phoenix, 1998).

Chapter

Vision and values before and after acquisitions

Overview

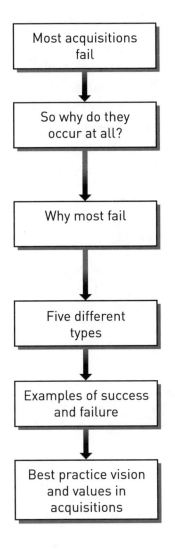

Most acquisitions fail	• Failure rate is 50%–70%
So why do they occur at all?	• Competitive pressure • CEO ego • Acquisitions as sport and fun • Investment banks stimulate • Easier and quicker than new product development
Why most fail	• Companies overpay • Benefits overestimated • Not enough focus on customers, employees • Cultural issues not prioritized • Weak planning, integration
Five different types	• Identify your type • Each has different effect on values
Examples of success and failure	• To date: Failures – Daimler Chrysler, Sony Columbia • Successes – IBM and Lotus, BP Amoco
Best practice vision and values in acquisitions	• Identify cultural differences early • Walk away if culture clash likely • For big deals, agree key people early • For small deals, train people in vision and values • Treat acquired people like long-term employees • Integrate quickly

13.1 CLUNK!

How acquisitions can destroy vision and values

Your organization has spent decades building up and refining its vision and values. It's one of the few to follow all seven best practices. Customer loyalty has never been higher. Employees are highly motivated. And finance providers are very satisfied. Then suddenly... clunk!

Company B, a larger rival, has made a hostile bid. After months of haggling, you are acquired. Company B's main rationale is cost reduction. It reckons that 10 000 jobs can be 'saved', and moves rapidly to integrate. Many of your friends and colleagues disappear. The best ones move out fast, and others are made redundant. Your customers complain about poor service and communication. Operationally, Company B is very efficient, but its outlook is short-term, and it has no interest in vision and values (see **Chart 13.1**).

So, was all the effort Company A devoted to building commitment through vision and values a waste of time? No. It resulted in the profitable growth, loyal customer base and high calibre workforce that led Company B to pay a high price. Company B, though is in danger of destroying these assets through clumsy short-term management.

Acquisitions are usually disruptive. They often involve a change in vision for the new combined enterprise. They can erode deeply held values. And when vision and values clash, both companies become unhappy places to work in or do business with.

This chapter will examine why acquisitions take place at all, why most fail and how success can be enhanced by following best practice in managing vision and values.

CHART
13.2 Most acquisitions fail... so why do them?

Certificate of Award

* CEOs like publicity, bigger business, more money, buzz
* Executives view acquisitions as sport
* Acquisitions are fun
* Investment banks stimulate big deals
* Executive delusion that failure is success
* Acquisition is easier than building ... and quicker

THE SOURCE

1 Ronald Askenas and Suzanne Francis, 'Integration Managers: Special Leaders for Special Times', *Harvard Business Review*, November/December 2000.
2 *Unlocking Shareholder Value: The Keys to Success* (KPMG, 1999). Study of 700 cross-border deals in 1996–8.
3 Nancy Hubbard, *Acquisition Strategy and Implementation* (Palgrave, 2001).

Why do acquisitions occur at all?

This is not a stupid question, though it isn't often asked. Objective studies show that half to two-thirds of acquisitions fail to meet their financial or strategic goals,[1] and the majority do not achieve significant gains in value for acquiring shareholders. The figure is much higher for cross-border acquisitions – a recent study by KPMG concluded, "83% of mergers were unsuccessful in producing any business benefit as regards shareholder value".[2] Yet the long-term trend in acquisitions spending is upwards.

In 1999, world-wide spend was $3.3 trillion, up 32% from the previous year, and equivalent to 35% of American GDP. It has since declined sharply, as share prices have fallen, but will eventually resume the upward trend.

There are two answers to why acquisitions occur at all. The first is the official one, which goes something like this:

Many companies are stuck in static markets. But shareholders still expect profitable growth. Costs have probably already been cut to the bone, while new product development or home-grown expansion into other categories is slow, expensive and risky. Acquisitions enable us to:

- buy competitors, so saving costs and increasing market share;

- enter new markets at low risk;

- expand geographically;

- acquire new people, products or technology;

- use acquired brands, people and resources more effectively.

This official answer does not explain the continued pursuit of acquisitions, despite a high failure rate. The unofficial one (see **Chart 13.2**) does:

- **CEOs like publicity, bigger businesses, more money, buzz.** Few chairmen and CEOs are shrinking violets. They like to see their pictures in business magazines, to be talked about by peers. A major acquisition will result in a larger company, more power for the CEO, and higher remuneration.

- **Acquisitions as sport.** Acquisitions are a form of conquest. A merger of equals rarely occurs.[3] It is a myth put around by winners to persuade losers to merge or make them feel better about it afterwards. The winner in the short-term is the acquirer, even though he may have overpaid. Executives enjoy sport, and acquisitions are the nearest thing to it in business.

- **Acquisitions are fun,** although they often involve work and pressure to the point of exhaustion. It's more fun to work on acquisitions than on budgets, planning or the everyday slog of management.

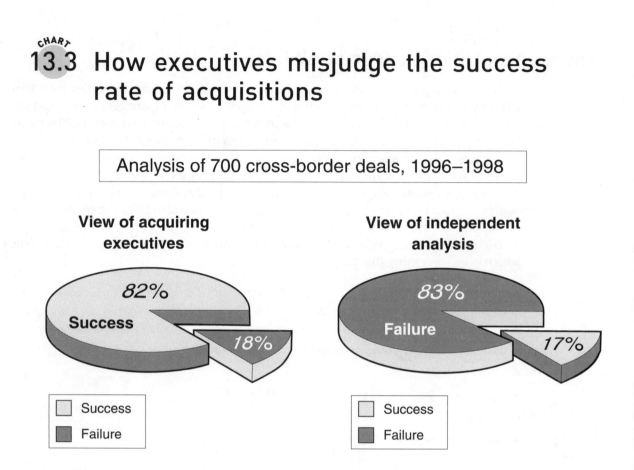

13.3 How executives misjudge the success rate of acquisitions

Analysis of 700 cross-border deals, 1996–1998

View of acquiring executives

82%
Success
18%

Success
Failure

View of independent analysis

83%
Failure
17%

Success
Failure

Source: **Mergers and Acquisitions – A Global Research Report** (KPMG, 1999)

- **Investment banks stimulate big deals**, because they build client relationships, and generate large fees. Every bank wants to top this year's table of acquisitions revenue.

- **Executive delusion that failure is success.** The KPMG study of 700 cross-border deals showed that 82% of acquiring executives thought their deal was a success, whereas objective analysis suggested a success rate of only 17%[4] (see **Chart 13.3**). Acquiring-minded executives wear rose-tinted spectacles and only 45% had carried out a formal post-deal review.[5] However, a minority of companies, like GE or ABB, are very good at acquisitions.

- **Acquisition is easier than building ... and quicker**. Acquisitions can be completed in weeks or months. Home-grown revenue building, through new products, takes years, is very expensive, and has a higher failure rate than acquisitions.[6] Speed is important to CEOs. Their average tenure is now 4–5 years, and they have little time in which to make an impact.

If acquisitions give acquiring executives more power, fame, money and fun ... quickly, their continuing popularity is not surprising. Nor is the fact that longer-term issues, like vision and values, get overlooked in the frantic rush to establish synergies, agree a price, arrange financing and fix a myriad of legal details, *before* the deal is struck. By then it may be too late to rescue the vision and values, even though their loss can wreck all the 'hard' numbers supporting the deal, and render them illusory.

Professor Bower, who recently headed up a year-long study of acquisitions, sponsored by Harvard Business School concluded:

Our collective wisdom [about acquisitions] can be summed up in a few short sentences:

- Acquirers usually pay too much.

- Friendly deals done using stock often perform well.

- CEOs fall in love with deals, and don't walk away when they should.

- Integration's hard to pull off, but a few companies do it well, consistently.[7]

Why most acquisitions fail

- **Companies overpay.** Most acquirers pay 25% to 50% above the pre-bid share price. This premium is rationalized as representing the benefits of the acquisition. Buying a company is a cross between buying a house and attending an auction. People get emotionally involved and competitive instincts become inflamed. Reason can fly out of the window.

___ THE SOURCE ___

4 Ibid.
5 Ibid.
6 Most studies show that the failure rate of new products is between 75% and 90%.
7 Joseph L Bower, 'Not All Mergers and Acquisitions Are Alike – and That Matters', *Harvard Business Review*, March 2001.

13.4 Why most acquisitions fail

- Companies overpay
- Benefits of acquisition overestimated
- Too much focus on shareholders
- Too little focus on employees and customers
- Cultural issues not prioritized
- Weak planning and integration

- **Benefits usually overestimated.** Everyone gets drawn into the excitement of the chase. If the CEO appears keen on the acquisition, executives will make 'best circumstance' estimates of cost savings and revenue gains, cheered on by investment bankers and consultants. These usually look most attractive at a distance, because the irritating details of people, customers and markets are invisible or ignored. And the high-flying team that calculates the gains is different from the practical people who implement them. Skeletons will fall out of cupboards, and surprises will occur. "I've never seen a positive due diligence surprise," said David Coulter, former President of Bank of America. He resigned in 1998 after the discovery of $1.46 billion of unexpected losses following the merger with Nations Bank.[8]

- **Too much focus on shareholders, not enough on employees and customers.** The balance between the three main stakeholders of the Committed Enterprise can be badly disrupted by acquisitions. The acquirer focuses on convincing Wall Street that the deal is positive, with a very strong emphasis on financial results. This is necessary but often downgrades the interests of customers and employees.

"There's a saying in the acquisitions world that integrations would be easy if no people were involved... unfortunately, too many organizations fail because they treat integration as an engineering exercise, not one that affects people's lives and futures."[9]

Acquisitions are unlikely to succeed unless they consider both employees and customers. For people in the acquired company, life can become a negative question mark. For customers acquisitions often disrupt relationships and service levels.

- **Cultural issues not prioritized.** Before acquisition, emphasis is on the deal, the price, and the host of mechanical details. After acquisition, focus shifts to structure, strategies, systems, remuneration, cost savings and branding. All these issues usually have to be resolved fast, often between relative strangers in an emotionally charged atmosphere. They are best decided within an agreed framework of vision and values. Unfortunately, this is rarely the case. Vision, values, people and customers, are either trampled in the stampede for change, or suffocated by inaction.

A 1996 study showed that failure to address cultural differences was the No. 1 reported cause of acquisition failure.[10]

"What's most important in any deal is that the two companies share a common culture on how to conduct business... if people in the trenches don't like it, they will treat the coming together as an alien virus."[11]

THE SOURCE

8 John Wilman, 'The Perpetual Triumph of Hope Over Experience', *Financial Times*, n.d., 2000.

9 Askenas and Francis, 'Integration Managers'..

10 Mitchell and Holmes, *Making Acquisitions Work: Learning from Company Successes and Failures*, Research Report, 1996.

11 Rance Crain, 'Why Mergers Turn Sour; They're Not a Natural Combo', *Advertising Age*, n.d., 2000.

13.5 Five different types of acquisition and their effect on values

Type	% of total	Example	Effect on values
Overcapacity	43	Daimler Chrysler	If similar size, different values, expect trouble
Category expansion	42	Quaker Snapple	Expect difficulties in integration
Geographical expansion, same industry	10	Banc One	Integration of values less urgent
Industry convergence	4	Aol, Time Warner	Integrate cautiously over time
People and technology	1	Cisco buys 62 companies	If values different, you'll lose the people

(This table excludes sales of businesses to financial acquirers)

Source: Adapted from Joseph L. Bower's 'Not all Mergers and Acquisitions are Alike – and that Matters', *Harvard Business Review*, March 2001

- **Weak planning and integration.** This was highlighted by the KPMG study of 700 cross-border deals as a major reason for failure.[12]

Five different types of acquisition and their effect on values

While the segmentation of customers and markets has become very sophisticated, the segmentation of acquisitions by type remains rudimentary. There are signs of improvement, mainly from academics and the international accounting firms. **Chart 13.5** is an example, demonstrating five different types of acquisition and their effect on values, and based on an analysis by Joseph Bower.[13]

1 **Overcapacity.** This is the most common type of acquisition, especially in mature categories like chemicals, energy, consumer goods and automobiles. These markets are growing slowly or not at all, there is spare capacity, and large companies think bigger is better. Their solution is to buy competitors, thereby raising market share, and removing costs and capacity. This usually leaves lots of blood on the carpet, since people have to go.

Success in this situation can be achieved if the two companies develop similar vision and values, pre-plan the acquisition carefully and integrate skilfully. If not, expect trouble.

This type is usually a Win–Lose game, and acquirers tend to impose their own vision, values and processes.[14]

2 **Category expansion.** The acquiring company wishes to enter a new market or sector, and does so by buying brands and skills. Quaker Snapple is an example of a disastrous acquisition of this type, while PepsiCo Tropicana was a success. Cultural issues are very important. Acquirers lack the confidence and know-how to enter the new category on their own. They are buying new customer franchises and people. Imposing inappropriate values risks destroying what has been bought.

3 **Geographical expansion.** The objective here is growth, not capacity reduction. Friction is therefore less likely, and it is tempting (though often unwise) to delay integration of vision and values.

4 **Industry convergence.** This type of acquisition is usually dependent on a distinctive vision. It is high risk, since the vision may be flawed. To have any chance of success, both the vision itself, and the way it is to be implemented, must be shared by each party.

5 **People and technology.** Shared vision and values are critical to the success of this type of acquisition, which is growing in importance. If you lose the people, you've wasted your money.

THE SOURCE

12 *Unlocking Shareholder Value.*
13 Bower, 'Not All Mergers and Acquisitions Are Alike'.
14 Ibid.

13.6A Typical effect of acquisition on stakeholders

Stakeholder	Acquirer	Acquired
Shareholder	Lose	Win
Employee	Win	Lose
Customer	Neutral	Neutral
Suppliers	Win	Lose

13.6B How acquisitions can unbalance the Committed Enterprise

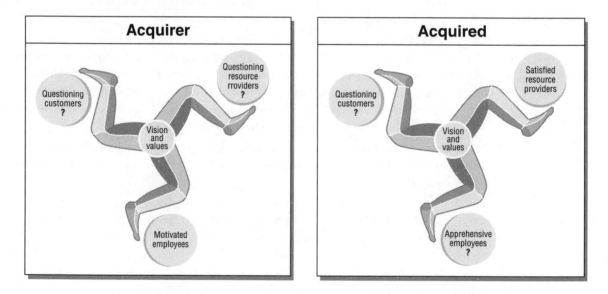

THE SOURCE

15 David Waller, *Wheels on Fire: The Amazing Inside Story of the Daimler Chrysler Merger* (Hodder & Stoughton, 2001).

16 'Daimler Chrysler Agrees Radical Restructuring', *Financial Times*, 24/25 February, 2001.

17 'Breakdowns', *The Economist*, 21 April 2001, p. 106.

This section has used one particular type of segmentation, but acquisitions can be segmented in many other ways. In general, larger and cross-border acquisitions provide the biggest challenges in vision and values management, and are the most difficult to pull off successfully.

Typical effect of acquisitions on stakeholders

Chart 13.6 demonstrates the different effect of acquisitions on **stakeholders**. It shows how acquisitions can unbalance the Committed Enterprise, causing disruption between acquirer and acquired, and between stakeholders.

Most acquisitions are advantageous to the acquired company **shareholder** because the acquirer has overpaid. Despite this, the acquirer's **employees** are likely to be happy, since at a senior level they may gain money and power, and at more junior levels, greater opportunities. **Employees** of the acquired company are likely to be apprehensive, except those negotiating personal deals. **Customers** will have many questions, and plenty of memories of poor service and disruption from past acquisitions. They need and desire strong communication from both companies. **Suppliers** will experience a mixture of hope for new contracts, worry about business loss, and price reductions.

The Committed Enterprise will avoid sole focus on shareholders, and consider the interests of all stakeholders, especially those of the company to be acquired. This is the way to succeed with acquisitions.

Example of failed acquisition due to vision and values clash

Daimler Chrysler.[15] In May 1998, this was trumpeted as a merger of equals. Chrysler was the world's most profitable car maker. Daimler Benz the most prestigious. The assumption was that technologies would be shared over higher volumes and a more global product base. This spanned two types of acquisition – overcapacity and geographical expansion (see Chart 13.5).

In February 2001, Daimler Chrysler announced a 49% fall in underlying operating profits, 26 000 job losses, and 6 plant closures at Chrysler.[16] Daimler Chrysler's stock price plummeted from $108 in early 1999 to $42 in late 2001. A number of things had gone wrong, many related to differences in vision and values:

Opaque positioning. Daimler sold the deal as a merger of equals, but in reality it acquired Chrysler. Influenced by this, many of Chrysler's best people left, and others 'were fired ... as the red ink flowed'.[17]

Different styles and values. Chrysler had an open, empowered, fast-moving style, and was sales/marketing-focused. Daimler was more hierarchical, and numbers-driven, with a strong engineering bent.

CHART
13.7 Failed acquisitions influenced by vision and values clash

Language barriers and lack of cultural understanding added to the difficulties:

"The Americans earned two to four times as much as their German counterparts. But the expenses of US workers were tightly controlled... Daimler-side employees thought nothing of flying to Paris or New York for a half-day meeting, then capping the visit with a fancy dinner and a night at an expensive hotel. The Americans blanched at the extravagance."[18]

Slowness in integrating the two businesses. In 1998, Daimler Chrysler's vision (called 'Mission') was 'to integrate two great companies to become a world enterprise that by 2001 is the most successful and respected automotive and transportation products and services provider'. That certainly hasn't happened yet.

Examples of how successful acquirers manage vision and values

IBM and Lotus.[19] IBM decided to acquire Lotus in the mid 1990s, in order to build its software business through networks. After months of fruitless negotiations, IBM made a successful hostile bid in June 1995, paying $3.3 billion for a business with revenues of only $970 million a year, and modest profit levels. This was a 'category expansion' type of acquisition, but it also involved 'people and technology' (see Chart 13.5).

Both sides knew there was a big difference in cultures. Lotus was only 13 years old, irreverent, hard-driving and fast-moving. IBM was a long-established colossus. When IBM's senior software officer first opened negotiations with IBM, he dressed down in jeans and T-shirt. To his surprise, Lotus did the opposite – their people wore dark suits and ties.

It was essential for IBM to retain most of the Lotus people. Lou Gerstner, the IBM Chairman, therefore promised to allow Lotus to continue as a separate entity, and kept the promise. Lotus retained the identity of a medium-sized software house, and using IBM's cash and distribution muscle, increased its user base from 2 million in 1995 to 22 million in 1998. By 2000, many IBM people had moved to Lotus, and vice versa.

IBM's strategy with acquired companies is to quickly apply its key metrics – e.g. customer satisfaction, market share, employee satisfaction, financial performance – and strategic planning processes, while being sensitive to cultural and branding issues. It has retained the Lotus brand.

IBM's key values of customer focus, winning, respect for the individual and teamwork, are relevant to all acquisitions, but an effort is also made to retain existing positive values and processes in acquired companies.

THE SOURCE

18 Bill Vlasic and Bradley Stertz, *Taken for a Ride: How Daimler Benz Drove Off with Chrysler* (HarperCollins, 2000).
19 Robert Slater, *Saving Big Blue* (McGraw Hill, 1999).

13.8 How successful acquirers manage vision and values

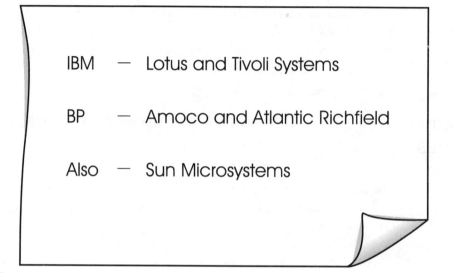

IBM — Lotus and Tivoli Systems

BP — Amoco and Atlantic Richfield

Also — Sun Microsystems

13.9 Five keys to successful acquisition

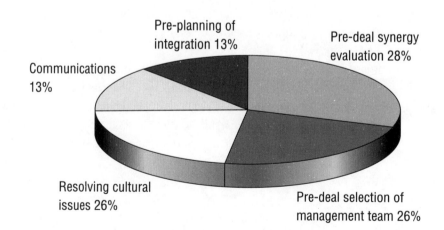

Pre-planning of integration 13%

Communications 13%

Pre-deal synergy evaluation 28%

Resolving cultural issues 26%

Pre-deal selection of management team 26%

BP Amoco. BP meets most of the criteria for the Committed Enterprise, and its acquisitions of Amoco and Arco are considered a success by analysts. Like Daimler Chrysler, these were partly 'overcapacity' acquisitions, partly 'geographical expansion' (see Chart 13.5). Aims were higher market share and reduced cost.

Amoco's vision and values appeared bland and by no means identical with BP. However, BP studied issues of cultural fit closely before acquisition. Amoco was initially sceptical about some BP values, especially its environmental ones, but ultimately bought in, because BP people were so committed. BP adapted its values and business policies to incorporate Amoco views and thinking.[20]

High technology companies. Microsoft, Oracle and Sun Microsystems have succeeded without making large acquisitions, not least because they are concerned at diluting their culture. Sun makes very small acquisitions, mainly for technology, and is put off by the digestion problems of big deals.[21]

Cisco Systems has been built on friendly acquisitions, "designed to accommodate the people first, then the product". It aims to buy people and technology, and bad chemistry with the management team or conflicting values are deal-breakers.[22]

Five keys to successful acquisition

The KPMG study of 700 cross-border acquisitions identified five keys to success (see **Chart 13.9**). They boil down to pre-planning – understanding what you are buying, and how you will generate extra value – and sorting out people and cultural issues early.

"Deals were 26% more likely than average to be successful if they focused on resolving cultural issues."[23]

Sony's 1989 acquisition of Columbia Pictures[24] is one example of a failed deal that broke all five keys:

- **Lack of pre-deal synergy evaluation.** The vision – synergy between Columbia film and Sony's existing music business – was vague. Film was a new business that Sony knew nothing about. There was a lack of due diligence, and Sony overpaid. Post acquisition, it discovered that the 'production pipeline was nearly empty'.[25]
- **Selection of unsuitable management team.** Sony did pre-select the top management team, but put itself in the hands of traditional Hollywood big spenders. Subsequently there were many changes in key personnel.

THE SOURCE

20 Interview with Lord Browne, CEO, BP, and with Chris Gibson-Smith, Managing Director.
21 Interview with Robert Youngjohns, Vice President, Sun Microsystems.
22 David Bunnell, *Making the Cisco Connection* (John Wiley, 2000).
23 *Unlocking Shareholder Value.*
24 John Nathan, *Sony, The Private Life* (HarperCollins Business, 1999). This section derives mainly from this book.
25 Ibid.

13.10 Best practice vision and values in acquisitions

1. Identify cultural differences **before** acquisition

2. Walk away if major culture clash is likely

3. Agree people, vision, values, before big deals

4. For small deals communicate acquirer's vision and values and integrate

5. Treat acquired people like long-term employees

6. Integrate most acquisitions quickly

THE SOURCE

26 Ibid.
27 Hubbard, *Acquisition Strategy.*
28 Interview with Richard Currie, President, George Weston Ltd; Former President, Loblaw Companies.

- **Cultural issues.** There were problems of expectation and management style.
- **Communications** with the outside world and between Sony USA and Sony Japan were weak, and 'the spectacle of Japan's apparently most sophisticated company being eaten alive by Hollywood was reported with uncontainable glee'.[26]
- **Integration**. There was little attempt to integrate Columbia with Sony's existing American businesses in the early years.

Sony paid about $6 billion for Columbia in September 1989. By mid 1993, it was losing $250 million a year, and in mid 1994 took a massive write-off of $3.4 billion, related to Columbia. The Columbia name has now been dropped.

Sony is one of the world's most exciting companies, and the original vision, which motivated the Columbia acquisition, may still succeed in the long term, but overall, this was a lesson in how **not** to do it.

Best practice vision and values in acquisitions

Identify cultural differences before acquisition

A cultural due diligence is at least as important as a financial one. The two can be run together. Questions to ask include:

- Do the two companies have similar or different visions? If different, who changes? Is a totally new vision needed? To answer these questions, acquirers need to have a clear understanding of their real vision and values, and an ability to communicate them clearly. This understanding is often lacking.[27]
- What are the values and practices of each company? Similarities, differences, conflicts? Speed and manner of integration?
- How does the acquiring company embed and measure vision and values? What changes need to be made, and how quickly?
- If redundancies or company name changes are planned, how will they be handled? These are high profile tests of the culture of the acquiring company.

Companies in the same industry often have different cultures:

Loblaw is one of the most effective retailers in North America, with around 35% share of the Canadian grocery market. It bought Provigo, another grocery chain, mainly to strengthen its position in Quebec. Loblaw spent a lot of time in Provigo stores pre-acquisition, looking closely at both culture and performance. They concluded that the stores were well located but the people were not well tended. The CEO said, "It's never sensible to make an acquisition and let the acquired company continue independently – in that case you're just acting as a banker. You don't need to change culture instantly, but must get in your own key managers early."[28]

13.11 Assessing differences in values

DEAL BREAKERS

Differences in ethics, treatment of people, openness, customer focus

MANAGEABLE DIFFERENCES

Differences in speed, innovation, enterprise

Attitude to risk, quality and performance

THE SOURCE

29 Interview with Edward Whitacre Jr, Chairman/CEO, SBC Communications.
30 Author's interview, identity withheld.
31 Interview with John McGrath, founding CEO of Diageo.
32 Interview with Sir David Barnes, founding CEO of Zeneca; Deputy Chairman, Astra Zeneca.

Companies like GE or SBC with an excess of effective managers have a better than average chance of success with acquisitions, by transplanting their cultures:

At SBC Communications, we do look at culture pre-acquisition. We're based in Texas, which is somewhat different from the West Coast (where we acquired Pacific Bell) and the mid-West (Ameritech acquired). In some cases senior executives of acquired companies leave, influenced by the size of their old company's change of control packages, but this is not a problem for SBC because we have many excellent managers and promote from within."[29]

Walk away if culture clash is likely

A Chairman with a successful record of major acquisitions said:

"Before any acquisition, we always find out about the target's behaviour and screen its culture. If cultures are different, we would not acquire, because the idea that you can easily convert people is unrealistic."[30]

Much depends on the type of difference (see **Chart 13.11**). If there are fundamental differences in attitudes to ethics, people, or customers, you walk away. Equally an organization built around highly incentivized individuals would clash with one committed to teamwork. But differences in values like fast/slow, entrepreneurial/cautious or innovative/pedestrian, can often be bridged, as at Diageo:

Diageo was a merger of Grand Metropolitan and Guinness. Grand Met people were fast-moving, entrepreneurial and didn't overanalyse things. Guinness people were thorough, analytical, and deliberate. They viewed Grand Mets as 'hip shooters in a data free zone', but were seen by Grand Mets as suffering from 'analysis paralysis ... and if they ever did make a decision, it was probably wrong'.

These value and style differences did prove bridgeable at Diageo, with Guinness people becoming more entrepreneurial, and Grand Mets more considered, though the Grand Met culture generally prevailed."[31]

In the Astra Zeneca merger, there were known differences in culture, but these were manageable:

"Astra was more hierarchical than Zeneca, and Zeneca was more effective in translating values into practices. There were also differences between Swedish (Astra), UK (Zeneca) and USA (both Astra and Zeneca) cultures.

However, there were many similarities. Scientific thinking in US, UK and Swedish pharma companies has much in common (whereas German and Japanese have a different approach). And fit by type of drug area and geography was good.

Astra Zeneca developed a new vision, and blended the values of the two companies into one."[32]

For big deals, agree the people, vision and values early

It's preferable to decide who will do the top jobs before acquisition, especially in big deals between companies in the same industry. This prevents damaging clashes later, and, if fairly done, will reassure less senior managers, especially in the acquired company.

If there is to be a change in vision, it should be agreed in outline pre-acquisition. Differences in values should also be discussed candidly, and a judgement made as to whether they can be successfully bridged. For example, Cisco Systems insists that the management of target companies believe in employee ownership.[33]

For small deals, communicate acquirer's vision and values, train and integrate

Small deals will not change the acquirer's vision and values, and the only issue is how far and how fast to integrate.

Treat acquired people like long-term employees

This means fairness in deciding who will go, who will stay, who will be promoted and avoiding the colonial approach of always giving preference to your own people. Such preference is tempting because it is natural to opt for those who have already proved themselves and know how the company works. Some organizations, like Unilever and GlaxoSmithKline, use executive-search firms to interview and recommend candidates for each senior job in newly merged companies. This builds objectivity and makes it manifest.

Integrate acquisitions quickly

A key issue is the trade-off between speed of integration, which maximizes savings, and the need to build a common culture.[34] In practice, post-acquisition effort is often concentrated on cost reduction and revenue building, while vision and values are deferred. This can be damaging, and it's essential to give vision and values the highest priority, since resolving them will make change easier, and quicker to achieve. Many CEOs said that they favoured much faster integration, to generate acquisition benefits early, and to reduce uncertainty.

THE SOURCE

33 Hubbard, *Acquisition Strategy*.
34 Wilman, 'The Perpetual Triumph of Hope Over Experience'.

Chapter

Aligning individuals and organizations

Overview

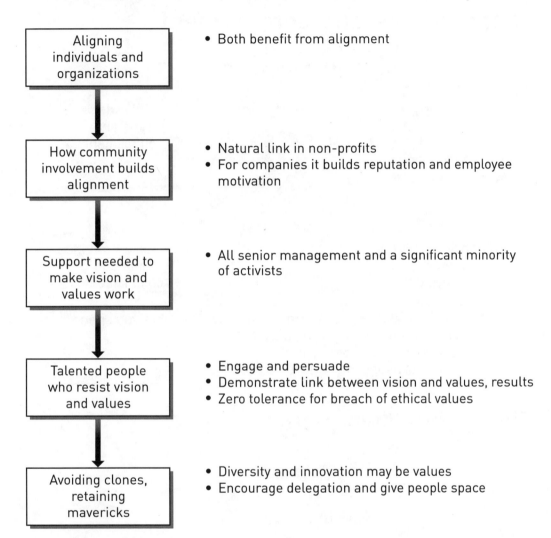

Aligning individuals and organizations	• Both benefit from alignment
How community involvement builds alignment	• Natural link in non-profits • For companies it builds reputation and employee motivation
Support needed to make vision and values work	• All senior management and a significant minority of activists
Talented people who resist vision and values	• Engage and persuade • Demonstrate link between vision and values, results • Zero tolerance for breach of ethical values
Avoiding clones, retaining mavericks	• Diversity and innovation may be values • Encourage delegation and give people space

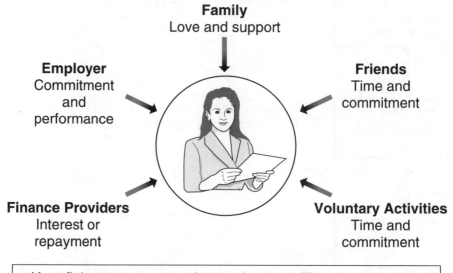

14.1 Work organizations only get part of people's time and commitment

Family
Love and support

Employer
Commitment
and
performance

Friends
Time and
commitment

Finance Providers
Interest or
repayment

Voluntary Activities
Time and
commitment

- Your finite resources are time and money. The more you spend with one group, the less you have for others
- These needs therefore conflict
- Successful people manage to balance them

14.2 Fill in your own picture

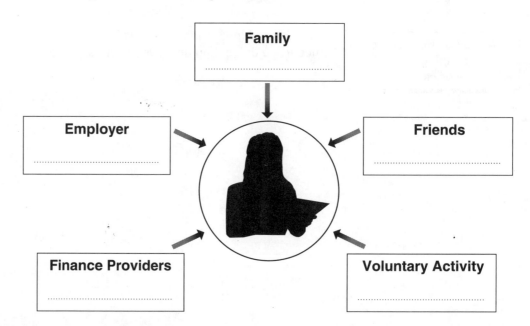

Family

....

Employer

....

Friends

....

Finance Providers

....

Voluntary Activity

....

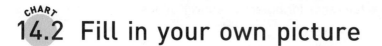

Linking people and organizations

Both individuals and organizations have a need to answer the basic questions of life:

- What are we here for (*Purpose*)
- Where are we going? (*Vision*)
- What are our principles? (*Values*)

They will inevitably come up with different answers. The more closely the vision and values of organizations reflect the personal aspirations of their members, the more effective they will be. Alignment is generally easier to achieve in non-profits than in companies, as with Greenpeace:

"There is a unity between Greenpeace values and the values of the individuals joining it."[1]

Organizations benefit by understanding the power of this unity, which involves seeing work in the context of an individual's whole life. How does it fit with spiritual values, aspirations, and family? These questions penetrate far beyond the traditional ones of home/work balance.

Like organizations, individuals have stakeholders. Who are they? Look at **Chart 14.1**, which illustrates a typical set of relationships, then fill in your own picture in **Chart 14.2**.

Chart 14.2 shows you at the centre of a web of needs. Others in your web also have their own charts, and they are at the centre. You look different to all stakeholders. Your employer may see you as a committed high flier, your family as a neglectful parent and partner. 'Success' in this chart is not material wealth, but balanced achievement.

Organizations do not own individuals, whose resources of time and commitment are limited. You can prove that by filling in Table 14.1:

Table 14.1

Your weekly allocation of time	
Activity	Time (hours)
Family Friends Employer Voluntary work Sleep Other	
TOTAL	168 hours

Someone sleeping 7 hours a night has 119 waking hours a week. If 50 hours of this are spent at work, this only occupies 42% of the waking time.

Combine Table 14.1 with Chart 14.2 and consider three questions:

THE SOURCE

1 Interview with Lord Peter Melchett, Director, Greenpeace UK.

14.3 Not many CEOs describe alignment this boldly

" I tell people that their job is not the most important thing. Spiritual life (however defined by the individual) is number one, family and friends number two, job number three, and then comes hobbies and community service.

I really believe that a person with balance in life is much more focused and productive at work."

Joe Weller
CEO, Nestlé, USA[2]

14.4 Can this individual and organization become aligned? (Spot the mismatch)

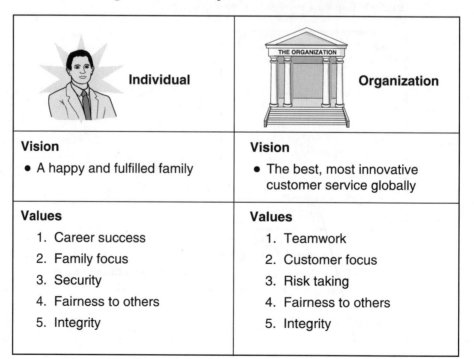

Individual	Organization
Vision	**Vision**
• A happy and fulfilled family	• The best, most innovative customer service globally
Values	**Values**
1. Career success	1. Teamwork
2. Family focus	2. Customer focus
3. Security	3. Risk taking
4. Fairness to others	4. Fairness to others
5. Integrity	5. Integrity

1 How does each stakeholder feel about you?

2 How well are you meeting their needs?

3 What future changes will you make?

These are exactly the same questions that organizations need to ask themselves. Some individuals choose the unbalanced approach through ambition, fear or work absorption. Others are forced into it by peer pressure, job demands, limited competence or financial need.

Overwork can affect quality, impair judgement, weaken creativity and erode relationships. It is arguable that 50 hours of intelligent and committed work is worth 100 hours on the job treadmill. Many recognize this, but find it hard to change.

Time allocation is a critical issue in aligning individuals and organizations, and affects commitment. Some organizations expect blood; others encourage balance, like Joe Weller, CEO of Nestlé USA[3] (see **Chart 14.3**) and Terry Leahy of Tesco:

"Work pressures are increasing exponentially, and helping people get the work/life balance right is a key issue for CEOs. It's a lot easier for people if their own vision and values are closely aligned with the company's."[4]

Chart 14.4 probes for possible conflicts between an individual and his organization. The two visions shown are compatible, though different.

Value No.1 is compatible if this individual pursues career success through teamwork. There is no conflict between Value No. 2 – family and customer focus. Value No. 3 is problematic. This individual values security, but his organization wants risk-takers; a clash, as this example from Diageo shows:

"Our value of 'Freedom to Succeed' is designed to encourage an entrepreneurial approach – more testing, early decisions, and then cutting or running fast. But for many individuals who personally value security, this value means risk, and therefore clashes."[5]

Values No. 4 and 5 are identical. The big issue for this individual is whether he can flourish in an organization that encourages risk-taking.

Individual and corporate vision and values will always differ, and may be reconcilable. But they can create conflict, and this needs to be recognized candidly, as one CEO commented:

"Corporate and individual values may sometimes differ. Values, like equality of opportunity or no racial discrimination, may be difficult for some people in some countries to accept. Or the company's performance expectations may be hard to take if you lack confidence."[6]

THE SOURCE

2 Interview with Joe Weller, CEO, Nestlé, USA

3 Interview with Joe Weller, CEO, Nestlé, USA.

4 Interview with Terry Leahy, CEO, Tesco.

5 Interview with Paul Walsh, CEO, Diageo, John McGrath, former CEO, Diageo.

6 Author's interview, identity withheld.

- Nestlé has adopted 49 schools nationally, offering funds and employee skills

- Its criteria for adopting a school include the school's need and the presence of Nestlé employees working in the community.

- 40% of Nestlé HQ staff, and thousands of Nestlé employees nationwide, now volunteer and are given paid time off to spend with children

- Activities include local tutoring, mentoring, field trips, book fairs, reading and 'pen friends' program

However well aligned, vision and values are not the only ingredients in job satisfaction. Recognition, rewards, relationships and professional pride also have a role. Some people may prefer to work for an excellently managed tobacco company rather than a badly run children's charity.

How community involvement builds alignment

In many non-profits, the purpose is to benefit the community, so the aspirations of the organization and the *whole* individual are linked. The purpose of companies, however, is to build shareholder value, and the link with the community is incidental. Companies can extend this by helping individuals fulfil their personal visions outside work.

For example (**Chart 14.5**), Nestlé USA has developed strong links with schools, because this is motivating to many employees, and builds company reputation.

Home Depot has adopted community involvement as a specific value, for the same reason – a mixture of altruism and commercialism:

One of Home Depot's values is 'giving back'. Both the founders of Home Depot and the company give away a lot of money, quietly. And if there is a local community need, a store can decide to attend to it, without authorization. Here are two examples:

- In 1999, there was a huge ice storm in parts of the USA. It was disabling because there was no power or heat. Store people picked up lanterns and generators and gave them away, took cutting tools and removed fallen trees. No one ordered or co-ordinated this and the stores still had to hit budgets. Head Office heard about it later.
- When there were hurricanes in the southeast, Atlanta stores loaded trucks and sold product at cost to the community.[7]

Here lies a trap for some companies. They exist in order to create wealth, and achieve this through building committed customers and motivated employees. Community involvement is a means to this end, but not an end in itself. If Body Shop wants to save whales and better the lives of poor people, it should build wealth. This will enable the founders to establish a Foundation for whales and people. Andrew Carnegie, Bill Gates and David Packard took this approach. They did not confuse business and philanthropy.

One realistic CEO, whose company is a generous giver, expressed this point succinctly:

''Community giving is a *consequence* of shareholder value creation, not a specific corporate objective.''[8]

THE SOURCE

7 Interview with Faye Wilson, Senior VP, Home Depot.
8 Author's interview, identity withheld.

CHART

14.6 Will vision and values work with this support level?

Activists	Supporters	Neutral	Blockers
		?	
Organization A			
15%	15%	50%	20%
Organization B			
5%	10%	55%	30%

How much alignment is needed to make vision and values work?

Chart 14.6 breaks down attitudes to vision and values into four categories – activists, supporters, neutrals and blockers. It illustrates level of support in two different organizations. How much is needed to make vision and values work?

In Organization A, 30% are activists or supporters, 20% blockers. This is probably a winning situation, because many of the blockers will become disaffected and leave, while neutrals will slowly gravitate to the winning side. Organization B faces a much tougher situation.

Recent research by ORC[9] among 363 companies in 1999 and 2000 showed that about 50% agreed with the statement, 'The brand mission, vision and values are understood by all employees, most of whom believe in them strongly.' Fifty per cent support sounds on the high side.

Many organization leaders felt that 30% active support was enough to make vision and values work, as long as senior management and key opinion-formers were committed. If not, there is little hope. It is difficult to live vision and values in action, even with strong commitment from senior people.

Key action points to build support are as follows:

- Ensure that all senior managers are fully committed to the vision and values. They are the evangelists, and their example will be closely watched by everyone else.
- Those not committed will have to change or go.
- Target key opinion-formers and consult them early on. Front line people, with customer contact, are important to convince. So are influential cynics. Scotland Yard (the Metropolitan Police) understood this well:

"We set up Focus Groups on our vision and values with people on the front line. Police are very hands on, pragmatic, and can be severe critics. We involved some of our most cynical people, since they were the ones who needed to be convinced."[10]

- View vision and values as a continuing programme, not a 'one-off' initiative. At first, you may only gain 20% active support, and this will be enough if it is regularly built upon. There will always be a large group of 'neutrals'.
- Monitor level of support at least annually through Employee Surveys, and estimate what proportion of people are in each of the groups shown in Chart 14.6. Develop plans for moving people to the left.

THE SOURCE

9 Milorad Ajder, *Global 250 – Exploring Attitudes and Practices in Corporate Branding*, ORC International, 2000. Study conducted in 1999 and 2000 among USA, European and Pacific Rim countries.

10 Interview with Sir John Stevens, QPM, Commissioner, Metropolitan Police (i.e. London Police).

CHART 14.7 Talented people who don't buy into vision and values – the silent saboteurs

> " Those who openly disagree with your vision and values can be engaged and often persuaded. Those who disagree and stay silent are a bigger problem and hard to spot – silent saboteurs."
>
> **Paul Walsh**
> **CEO, Diageo**

CHART 14.8 Talented people who don't buy into vision and values – trade-offs

> " Alignment with our four core values is essential at DuPont. However, we encourage strong debate. This means things may take longer, but it's a worthwhile trade-off to retain diversity and innovation.
>
> People may question the balance of business between chemicals and biology or dislike our 'miracles of science' advertising, and those issues are open to debate. But the primacy of our values – like safety, ethics, and treating people right – is not."
>
> **Charles Holliday Jr**
> **Chairman and CEO, DuPont**

Dealing with talented people who resist the vision and values

In practice, people who lack ability and don't buy into the vision and values will be encouraged to move on. Talented people who are lukewarm may leave, but should be encouraged to stay. The problem group is talented individuals who don't live the vision and values. What do you do with them? Most organization leaders said that efforts would be made to understand their views, try to persuade them, offer training. But they were emphatic in saying that anyone breaking the *moral* values of the organization (i.e. ethics or treatment of others) would be dismissed, however talented, and examples were given.

Chart 14.7 highlights some of the issues and **Chart 14.8** demonstrates the opportunity for legitimate trade-offs outside the core values. Here are further comments from Procter & Gamble, General Mills, Dow Chemical and Denby Pottery:

"There's zero tolerance at **P&G** for those who lack integrity or treat people badly. In a company where you only promote from within, it's very important to be able to trust people."[11]

"**General Mills** coaches and advises people who don't live our vision and values. But if they remain outside our value system, they have to go, however talented. We have a very low tolerance for harassment, fraud or cheating."[12]

"In any trade-off between values and talent, [at **Dow** Chemical] values must win."[13]

"If you didn't care about quality, you couldn't live in the **Denby** business because peer pressure would force you out."[14]

And here's the approach of a leading head teacher:

"You need brilliant teachers, and some are difficult colleagues. I'm quite prepared to talk in private with those who disagree with policies, even after extended staff discussion. But I've got one member of staff who opposes policies even after they've been discussed and agreed, and she tells pupils she disagrees. I won't tolerate that because it's destructive for the school."

Not every organization takes such a strong line. Consider the reaction of a great company like Sony (suspending two senior US employees for 30 days) to revelations that 'its marketing executives were making up comments' about its own new movies 'and attributing them to a fictitious critic named David Manning'.[15]

'Additionally it was discovered that Sony used its own employees in on-air testimonials to promote... the movie *Summer Patriot*'. As *Advertising Age* stated in a leader: 'Sony's other ploy – creating phoney reviews by a phoney critic – can't be excused'... and 'passing off studio employees as unbiased film fans in TV ad commercials is flat wrong'.

THE SOURCE

11 Interview with Durk Jager, former CEO, Procter & Gamble.
12 Interview with Stephen Demeritt, Vice Chairman, General Mills.
13 Interview with Dr William Stavropoulos, Chairman, Dow Chemical.
14 Interview with Nigel Worne, Managing Director, Denby Pottery.
15 *Advertising Age*, 25 June 2001. This publication consistently takes a strong line on ethics in advertising and marketing.

14.9A Aligning teams of people

> " At SmithKline Beecham, people who didn't follow the "Facts and Data" approach would never get things approved.
> Even if they were very successful, but kept upsetting people, they'd run into difficulty.
> The key is to have a team of people with fully aligned attitudes and values. Then you spend your time getting things done and don't waste it explaining *why* you're doing it."
>
> **Peter Jensen**
> **Former President WSO, SmithKline Beecham**

14.9B Avoiding clones, retaining mavericks

Individual	Company
Behaviour of individual	**Values of company**
• Short-term performance	• Short-term performance
• Independent, courageous	• Centralized/controlling
• Big spender	• Cost conscious
• Quality of execution	• Quality of execution
• Inspirational leader	• Hard on non-performers
• Big risk-taker	• Cautious, analytical

Avoiding clones, retaining mavericks

A typical CEO comment is: "We want everyone to be fully committed to our vision and values, and to be really innovative." Is there a conflict here? Not necessarily, since innovation and continuous improvement may be core values. There is a concern, though, that strong values can squash individuality and stifle creativity. And in some organizations with strong vision and values, people rush over the cliff like Gadarene swine, in perfect formation. Values may also be misrepresented to prevent change.

Let's consider an analogy – a football team. The area in which it operates – the pitch – is marked out with white lines. If the ball goes outside these, the game stops. Every player wears a 'uniform', which is tightly specified. The vision is clear and simple: to win every game. The rules are well understood and policed by referees. Yet, in this very tightly controlled environment teams regularly develop new tactics, and perform with flair. This applies equally to all types of football: American, rugby or soccer. And every year, innovative new players emerge. The quote in **Chart 14.9A** demonstrates the importance of alignment for teams.

Businesses and non-profits operate in a much less restricted environment, and in theory have an easier task. However, they tend to be larger organizations than football teams, and can frustrate innovators:

"Brilliant mavericks don't feel comfortable in big organizations. However, they do represent agents for change, and it's worth trying to keep them via delegation. At Unilever, there is a tradition of delegation down as far as possible, since in the old days of communication by steamship, delegation was a necessity."[16]

Although rules affect everything a footballer does, they only affect a small proportion of an executive's activity, as these two CEOs observe:

"A company must tolerate a wide range of opinions. Strong vision and values is not about looking, thinking, and sounding the same. Values only address a limited number of topics, and there's room for great diversity in behaviour on other issues."[17]

"There's a preferred pattern of behaviour, but you'd lose a lot of good people if you insisted upon it in detail. Some very talented people are mavericks, and you need them for challenge, innovation, inspiration."[18]

Chart 14.9B outlines the behaviour of a brilliant maverick, and asks whether he and the company can stay together.

The individual was managing director of a large company within a major multi-national. He drank too much, sometimes played ping-pong on weekday afternoons, was highly entrepreneurial, and disliked planning, "because it takes all the excitement away".

THE SOURCE

16 Interview with Sir Michael Perry, Chairman, Centrica, former Chairman of Unilever.
17 Interview with Terry Leahy, CEO, Tesco.
18 Interview with Sir Brian Pitman, former Chairman, Lloyds TSB.

CHART
14.10 Building individuals into a brand

" Mayo clinic is a complete brand where the organization outranks the individual. Anyone there is assumed to be of Mayo class.

For second opinions, I send my patients to the Mayo, and don't specify a doctor. Cleveland and Johns Hopkins are also in this league. Anywhere else, I'd look at the doctors there and pick one.

It's a long and hard transition from a collection of individuals to a brand, and we're moving in that direction, but we're not there yet."

Leading physician from a major American hospital

THE SOURCE

19 Interview with Sir Michael Perry, Chairman, Centrica, former Chairman of Unilever.
20 See page 131.

In one year, he increased sales by 80% and almost doubled market share. In the process, he developed a new business system, which was successfully applied to many countries. But there was a fundamental mismatch between an entrepreneurial free spirit and a highly centralized global company. As soon as he had a run of weak short-term performance, he paid the price.

Key action points for building strong values, yet driving innovation are:

- Ensure that both vision and values include a strong customer focus. Customers and markets change constantly, forcing organizations to do so too.
- Include innovation or continuous improvement as a core value.
- Regularly review the vision, and the practices supporting the values, updating as necessary.
- Emphasize how strong vision and values provide more opportunity to delegate responsibility.

"The closer the decision is to the customer, the better it will be."[19]

Are organizations now responsible for providing moral leadership?

As we have seen, many organizations are strongly committed to their values. And, on average, almost 50% of values have moral rather than performance implications, affecting ethics and attitudes towards people.[20] Does this mean that organizations have a responsibility to lead society towards better moral values? Traditional upholders of morality – e.g. churches, parents and schools – are losing influence, and it has been argued that work organizations should take more of a moral lead. Indeed some corporate values, like treating others as you would like to be treated, are biblical in tone.

Let's take companies first. On a narrow view, their purpose is to create wealth for shareholders, acting within the law. To achieve this, they need to be trusted by customers and employees. Moral values strongly influence trust, and companies therefore have a commercial interest in pursuing them. While companies have no specific responsibility for moral leadership, commitment to it helps them achieve their purpose.

Secondly, non-profits. Schools and colleges have always had a leadership role in moral values, although their primary purpose is education. The medical and caring professions, like teachers, have professional standards, with some moral implications. Moral and performance values are therefore closely intertwined.

Building individuals into brands

The Mayo Clinic illustrates how individuals can be built into a strong brand (see **Chart 14.10**). In the days when most brands were products, the best built trust through consistent high quality. The customer didn't know who made a particular pack of Tide or Budweiser, and didn't need to, because the brand name guaranteed quality.

CHART

14.11 Brands where organizations outrank individuals

Sony

United Parcel Service

FBI

USA Marine Corps

Caltech

Berlin Philharmonic

Goldman Sachs

The Economist

Harvard University

McKinsey

Today, most brands are either services, or combinations of products and services. This applies particularly to business-to-business brands and to non-profits. In many cases the people are also the product, and they often have face-to-face contact with the consumer.

The ideal for a service organization is to build a brand which outranks the individual, like the Mayo Clinic. In such cases, customers and their friends have many high quality experiences over a long period, leading them to believe future quality will be similar, irrespective of who delivers it. A few service brands such as UPS or Harvard University build a reputation which transcends that of the people working there. **Chart 14.11** lists others – there aren't many. To get to this level, you need strong, consistent vision and values, plus excellent execution.

A final word on alignment – recruitment

The easiest way to align individuals and organizations is at the beginning, through recruitment. A clear exposition of vision and values will tell people whether your place is their kind. Organizations need to be very clear who they are looking for, like New York Central Park, which seeks people with empathy, and an interest in horticulture. They will invest in training but don't want skilled horticulturalists who are uninterested in people.

''People who are just top flight horticulturalists and don't want to work with colleagues, volunteers or the public won't fit here and they leave. They prefer to prune trees, grow borders, and see the public as a nuisance. New York Central Park has outgrown them.''[21]

An organization lacking clear vision and values can expect to hire too many of the wrong kind of people.

THE SOURCE

21 Interview with Doug Blonsky, Chief Operating Officer, Central Park Conservancy.

Chapter

A renewable process for vision and values

Overview

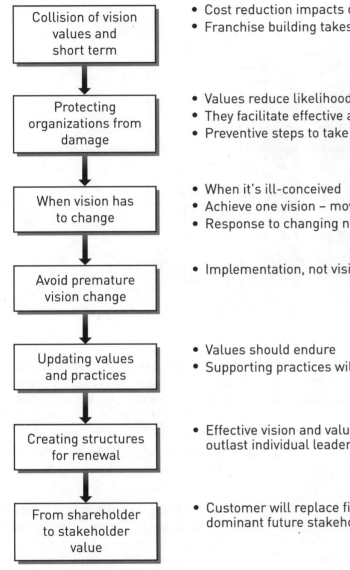

Collision of vision values and short term	• Cost reduction impacts quickly • Franchise building takes much longer
Protecting organizations from damage	• Values reduce likelihood of crises • They facilitate effective action • Preventive steps to take
When vision has to change	• When it's ill-conceived • Achieve one vision – move to next • Response to changing needs
Avoid premature vision change	• Implementation, not vision may be the problem
Updating values and practices	• Values should endure • Supporting practices will change
Creating structures for renewal	• Effective vision and values structures outlast individual leaders
From shareholder to stakeholder value	• Customer will replace finance providers as dominant future stakeholder

15.1 Average time spent with US company by major stakeholder

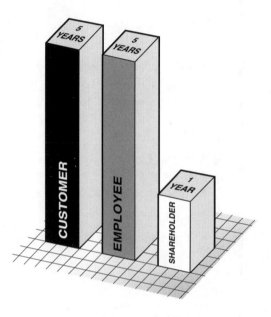

Technical note:

This chart is illustrative rather than exact, since comparable data on the loyalty of the three major stakeholders is unavailable. However, its basic message – that customers and employees are more loyal to companies than shareholders in the USA and UK – is sound.

- The shareholder loyalty figure of 1 year is based on the 1999 Bain study in the USA.[1]

- The employee figure of 5 years is average job tenure in the UK in 1999 ('Job Tenure 1975–98' by Paul Gregg and Jonathan Wadsworth, in *The State of Working Britain*, 1999, Manchester University Press).

- The customer loyalty figure of 5 years is an educated guess, because this is a very complex area, and there is no commonly accepted definition of 'loyalty'. Discussion with experts confirmed wide differences in loyalty between individual product and service categories, making a single generalized figure unfeasible to calculate. The most demanding categories for loyalty are fast moving consumer goods (FMCG, e.g. detergents, coffee) since consumers vote through their purchases every few weeks. A 3-year study of 113 UK FMCG brands in 2000 projected that customers initially loyal to a particular brand, continued to include it within their purchasing portfolio for 8–10 years.[2]

When vision, values and short-term pressures collide

Many Chief Executives said there was no conflict between long-term vision and values, and short-term performance demands. This may be true from their perspective, but pragmatic moves can be seen lower down the organization as eroding vision and values. One reason for such conflicts is the difference in time lines between the main stakeholders.

Shareholders tend to a short-term view. In the USA (1999), the average share on the New York Stock Exchange was held for 1.2 years (down from 8 years in 1960). On the NASDAQ, where more high-tech firms are listed, shares were held for only 4 months and for Amazon, the figure was 7 days.[1]

Both customers and employees stay with organizations much longer than shareholders. Chief Executives last for 4–5 years. **Chart 15.1** illustrates time spent with companies by major stakeholder.

The principal reason for conflict between vision, values and short-term results is the time effect of different decision types. Cost-reducing decisions impact the bottom line quickly, especially if they involve cutting people in either the USA or UK. By contrast, most revenue-building decisions (e.g. increase in capital investment, new product or business development) takes years to pay back, as Table 15.1 shows:

Table 15.1

Time impact of different decision types	
Decision type	Payback period (years)
Most cost reductions	0–1
Major advertising increase	1–3
Training and development	1–3
New vision and values	2–5
New brand, consumer goods	4–6
New market entry (green field)	4–6
Basic or applied R&D	3–10

For a Chief Executive under profit pressure, it is tempting to focus on cost reduction, and to cut back on revenue-building programmes, since the payback on the latter is often longer than the CEO's job tenure. Such actions build up problems for their successors.

THE SOURCE

1 Data: K. Darrell Rigby, Bain & Co., in study for *Business Week*, 20 September 1999.
2 Study was conducted by Andrew Roberts, Group Technical Director, Taylor Nelson Sofres.

15.2 How short-term actions can damage vision and values

Vision or values	Damaging short-term actions
Vision	
Enter new markets	Postpone entry for 2 years
Become No.1 in category	Cut marketing and capital spend
Develop best customer service	Cut training budget, downsize
Values	
Respect for people	Make good people redundant
Teamwork	Disproportionate rewards for senior managers
Superior quality	Disruptive changes affecting quality
Innovation	Cut R&D budget

All the short-term actions in **Chart 15.2** conflict with the vision and values. Such actions should be openly and convincingly explained. Otherwise they will be interpreted unfavourably. The best approach is never to trade off vision and values against short-term pressures, because the very process of trade-off is both corrosive and addictive.

An example of pursuit of long-term vision despite an adverse effect on short-term share price comes from SBC Communications. It is one of the world's most successful telecom companies, with sales of over $50 billion, net income of around $8 billion.

SBC's vision is to provide a full service to customers for communications, entertainment and information – "The only telecom company our customers need." Key strategies to deliver this are more customers, more services per customer, and state of the art technology:

"You have to walk a hair-thin line between pursuing the vision and delivering short-term results. One of our major growth motors is building broadband networks to exploit the Internet. This has cost $6 billion in capital spending, with little short-term return, and our stock was downgraded as a result.

Shareholders take a short-term view and SBC has to balance this with its long-term attitude towards employees and investment. These sometimes clash, but if SBC had not built a clear long-term vision when deregulation began in 1986, it would not now exist as an independent company."[3]

Sir David Barnes, founder CEO of Zeneca, and a key player in the Astra–Zeneca merger, has a similar attitude towards short-term pressures:

"It's a big mistake to move away from vision and values at the first sign of trouble. You must retain them, and communicate why the problem has occurred, how it will be tackled."[4]

Protecting organizations from damage

Most organizations beaver away in relative obscurity. They serve customers, control spending and produce goods or services. Their activities are reported, if at all, on the business pages or in trade magazines, but a few are propelled overnight into front-page news. The lightning strike may be a single event, like an act of discrimination, or a series, such as taking bribes. The crisis may happen to a global company in a country nobody has previously heard of. The better known the organization, the bigger the story.

Values have two influences on this picture. First, they reduce the likelihood of crises occurring. Secondly, they facilitate fast and decisive action. Constant renewal of values acts as both a preventative and a protective coating.

Here is a disguised story about a boarding school not listed among those interviewed, which demonstrates the risk inherent in weak values – and a nightmare start for a new headmaster:

THE SOURCE

3 Interview with Edward Whitacre Jr, Chairman and CEO, SBC Communications.
4 Interview with Sir David Barnes, Deputy Chairman, AstraZeneca.

15.3 Problems which strong values may prevent

Crisis causes	Examples or allegations
1. Treatment of employees	• Pay and conditions of workers in Asian countries making sports shoes • Coca Cola racial discrimination case
2. Treatment of customers	• Overcharging or price fixing • Exploitation by those in trusted positions • Fraud or harassment
3. Safety	• Plane or rail crashes • Unsafe food or drugs • Unsafe hospital practices
4. Ethics	• Alleged bribes paid by Elf Aquitaine • Insider trading
5. Environmental or social damage	• Exxon Valdez oil spill • Effect of Wal-Mart on communities

"When I took over, it was obvious that the school had lost its way some years ago. The original values, which had been strong, were neglected. Staff quality was variable, the school was in debt, and student numbers in decline.

My plan was to upgrade staff and curriculum, sort out the finances, create a new vision, and re-establish the old values. This was blown away as soon as I arrived. A sex scandal erupted, involving a pupil who had left 15 years ago, and a former staff member. It took six months to settle with the pupil's mother.

Shortly afterwards, another sex scandal hit us. I'd assembled a crisis management team early on, and this incident was handled quickly. The teacher involved went, and letters were sent to parents, colleagues, old boys and the community, explaining the situation and our future plans. Today the school values and standards are high and pupil numbers are up by 60% since I arrived. But the early crises impeded progress, diverted our energies and damaged our reputation."

Most of the literature on crisis management deals with handling crises rather than preventing them. Can strong values prevent them? Let's consider the causes of crises in tackling this question. Most fall into five categories – treatment of employees, treatment of customers, safety, ethics and environmental or social damage, as **Chart 15.3** shows. Each of these five areas is prime territory for values. Best practice management of values would have prevented some of the crises.

But not all. Every organization consists of fallible human beings. Even though strongly committed to exemplary values, they will make misjudgements. The best police forces have pockets of poor practice, and don't always achieve the right balance between firmness and restraint. And certain crises, like kidnapping of bank managers at home or deliberate contamination of food by store customers, are very difficult to guard against.

Here are specific steps an organization can take to protect itself from unexpected crises. Most relate to values rather than vision, and to moral rather than performance values:

- Set up a powerful Crisis Management Committee, consisting of influential people who understand the organization and its customers, are familiar with change in the outside world, and skilled communicators. The CEO, Head Teacher or Hospital President would lead this committee. It should include younger, front line people, prepared to speak their mind. Don't make the mistake of packing the committee with senior 'nodders' who are out of touch.

- Give the committee responsibility for prevention as well as management of crises. This would involve ensuring that values, practices and processes covered all five major crisis causes (see Chart 15.3), as well as auditing their application. Possible areas of concern would be highlighted. Systems for spotting value breaches early, dealing fast with causes, and preventing recurrence would be set up.

- Identify possible crisis scenarios, and rehearse how they would be handled, like fire drills, using real external critics.

CHART 15.4 Home Depot[5]

> **Home Depot – four channels for employees to bring concerns to management's attention**
>
> - Annual Associates Survey
> - 360° personnel appraisals
> - Directors store visits
> - Open door policy which encourages calls to management

CHART 15.5 Diageo[6]

> **Diageo – four ways to identify problems early**
>
> - Free call line that everyone can use. (*When Paul Walsh was President of Pillsbury, he personally saw all callers.*)
> - Code of Practice that has to be signed, increasing awareness of ethics.
> - Senior management presence in the field to build trust with front-line operators. (*The CEO spends half his time in the field and encourages his top 50 managers to be very mobile.*)
> - Active round of social activities where things can be raised informally.

CHART 15.6 Ill-conceived vision[7]

> **Monsanto's vision, 1999**
>
> "We face a business environment that will change radically and unpredictably. Accordingly, we need to be flexible and responsive. Intense competition will make it unlikely that we can achieve price increases. Therefore, we need to achieve substantial and continuous gains in operational excellence, and increases in margin, driven by eliminating waste, not value."
>
> **Robert Shapiro**
> **CEO**

THE SOURCE

5 Interview with Faye Wilson, Senior VP Values, Home Depot.
6 Interview with Paul Walsh, CEO, Diageo.
7 Robert Shapiro, article on Shareholder Value, included in William Dauphinais and Colin Price, *Straight from the CEO* (Nicholas Brealey, 1999).
8 Kerry Cooper, 'An About-Face at Aventis', *Business Week*, 27 November 2000.

- **Charts 15.4 and 15.5** illustrate the internal alarm systems at Diageo and Home Depot that help surface problems early, and minimise nasty surprises.

- Always view crises from the viewpoint of key stakeholders, especially customers.

- Once a crisis emerges, follow the organization's values. Act quickly and openly. Use of sophisticated marketing or PR techniques can misfire. Success is achieved by organization leaders demonstrating their concern, personally taking the lead, and telling the truth. The classic case example (which is well documented) is Johnson & Johnson's response to the Tylenol crisis:

A number of people died due to criminal tampering with bottles of Tylenol, an analgesic, in store. The brand was withdrawn, all stocks destroyed, and it was only re-introduced months later when a tamper-free bottle had been developed. Jim Burke, the then CEO, led from the front, was totally open and acted quickly. In managing the crisis, he closely followed Johnson & Johnson's 'Credo', putting the interests of the customers first.

When vision has to change

Visions have a life cycle like products or strategies. They wear out and need updating. Values are like strong brands – they should endure forever. The practices surrounding values require constant sharpening and updating, just like the products and services supporting brands.

There are three main reasons why vision has to change. First, it may prove to be ill-conceived. Second, the vision may be achieved, so a new one is called for. Third, major changes in customer needs or markets may force change.

Ill-conceived visions   Getting the vision right is a difficult and challenging task, as the Monsanto example in **Chart 15.6** illustrates. This vision didn't mention customers. Monsanto hit a brick wall by failing to understand customer response to genetically modified foods and was acquired by Pharmacia in 2000.

Bold visions involve taking a calculated risk on future trends. Aventis, a merger of France's Rhône-Poulenc and Germany's Hoechst, did this, got it wrong and, to its credit, changed quickly. The vision for the new company was to be the world leader in life sciences. It must be one of the shortest-lived visions on record. 'By applying gene-based technology used in drug discovery to agriculture... Aventis could realize major cost savings and a host of promising new products, including enriched seeds and disease-resistant grains. Nearly a year later, it's clear the life sciences model is dead.'[8] Its future vision is now based on pharmaceuticals, where it is No. 6 in the world, but only No. 12 in USA.

Evolution   Achieve one vision, move to the next. The analysis of vision statements in Chart 5.9 (page 89), revealed six recurring words. The most important were 'global, best, leader and customer'. So, the organization achieves its vision of becoming global or category leader. What next? A new vision is required.

15.7 Achieve one vision, move to the next

Successive visions of Dallas Symphony Orchestra (DSO)	
Vision 1	
1900–1920	Become paid, professional ensemble
1920–1970	Consolidation
1974	DSO almost bankrupt
Vision 2	
1977–1990	Re-establish national prominence
Vision 3	
1990 onwards	Become one of world's best orchestras

Changes in vision may evolve smoothly, or involve abrupt deviations. In great companies like Estée Lauder, vision evolves:

Estée Lauder vision has evolved three times since it was founded by Joseph and Estée Lauder in 1946. As each vision was achieved, a related but more ambitious one followed. Like UPS, Estée Lauder anticipated the future, and changed its vision before it had to:

Vision 1 (1946–60): To build a high quality cosmetics brand in the USA, offering, as Mrs Estée Lauder said, "The most wonderful beauty products in the world".

Vision 2 (1960-late 1990s): To build a multi-branded global beauty business, offering the very best – in people, products, advertising, and selling environment.

Leonard Lauder felt the most important decision he ever made was to go multi-brand and global very early, at a time when his major competitors – Helena Rubenstein, Revlon and Elizabeth Arden – were all single brand. Clinique was introduced to compete with Estée Lauder and Aramis later. A London office was opened in 1960. Focus on high quality was sustained and extended.

Vision 3 (late 1990s onwards): Bringing the best to everyone we touch, globally, across a range of brands and distribution channels (see page 118).

Estée Lauder went public in 1995, and now had very different major competitors – Unilever, Procter & Gamble and L'Oreal. The company made a number of acquisitions, such as Bobbi Brown Essentials, botanical beauty company Aveda, and teen marketer Jane Cosmetics, entering mass-market distribution channels.

To reflect these changes in 1999, the vision was updated to 'Bringing the best to everyone we touch', and this applied to all brands whether expensive perfume sold at Nieman Marcus or budget-priced cosmetics offered at Wal-Mart. The new vision was supported by a set of practical Commitments and Principles.[9]

By contrast, the Dallas Symphony Orchestra has had a rougher ride (see **Chart 15.7**). It also had three changes in vision, but over a 101-year period. The DSO has been close to bankruptcy at least once, and has survived through the vision and courage of a few determined individuals, to become one of the world's top ten orchestras:

The Dallas Symphony Orchestra was founded in 1900 and its early vision was to become a paid, professional ensemble. This was achieved in the 1920s. It almost went bankrupt in 1974 and in 1977 a new vision was set – to restore the orchestra to national prominence and to create a first class concert hall.

This was achieved, and in the early 1990s a new vision was set: to build an orchestra ranked among the best in the world in artistic quality. It's now probably at the bottom end of the top ten. Strategies for reaching this new vision include:

━━ THE SOURCE ━━
9 Interview with Leonard Lauder, Chairman, Estée Lauder.

15.8 Customer vision

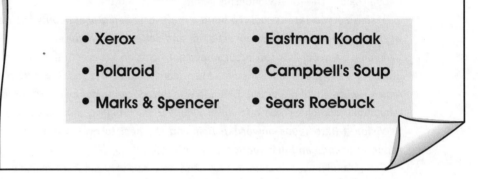

*Companies with a great past and questionable future –
they failed to change their customer vision*

- Xerox
- Polaroid
- Marks & Spencer
- Eastman Kodak
- Campbell's Soup
- Sears Roebuck

- Further upgrading artistic quality.

- Building the next generation of players through education.

- Becoming a leader in electronic delivery.

- Making the DSO an exciting place to work.[10]

Response to changes in markets and customer needs   Twenty years ago, being a CEO was like driving a family car along fairly familiar roads. Today it is like handling a Formula 1 racing car, taking bends at 200 mph, and never quite sure what's round the corner or who's about to overtake.

Accelerating changes in customer needs affects non-profits as well as companies. However, market selection is more straightforward for most non-profits. Schools and colleges will still be in education, hospitals in patient care in 50 years time.

By contrast, companies may find their present markets become unattractive or even disappear. Who wants to be world leader in instant camera photography, like Polaroid, when digital and Internet images are taking over? Is there a future for 'The Document Company' – Xerox? And will markets like mid-sized cars, agricultural equipment or railways ever deliver reasonable returns again? You could buy most of the USA's railway system for under $30 billion, less than the present capitalization of Orange, founded in 1994.

Vision points to future destination. Selecting the right markets and anticipating changes in customer needs is a vital ingredient in this. Successful companies match their skills and resources to the best *future* opportunities. This may involve leaving existing markets, entering new ones, developing new skills and envisaging new customer propositions for the future. Such difficult decisions require courage and imagination.

AOL and Time Warner merged due to a vision where Time Warner's creative content (e.g. movies, books, magazines) combined with AOL's global access to 90 million Internet users. AT&T, a world leader in telecommunications, spent over $100 billion buying cable TV companies, because it envisaged a link between the two, but this bold vision now looks unlikely to succeed.

Changes in vision often occur when organizations run into difficulties such as lack of growth or shrinking markets. By then it may be too late. It's much easier to list companies who fail to change their consumer vision fast enough (see **Chart 15.8**) than the few which change when they're healthy, ahead of market pressure to do so. UPS (page 114) is one of the few.

UPS, in modifying its vision in 1999, responding to anticipated future changes and new opportunities, retained its original values established by founder Jim Casey. These have not changed in 93 years and remain the bedrock of UPS's business – integrity, excellence, employee satisfaction and development, and innovation.[11]

THE SOURCE

10 Interview with Dr Eugene Bonelli, President, Dallas Symphony Orchestra.
11 Interview with Jack Duffy, Senior VP Strategy, United Parcel Service.

15.9 Weyerhaeuser Company Roadmap for Success

	Objectives Where we're going	Processes How we'll get there	Goals How we'll know we're there
Vision The best forest products company in the world			
Values • Customers • People • Accountability • Citizenship • Financial responsibility			
Behaviours • Operate as one company • Safe from the start • Speed, simplicity, decisiveness			

Note: This is a simplified chart. In Weyerhaeuser's Roadmap for Success, all the boxes are filled in.

- Vision, values and behaviour columns unlikely to change.
- Objectives, processes and goals need regular adjustment.

Don't change the vision when implementation is the problem

Organizations sometimes change visions prematurely, mistaking flaws in implementation for lack of vision. Clear future direction may be absent, despite a strong vision, because the strategies and processes for executing the vision are not in place. This used to be the case at Weyerhaeuser:

Steve Rogel was appointed Chairman/CEO of Weyerhaeuser, one of the world's largest forest products companies, in 1997. The Board felt Weyerhaeuser was too fragmented, preventing it from achieving maximum shareholder value. But it wanted to retain the company's values, good name, customer focus and community goodwill.

The vision was to be 'The best forest products company in the world'. Did it need changing? No. It had been in place since the early 1990s and remained valid. But there were no goals for measuring progress towards it. The values were strong and relevant – with safety No. 1, and customer focus a particular priority. However, Weyerhaeuser was operating as a number of separate companies, with duplication of services and few common processes. Each business did its own purchasing, and the whole organization was too slow-moving.

After 6 months, Steve Rogel decided his top team was capable of changing and wanted to. He kept the 55 senior people. The original vision and values were retained, but new 'behaviours' added, and objectives, processes and goals set to ensure implementation (see **Chart 15.9**).

Common processes were established, and compliance related to performance appraisal and rewards. There is now central purchasing, and duplication of services has been removed. Weyerhaeuser businesses are expected to 'think Weyerhaeuser', and to move decisively, with speed. In this case, the vision and values didn't need to change, but the way they were applied did.[12]

Updating values and practices

When drawn up effectively in the first place, as in Best Practice No. 3 (Chapter 7), values often endure for many decades. Chart 7.5 divided values into moral and performance ones. The moral values such as integrity, treatment of people and safety, are least likely to change. Performance values need to be modified if the vision, or key success factors change; values like superior quality, innovation, speed and customer focus will always be relevant in any organization, but their relative importance will change over time.

Dr Tom Everhart describes how values at Caltech, the leading American university, evolved during his decade as President (1987–97):

"When I first arrived at Caltech, it had a reputation of being a very intense place. Lights in the labs were usually on at midnight, and for breakfast meetings, a third of the students hadn't been to bed. People on the campus often passed you with their heads down and didn't speak.

THE SOURCE

12 Interview with Steven Rogel, Chairman and CEO, Weyerhaeuser.

15.10 A renewable process for managing vision and values

Best practice No. 1 Building foundations	• Who are our stakeholders? • What are their needs and how are they changing? • How effectively are these being met and linked? • What are the key lessons from the past? • How to align key skills, future opportunities?
Best practice No. 2 Strong vision	• How well does the vision stack up on criteria for measuring strength? • Where are we strong and weak? • How effective are the strategies for implementing vision? • Is central vision translated into local visions? • What changes need to be made?
Best practice No. 3 Strong values	• How strongly are values linked to key success factors? • How well do they support the vision? • How effectively are the practices being implemented? • Future changes and improvement targets?
Best practice No. 4 Communication	• How well are vision and values being communicated? • What are real versus stated values? • How can communication be strengthened? • What are targets for the future?

Another problem was teamwork and functional silos. A formal survey of faculty, students and staff showed that graduate students felt very isolated, rarely meeting people from other disciplines, while single faculty had few chances to mix with other people socially.

Caltech vision, established in 1921, was to stay at the forefront of Maths, Science and Engineering. How to do this required constant innovation, but the vision did not need to be changed. Supporting values were excellence, creativity, taking big risks, integrity and staying small (under 2000 students).

The challenge was to reinforce these original values and to add new ones to encourage more teamwork and respect for people. We pursued a gradualist evolution in values, because sudden change is usually not sustainable. Here are some examples of changes made:

- Graduate students social hour every Friday – same hour but always in a different place and department.

- Quarterly graduate seminar where one graduate gives a talk to which all are invited, followed by discussion and socializing.

- Athletic facilities, to be used jointly for undergraduates, graduate students, faculty and staff, were enhanced. This encouraged interaction among individuals in different groups. Previously they had rarely mixed and there was some fear on both sides. Most were aged 20–35, and in a T-shirt and shorts, you can't easily tell a mature undergraduate from a young professor.

- Teamwork across disciplines, and respect for others, regardless of their position, gender or ethnic background, was encouraged.

While still intense, Caltech is now viewed as a friendlier place, and working across disciplines has helped it get into several new fields, through interactions among people in Chemistry, Physics, Biology and Engineering."[13]

A common mistake in declining organizations is to assume that its values are wrong and need to be changed. Failure to follow the original values may be a prime reason for the decline. Lou Gerstner frequently said: "I want to take IBM back to its roots", and that's what happened from the mid 1990s, as Douglas Sweeney, an IBM employee for 30 years, describes:

"Since the 1920s, IBM followed values of best customer service, respect for individuals and pursuit of excellence (e.g. quality). In the late 1980s and early 1990s, these values became distorted. There was too much focus on selling products, not enough on customer solutions. Respect for individuals made IBM too inwards looking and technology driven, and things like arrogance, high cost, paternalism and over concentration on large customers crept in.

Lou Gerstner didn't change the three key values – he reinforced them, returning to:

- Strong customer focus and service as the key priority.

┌─ THE SOURCE ──
│ **13** Interview with Dr Tom Everhart, President Emeritus, Californian Institute of Technology (Caltech).
└──

15.10 *cont.*

Best practice No. 5 Embedding	• How strongly are vision and values reflected in recruitment and appraisal criteria? • How far does commitment to vision and values affect rewards and promotion? • What happens to those who breach the values? • Future improvement plans?
Best practice No. 6 Branding	• What is the organization brand? • Who is responsible for managing it? • What are 1- and 5-year targets for brand awareness, attributes and attitudes? • What is the brand proposition and how is it differentiated? • How is the proposition tailored to each stakeholder? • How well does the organization brand express the vision and values? • Are internal practices and external brand expression consistent, or is there hypocrisy?
Best practice No. 7 Measurement	• How is the strength of the vision measured? • How are the organization's real values identified? • How is progress towards realizing vision and values measured? • Is there clear measurement by type of stakeholder? • Are there regular and rigorous surveys of customer, employee and shareholder satisfaction? • What actions are taken as a result of measurement?

THE SOURCE

14 Interview with Sir Michael Perry, Chairman, Centrica.

- Respect for the individual, but more teamwork, speed and a competitive approach.

- Excellence, resulting in winning in the market place.

The practices used to implement values need regular updating, as the sharpening of IBM values shows. Values at the British Army, Du Pont, and the London Metropolitan Police have survived for nearly 200 years, but supporting practices have been continuously adapted to changing social conditions.

Creating a structure for renewal

Vision and values should be actively managed, as a continuous improvement process. Basic questions of responsibility and accountability need to be resolved. Who is responsible for ensuring that vision and values work? What are future objectives and targets in this respect? How will they be measured and by whom? Who is accountable for failure and success? Who is responsible for developing the organization brand? **Chart 15.10** provides a checklist for renewal, based on the Seven Best Practices.

Similar questions on marketing, finance and operations are easy to answer since they are organized on a functional basis. Vision and values management is cross-departmental, and therefore more difficult to tie down. To say that everyone is responsible usually means that nobody is.

The organization leader needs to establish a structure and a process for managing vision and values, which will renew itself and outlast individuals:

''You need to distinguish between vision and values created around individuals (like Bill Gates or Richard Branson) which may not survive them, and those built around organizations like Procter & Gamble, 3M and Johnson & Johnson, which endure through changes in CEOs.''[14]

One approach is to establish a Vision and Values Board, chaired by the CEO, and consisting of senior individuals with expertise in each of the seven best practices. To these could be added two or three more junior people with front line experience of shareholders, customers or other stakeholders. Each of the senior people would be responsible for making one of the best practices work. They would set annual objectives, and be accountable for achieving them. The Vision and Values Board would be collectively responsible for making vision and values work.

It is good discipline to review progress towards vision, and performance on values prior to the annual business planning cycle. In this way, they will receive a formal review, using integrated measurement and the organization's new 3-Year and 1-Year Plan will be developed in the right context.

From shareholder value to stakeholder value

Shareholder value is tied to yesterday's themes of scarce capital, compliant customers, pockets of weak competition and memories of seller's markets. As the twenty-first century progresses, the customer will replace the shareholder as the dominant stake

15.11 From shareholder value to stakeholder value

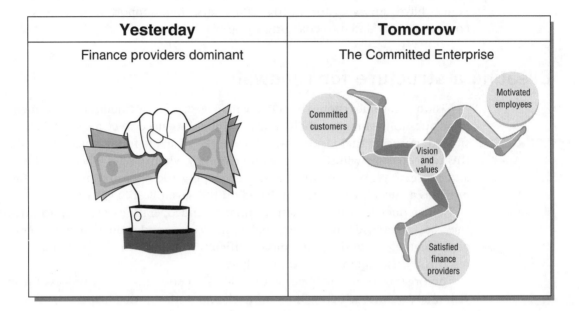

Yesterday	Tomorrow
Finance providers dominant	The Committed Enterprise

holder, powered by even more intense competition, and the ability of the Internet to highlight price discrepancies, give consumers a louder voice, and reveal buying opportunities.

Organizations, both businesses and non-profits, will be managed on a more balanced basis for all stakeholders. The Committed Enterprise, with committed customers, motivated employees and satisfied finance providers, will become the future model for success. Organization leaders will judge the success of their increasingly short terms of office by asking, "What have I contributed to building stakeholder value?", "Are customers more satisfied and employees more motivated than when I started?", "Have I helped build or sustain a Committed Enterprise?"

Strong and relevant vision and values are essential for long-term success. They have existed among groups of people for thousands of years, but have only been written about in recent decades. Some regard them as a short-term management fad. While they have been widely misused, they are no more a fad than organizations are.

Vision and values often fail to work because they are poorly managed. The basic disciplines of responsibility, accountability, targets and measurement are ignored. This book is intended to provide guidance in vision and values management, by using the processes implicit in the Seven Best Practices. Since you have stayed with it to the end, I wish you every success in making vision and values work.

Summary: 10 Keys to Failure

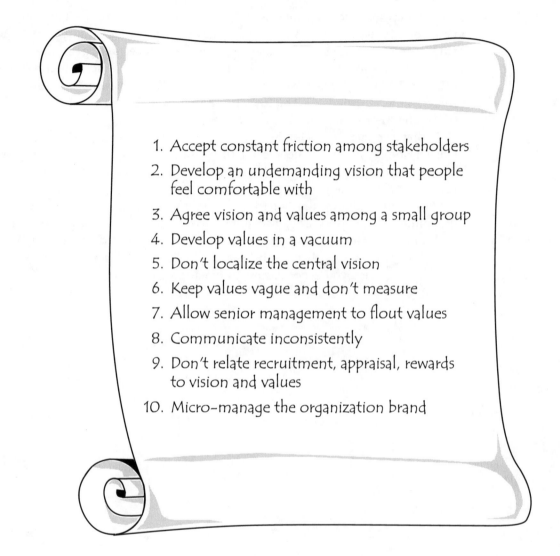

1. Accept constant friction among stakeholders
2. Develop an undemanding vision that people feel comfortable with
3. Agree vision and values among a small group
4. Develop values in a vacuum
5. Don't localize the central vision
6. Keep values vague and don't measure
7. Allow senior management to flout values
8. Communicate inconsistently
9. Don't relate recruitment, appraisal, rewards to vision and values
10. Micro-manage the organization brand

Summary: 10 Keys to Success

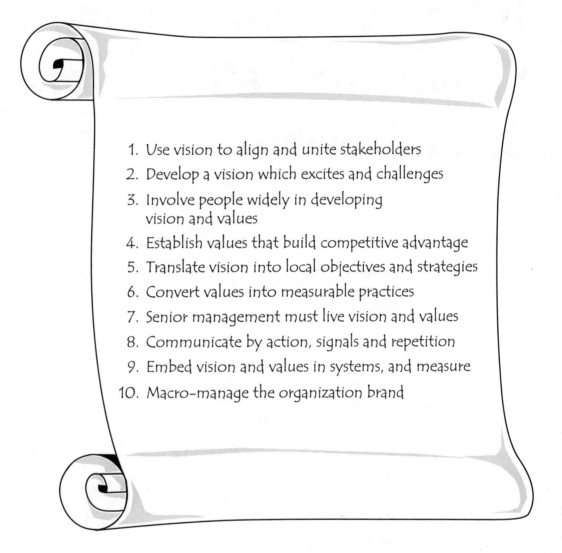

1. Use vision to align and unite stakeholders
2. Develop a vision which excites and challenges
3. Involve people widely in developing vision and values
4. Establish values that build competitive advantage
5. Translate vision into local objectives and strategies
6. Convert values into measurable practices
7. Senior management must live vision and values
8. Communicate by action, signals and repetition
9. Embed vision and values in systems, and measure
10. Macro-manage the organization brand

Appendix

Interview outline: making vision and values work in organizations

Background

This interview outline was used for all organizations. For companies, acquisitions/ mergers was also discussed, and for international entities, tailoring of vision and values to local cultures.

Introduction

I am interviewing a number of senior leaders of major organizations in the UK and USA, on the topic of *Making Vision and Values Work*.

Individual interviews are conducted in confidence.

Perhaps before we start the interview discussion, I could give you my definition of three terms and discuss whether you agree (although it doesn't matter if you use different words to describe these three areas):

- **MISSION** is the <u>purpose</u> of the organization, i.e. 'What are we here for?'
- **VISION** is a view of where the organization should be going in the long term future, i.e. 'What is our long-term direction?'
- **VALUES** are the <u>beliefs</u> which will guide us in pursuing our Vision, i.e. 'What are our <u>convictions or principles</u> regarding <u>how</u> we will operate?' These are not limited to ethical questions, e.g. a belief in offering <u>superior</u> quality or achieving world-class standards is a value.

MAKING VISION AND VALUES WORK – KEY QUESTIONS TO BE ASKED

1 Does your organization have both a Mission and a Vision?

2 What is your organization's mission or vision?

3 What difference would it make if you didn't have one?

4 Can Missions and Visions have a harmful effect? In what circumstances?

5 What are your organization's main values?

6 When were these Vision and Values developed? *(If relevant, influence of Founder or key individuals)*

7 How were they developed? Who was involved? Was there a process?

8 Who are the organization's main stakeholders? How are they prioritized?

9 How are Vision and Values communicated, and to whom?

10 How do you measure the effectiveness of your Vision and Values with employees and external stakeholders (e.g. the public, politicians, governments etc.)

11 Do you feel your organization's Vision and Values are accepted and acted upon?

12 What are the main barriers to full implementation of Vision and Values?

13 How often do an organization's Vision and Values need to be changed? Under what circumstances?

14 How are Vision and Values integrated into the organization's objectives and strategies, and linked to annual planning processes?

15 How do you respond to talented people who don't live your Vision and Values?

16 How are Vision and Values linked to personal appraisal and rewards?

17 Does your corporate brand proposition express your Vision and Values?

18 Which other organizations do you admire for having strong Vision and Values that are implemented in practice?

Index